Andrew Pettegree

SCOTLAND AND EUROPE

SCOTLAND
AND EUROPE
1200–1850

Edited by

T C SMOUT

Department of Scottish History
University of St Andrews

JOHN DONALD PUBLISHERS LTD
EDINBURGH

ISBN 0 85976 112 6

Exclusive distribution in the United States
of America and Canada by Humanities
Press Inc., Atlantic Highlands, NJ 07716,
USA.

Phototypeset by Quorn Selective Repro,
Loughborough.
Printed in Great Britain by Bell & Bain
Ltd., Glasgow.

INTRODUCTION

The essays published here were, with two exceptions, given before the Seminar for Scottish History at St John's House Institute of Advanced Historical Studies of the University of St Andrews. The exceptions were Anna Biegańska's important 'note' on the migration of the Scots to Sweden, which we were lucky enough to secure through the kind office of Dr Dukes, and Isabel Guy's paper on the Scottish export trade, which presents some findings and statistical material from her pioneering M.Phil. thesis at St Andrews. The latter should certainly be consulted by those wishing to take the subject further.

Of the remaining papers, five were given by British scholars, and five by scholars from continental universities. Some are concerned primarily with cultural and intellectual history, such as Donald Watt's study of the Scots who, before the founding of Scottish universities in the fifteenth century, had perforce to find their higher education in Europe; the same theme of intellectual contacts is developed in John Durkan's investigation into continuing French cultural connections after the Reformation, and Robert Feenstra presents a careful anatomy of the Scottish law students at the universities of the Netherlands in the later seventeenth and eighteenth centuries. James Cameron explores a little-known group of continental travellers in Scotland — very often themselves students — in the sixteenth century. Michael Ignatieff's masterly study of the clash of ideas over the consequences of economic growth between Adam Smith and Rousseau reminds us, however, that intellectual contacts, to be fruitful, do not always have to be face-to-face.

Another strong theme in the collection is economic. Apart from Isabel Guy's paper, Arnvid Lillehammer on Norway and Scotland, Thomas Riis on Denmark and Scotland and Elsa-Britta Grage on Sweden and Scotland have the common theme of trade and development, and as a group add very considerably to our knowledge of Scottish enterprise in, and dependence upon, the Scandinavian economies down to the beginning of the nineteenth century. Thomas Riis, who during the time he was undertaking his research was visiting Carlsberg Fellow at St Andrews, also covers political and cultural themes in his study of the sixteenth century as a trailer to his forthcoming book. A multi-faceted approach is also evident in Katia Kretkowska's lengthy and brilliant piece on Scottish economic and artistic influences on the Polish landed estate in the later eighteenth and early nineteenth centuries, an aspect of Scottish influence abroad hitherto quite unknown to English-speaking scholars.

One prominent theme of early modern Scottish-European contacts is, alas, under-represented in the collection — that of the mercenary selling his sword to the highest bidder. Paul Dukes alone investigates this field, in a study of the problems that confronted three leading Scottish soldiers of fortune when they attempted to leave the service of the Tsar: it was easier to embrace the hug of the bear than to disentangle oneself from it.

v

A seminar series of this kind — and, we must hope, the ensuing book — leaves the listener or the reader with a number of impressions. One is of the range and depth of the research being undertaken in the field both at home and abroad, to a degree of which the average Scottish historian too often has no inkling. Another is of one's appetite being constantly whetted to know more than can be conveyed in a couple of hours, or in the confines of a chapter: it is good to realise that many of these papers are the tips of a research iceberg of which much more will come to be revealed by their authors in full-length books or supplementary articles.

A third sensation is of all the other questions that might be asked as a sequel to the work presented here. It becomes immediately obvious, for example, that any scholar tempted still to regard Scotland before the Union of Parliaments as a cultural backwater devoid of intellectual and economic enterprise is completely and utterly wrong. How many other areas might there be which, like the fjord districts north of Stavanger, owed their first experience of international commerce mainly to the efforts of a group of Scottish merchants and skippers of the reign of James VI? Would a study of Scottish medical doctors and medical students in the 'republic of letters' of early modern Europe yield fruits as rich as the study of lawyers and divines? Is it not time to follow the leads first indicated by Thomas Fischer and others nearly a hundred years ago, and begin to think in terms of a series of volume-length studies of the Scots in the European world of the early modern period — not just Poland, Swden, Denmark and France, but Germany, the Netherlands, Norway, Russia and other areas not even attempted here such as Italy and the English colonies (to say nothing of Ulster)? Have we done more than skim the surface of the European archives that might yield material on the Scots, and on Scottish history itself? The horizon for scholarly endeavour is almost limitless.

The prospect for the century and a half after the Union is almost equally exciting. We have, thanks to the labours of Jacob Price and T. M. Devine, a lively awareness of the Glasgow enterprise that opened up Virginia to the Scottish tobacco traders: where is the equivalent study of the east-coast merchant houses that so vastly expanded Scottish trade to Russia? We have an understanding of the international effects of James Watt's steam engine: what about that item which increasingly occurs on the inventory of farms in Northern and Eastern Europe in the nineteenth century, the new Scots plough? Studies of the Enlightenment are an international academic industry, and the place of the Scots within it has long been honoured and is increasingly being understood: but what do we know in depth of the diffusion of popular Scottish ideas of the relationship between man and society as they became diffused through the European world down to, say, 1840?

We present these essays, therefore, in the same spirit as we established the seminar series, not as a set of homogeneous variations on the same theme but as an illustration of the diversity and excitement of current historical research on the inter-relationships between Scotland and Europe, and in the hope of inspiring further work that will be still more ambitious and comprehensive.

T. C. SMOUT

CONTENTS

1

SCOTTISH UNIVERSITY MEN OF THE THIRTEENTH AND FOURTEENTH CENTURIES

D. E. R. Watt

What were 'university men'? This study concerns those Scots who in the two centuries before the first native university was founded at St Andrews in 1410 sought a university education in England or on the continent, and thereafter formed a small but distinctive element in Scottish society. In round numbers about 1000 such adventurous and determined men can be traced today over this long period.[1] No doubt others have left no trace; but if we think of an average of just between five and ten young men starting out each year from the whole country, we are shocked right away into the right kind of thinking about a tiny élite. This figure may in fact be on the high side, for even when the much more convenient university of St Andrews had been founded, the number of students taking their first degree in the Faculty of Arts there was to average about only ten per year over the first forty years from 1410 to 1450.[2] 'University men' is now a fashionable phrase to describe those who are known to have studied for a while at university level. Some became graduates, attaining the degrees which from the thirteenth century became recognised as badges of attainment at different stages of study in the faculties of theology, medicine, law or arts; but many remained content with just a spell of study that did not end with a formal qualification, proud thereafter to style themselves 'Scholar in Arts' or 'Scholar in Law' and the like.[3] This custom among the Scots conforms to that noted in a recent study which suggests that a 'very large proportion' of students at Oxford and Cambridge in the Middle Ages, 'very possibly more than half', never took a degree.[4] To identify 'university men', therefore, we have to look not only for those who held specific degrees and those who attached the title *Magister* to their names on formal occasions, but also those who are only casually mentioned as having some university connection.

Magistri first appear in surviving Scottish sources in the mid-twelfth century. Apparently the term was then a mark of courtesy attached in formal documents to the names of men who were products of the distinguished cathedral schools of the period which were in process of turning into proto-universities. The men so described are found mostly in the service of the king or the leading bishops. A handful are additionally described as *medicus* or *physicus*, terms of indeterminate implication.[5] By 1200 there were enough of these men around for us to recognise them as a segment of society; and as the universities in England and on the continent became regularly organised thereafter, the holders of their degrees came to be styled Bachelor, Master or Doctor in accordance with their precise status (though it is noticeable that the style *Magiter* is quite often attached as a mark of respect to the names of men who had not studied beyond the stage of bachelor in one of the more advanced faculties such as law, and who had not technically qualified as masters or doctors). But as we consider the next two hundred years, we must take into account certain cardinal facts about the character of the available sources that control the kinds of study that are possible. No matriculation or graduation lists survive from the thirteenth-century universities, and it is only at Paris from about 1340 onwards that we have detailed information about students and masters from Scotland in the Faculty of Arts.[6] It hapens that from about the same date there survives in the Vatican Archives the series of Registers of Petitions to the pope.[7] While a scattering of papal graces conferring benefices and other privileges on individuals is available from 1198 onwards,[8] it is only with the Registers of Petitions that we find a comprehensive record of such acts of papal grace. Information is now available about many more people, and it is much fuller on matters like university qualifications as graduates everywhere press their claims on the popes at Avignon for provisions to benefices and dispensations for illegitimacy, pluralism and the like. For two reasons therefore the sources dictate that we know much more about Scottish university men after about 1340 than before. Some 600 of them can be identified between 1200 and 1340, but in most of these cases we have no means of knowing where, when or what they studied — indeed in only about one-sixth of these cases can the man's university be identified from some casual reference. On the other hand when we consider the 400 men identifiable between 1340 and 1410, we can trace their universities in nearly five-sixths of the cases. This makes a big difference to the quality of generalisation that is possible before and after 1340. There is very little scope for statistics in a study of this kind, and comparisons between different periods in the two centuries which we are considering are seldom valid.[9]

But we can try to be positive. How did these 1000 university men over 200 years fit into Scottish society? What about social origins? Recent writers on the English and French universities have been suggesting that most students in this period were not poverty-striken, whatever may have been the case earlier in the twelfth-century days of wandering scholars. Most students at Oxford and Cambridge, for example, are thought to have been supported by their families in relatively expensive circumstances,[10] and the conclusion has been drawn more generally that the majority of students at continental universities were of intermediate social status.[11] On the basis of fourteenth-century evidence from Paris at any rate it would appear that 'it was uncommon for Scottish students to be poor',[12] though this is not to say that none of them were ever short of cash at critical times, such as when university fees fell due. The very distance, time and expense involved in travelling outside the country for higher education must surely have normally made it a business which required careful planning and forethought. It was a more casual matter in England, where two universities were conveniently available and it seems likely that a sizeable number of men had the chance to go to study at them more than once at different stages of their careers.[13] Similar cases in Scotland can be traced,[14] but they were clearly exceptional. Most students went as young men, and so must have come from social circles that could provide the necessary resources for them. We do know about the parentage or at least the family connections of some who claimed the status of *nobilis*. These could be grand people, such as illegitimate sons of King Robert II, or sons of an earl of Ross or Dunbar, or members of leading families such as Comyn, Bruce, Douglas, Lindsay, or not so grand members of knightly landholding families such as Cunningham, Wishart, Macnaughton, Hamilton and Denniston;[15] but 'nobility' was a status based sometimes on a relationship in as little as the third or fourth degree from a distinguished personage, and seems to have been pretty diluted.[16] Kinship is mentioned also sometimes by *nepotes* of bishops.[17] Together the *nobiles* and nepotes constitute about one-quarter of the post-1340 group. Apart from them, however, we are left guessing on the matter of origins, with little to go on except surnames which appear to have been derived from place-names. There are many traps for the historian here: we know, for example, that in the later fourteenth century a John de Hawyk came from St Andrews diocese (when Hawick was a place in Glasgow diocese), and that a Thomas de Kingorn (presumably named from Kinghorn in Fife) came from Aberdeen diocese.[18] And then in the early part of our period some university men are found working in Scotland who were not of Scottish origin, but had come from France or England presumably because of family connections or in search of employment and betterment.[19] Things were very different in this respect after the War of Independence, when such foreigners are no longer found. All these suggestions about origins cannot be quantified: all we can do is to note the variety of possibilities that the sources suggest.

There is a clear contrast between the thirteenth and fourteenth centuries if we next consider where it was that Scots went for their university education. In the thirteenth century it was certainly to Paris and Oxford throughout the century, with a handful going to Cambridge under Edward I.[20] In addition we happen to know of a group of more than thirty Scots who studied at the great law university of Bologna between 1265 and 1294, because in the indexes to some notarial archives there which have been published there are allusions to them by name.[21] There is no reason to suppose that they had not been there earlier in the century as well. But Scottish students are not found south of the Alps in the following century. One reason for this important change is connected with the move of the papal court to Avignon for most of the century, for as a consequence it was much less common for Scots to have occasion to visit Italy. It was very different from the situation in 1301-2 when a famous embassy was sent from Scotland to Pope Boniface VIII in Rome to protest against the aggression of Edward I, when the two men sent with instructions from home could pick up their leader (Baldred Biset) at Bologna on the way.[22] Furthermore the fourteenth century brought also the foundation of new universities with law faculties north of the Alps. Here was another reason for a change of pattern, and we begin to find some Scots at least at Orléans, Avignon, Montpellier and Angers,[23] even if the German universities founded in the latter half of the century did not attract them as yet.[24] The popularity of Paris, however, was continuous and apparently increasing.

It was different in England where the connection with Oxford and Cambridge ceased abruptly for some decades after 1306 once England and Scotland were almost continuously at war. But then came an interesting development between 1357 and 1400, when at irregular intervals the English government issued general and particular letters of safe-conduct for Scots to come and study at the English universities for specific periods.[25] The first of these safe-conducts were issued when King David II was being released on ransom by Edward III. This was part of a deliberate policy on the English side, since free access for both Scottish and French students to the English universities was being encouraged in diplomatic agreements which were negotiated at this time.[26] The policy was strictly limited to periods of truce in the Anglo-Scottish wars: no safe-conducts were issued, for example, during a spell of open hostilities between May 1382 and October 1389. The names of ninety different Scottish students are specifically mentioned in a total of 117 safe-conducts issued over the whole period in question; but since in a few cases the person named was authorised to bring a number of unnamed fellow-students with him (as opposed to servants), and since in other cases advantage may have been taken of the safe-conducts which were issued from time to time for Scots in general to come and study at the English universities, we cannot be sure of the total number who sought to take advantage of this policy. It seems likely, however, that there were few besides the named ninety, since only one other Scot is now known to have studied in England at university level in the period.[27] Furthermore we must not assume that all the safe-conducts which were issued were in the end used, for it is a striking fact that when we study the careers of the ninety men whose names are known, only eleven fairly certainly made use of their safe-conducts, twenty-nine may perhaps have done so, but in fifty cases there is no corroborative evidence to prove that the safe-conducts were ever used — indeed for most of this last group there is not even confirmation that the persons whose names are given ever existed. The usefulness of the whole series of safe-conducts for the historian is therefore remarkably uncertain. It is hard to resist the conclusion that even though as many as ninety Scots in the last forty years of the fourteenth century may have had plans to go to Oxford or Cambridge, only a small minority of them ever went.

An interesting point of contrast emerges from this change regarding the accessibility of the English universities to Scots. In the mid-thirteenth century Peter de Ramsay is notable as a reforming bishop of Aberdeen 1247-57. He appears to have earlier studied theology at Oxford as a young man in the 1220s under Edmund of Abingdon, and in 1235 had certainly succeeded the great Robert Grosseteste as theological mentor of the members of the Franciscan house there. We have here a man thoroughly in touch with the latest ideas about both faith and order, and who returned to Scotland and had a chance to put some of these ideas into effect there. But there was no one like him in the later fourteenth century when John Wyclif was in his heyday at Oxford. No Scottish academics were swept off their feet by his fascinating logic and daring heresies, because hardly any Scots were then around. We should therefore not be surprised that no Scot has as yet been satisfactorily identified as having returned home from England with Wyclifite ideas. It was rather the nominalism of Paris in the age of John Buridan in the middle decades of the fourteenth century that academic Scots were to encounter and bring back to keep Scotland orthodox.

The phrase 'bring back' is the right one, because when we consider the various kinds of career achieved by Scottish university men, a cardinal point to note is that the great majority of those who did not succumb at an early age to perils or plague whilst abroad as students did sooner or later return home, bringing back their university experience with them. But first, those few who did remain outside the country for long periods deserve some notice. There were two main categories here — the academics and those who obtained employment at the papal court. Amongst the academics it is hard to distinguish the professional teachers from the perpetual students. The problem arises from the fact that all university courses in the Middle Ages were designed as a preparation for the trade of master or teacher, whether in theology, medicine, law or arts. Practice in lecturing and disputation was included in everyone's curriculum, and those who took the full degree of Master or Doctor in any faculty were expected to serve their *universitas* or corporation of fellow-masters or doctors by teaching as a 'regent' for at least a couple of years.[28] But in practice from an early date graduates tended to treat a degree merely as a passport to a variety of careers, and the universities had difficulty in ensuring that those who took the formal full degree did remain to perform their 'necessary regency'; and of course, as already explained, the majority of students never went so far as a master's or doctor's degree anyway. Yet some Scots did remain at some universities for long periods to teach there. Theologians were few and their teaching careers usually brief: a Matthew de Scotia at Paris in 1218; Peter de Ramsay at Oxford in 1235; John Duns Scotus at Oxford and Paris 1302-7; John de Rate at Paris in the 1340s; (1) Walter de Wardlaw there in the 1350s; William de Trebrun there in the 1380s; and Laurence de Lindores there in the early 1400s before moving to St Andrews in 1410. Two Masters of Medicine taught for a time at Paris — Thomas de Duns in the 1360s and John Gray 1409-16. Of the lawyers Walter de Coventre taught civil and canon law at Orléans in the 1350s, while William de Lawedre taught canon law at Angers in the 1370s. It is not a long list for all the advanced faculties, and only Duns Scotus and Laurence de Lindores made anything like a lasting name for themselves as scholars as well as teachers. But there were others who did spend up to twenty years of their lives in university studies, and often they taught in the arts faculty somewhere while studying themselves for a further degree in one of the other faculties.[29] It was a way to earn money through fees, and this made it practicable for them to remain at university. Such men were thoroughly imbued with the academic ethos of the time if and when they eventually returned home. At Paris at any rate they are likely to have made some impact on younger university men by acting as official sponsors for fellow-Scots as they were presented for degrees in the arts faculty. This relationship must have created a basis for the character of future contacts (for good or ill) in the careers of both masters and students. Probably the most influential of these long-time academics in the long run was Henry de Wardlaw, who between 1380 and 1403 is likely to have studied at Oxford or Cambridge as he certainly did at Paris, Orléans and Avignon before returning to Scotland as bishop of St

Andrews 1403–1440. It was he who from 1410 onwards had the opportunity to found Scotland's first native university in his cathedral city, attracting there an essential initial core of qualified teachers,[30] and associating many other Scots with experience of universities abroad in the planning and administration of an institution which must surely in its modest way have fulfilled a long-felt ambition among these university men in their student days.[31]

The second field of activity which kept some men overseas was what contemporaries knew as 'following the Roman court'.[32] In the thirteenth century the papal administration was indeed itinerant in Italy or elsewhere, visiting Rome only rarely. From 1308 it took on a new character when it settled down at Avignon, and stayed there almost continuously (so far as Scotland was concerned) until 1403. There were many reasons which might take a man on a visit to the papal court — to secure confirmation as a bishop, to obtain personal graces of dispensation or provision, to pursue litigation (especially over benefices), to act as proctor for some other person or body in obtaining appointments, paying fees and taxes, taking oaths, or fighting lawsuits. Once there, some university men stayed on for lengthy periods, sometimes living on their wits, but in other cases becoming professional proctors[33] or gaining paid employment in the household of a cardinal[34] or of the pope himself. Not surprisingly, only a very few can be traced in this last category in normal circumstances, though at least two Scottish canon lawyers in the mid-fourteenth century rose to be judges of the Rota, the supreme court of the church (Alexander de Kininmund in the 1320s and Gilbert Fleming in the 1340s). Less unexpected perhaps is the appointment of two Scots (William de Grenlaw and John de Peblis) as collector of papal revenues in Scotland over the long period 1352–86. With the coming of the Great Schism in 1378 the popes at Avignon had a narrower range of qualified clergy to choose from, and we find Scots not only as judges again, but also as clerks in the papal chancery and penitentiary, or more generally as members of the pope's household.[35] Employment at this level was particularly attractive, for it often led to ecclesiastical advancement by way of additional benefices or a bishopric back home. In fact not many bishops emerged this way, for usually proposals for episcopal appointments emanated from Scotland; nonetheless it is likely to have been the opportunities for advancement that kept university men hanging on at the papal court. Indeed of the 400 of them in the later fourteenth century, some twenty-five are known to have died there.

Apart from these academic teachers and followers of the Roman court, most university men came back to Scotland to find employment. From a review of the various kinds of job which they are known to have undertaken, we can learn how they fitted into Scottish society. There were probably no appointments at this time for which university qualifications were essential; and it is not practicable to estimate the proportion of university men to others in the various professions at different times; but at least we can form some picture of where in society these men who had done so much to prepare themselves for their careers are to be found, and we can begin to appreciate the possible ways in which they exercised an influence.

Those who served the king have left the fullest record of their activities. We find

Magistri among the clerks who witnessed royal acts from the late twelfth century onwards.[36] Though the king's chamberlain was usually a layman, some university men did fill this office.[37] The royal chancellor was normally a clerk, and from the mid-thirteenth century onwards it was usual for him to be a university man.[38] Once the office of secretary emerges in the mid-fourteenth century, it too was usually held by a graduate.[39] It is especially interesting to note that two holders of this last office (Duncan Petit 1379–90 and Walter Forrester c.1401–c.1406) were clerks who had begun their careers at humbler levels in the royal service and had then gone abroad for some years with financial help from their employer to better their academic qualifications in law before returning to take up this responsible post. A long list of other jobs in the royal service offered employment to university men from time to time — as king's clerk, or more specifically as clerk of the rolls, wardrobe clerk, audit clerk, or clerk to the chamberlain.[40] At nearly every annual exchequer audit at least one university man was among the changing group of lords, knights, bishops and clerks who acted as auditors, and sometimes there were several.[41] They were also employed in the more domestic offices of the king's and queen's households as stewards, almoners, physicians, chamberlains, clerks and chaplains.[42] The royal service attracted and embraced a wide variety of talents. A few university men retained employment in it for the best part of their lives; but most of them seem rather to have passed through it in the course of a more varied career.

On a more political level university men played a conspicuous part in official embassies sent from Scotland to deal with the pope or secular foreign rulers. Such envoys were, of course, often selected from people who were already in the royal service on a permanent basis. A long list of them can be compiled from at least 1215 onwards. At first we know of them just as *Magistri*; but by the early fourteenth century it is clear how highly qualified were the men being employed.[43] An analysis of some fifty envoys whose academic degrees are known identifies three Doctors and one Bachelor of Theology, twenty-three Doctors or Licentiates of Law, ten Bachelors or Scholars of Law, as well as thirteen qualified just in Arts. Here some of the best-trained brains in the country were in the service of the government. The 1360s are a particularly interesting period, when Edward III of England was using all his diplomatic wiles to persuade the Scots to accept one of his sons as a successor to the childless David II, and the Scots were wanting to appear to be co-operative without actually committing themselves. The most prominent envoy used by the Scottish king in these negotiations was Walter de Wardlaw, a Doctor of Theology and ex-university teacher, who could cope successfully with the most tortuous of diplomatic exchanges, and emerged with Scotland free (for good or ill) to have her own Stewarts on the throne.[44]

The king needed advisers as well as servants. We have little information from the period about the composition of the royal council,[45] though it is clear from the witness lists attached to royal charters that university men (not least the leading bishops) were regularly among the small group of people who were formally associated with day-to-day royal decisions. A broad spectrum of clerical advisers took part in the wider occasional discussions in parliament and general council.

Detailed records are available for only a handful of such meetings in the later fourteenth century, but more than forty of the 400 university men of 1340–1410 can be definitely identified as attending them. They came sometimes as royal officials or envoys, sometimes by right of episcopal office, sometimes as proctors for absent bishops or the diocesan clergy.[46] Again their academic qualifications tended to be high, with as many as half of the forty holding degrees of Doctor or Licentiate of Theology or Law. In 1369 and 1370 at any rate we have also examples of graduate clerks of non-episcopal rank taking part in the judicial and business committees of parliament;[47] this was probably quite usual by that date. And when in 1399 a council of twenty was chosen to assist the young duke of Rothesay as lieutenant of the realm, the five clerical members were all university men.[48] We can be sure that there was normally an academically-trained element among those who submitted advice to the king, whether or not this advice was taken.

The next area in which we find university men was in the service of magnates, both lay and ecclesiastical. Lay lords had households like the king's, and from the early thirteenth century onwards it was not uncommon for university men to be employed at least in the comital households and in those of other magnates of grand status, such as the lords of Galloway, Annandale, Badenoch or the Isles.[49] In the late fourteenth century the great earls of Douglas are notable for retaining university men for long periods in their service.[50] When their functions can be discerned, they are described under a long list of titles, such as chaplain, counsellor, doctor, clerk, chamberlain, chancellor, secretary, legal adviser; or they might act as witnesses to a series of charters granted by a magnate or as agents for executing his business. It is interesting that hardly any family tutors can be identified specifically,[51] though perhaps some chaplains fulfilled this task. No doubt the patronage at the disposal of these magnates was a factor in attracting university men to their service, and sometimes (as in the royal household) it was only after a period of service with a magnate that a young clerk was helped to start on university studies or to continue them after a pause.[52] It was common for men to move around during their careers: sometimes they started in a magnate household after university studies, sometimes they moved there in middle life as a stage in careers which eventually led to senior royal service or to bishoprics.

Service in episcopal households offered even greater opportunities. These too could in some cases be launching pads for university studies in the first place.[53] And then certainly from the later twelfth and early thirteenth centuries qualified university men can be traced in such households, as successive bishops (especially of St Andrews, Glasgow and Moray) issued documents in which the witnesses who were styled *Magistri* are regularly differentiated from those who were not. Such episcopal familiars were commonly described just as clerks when assisting the bishop in the responsibilities of his office.[54] On the legal side most dioceses are known to have had an official in charge of a court operating in the bishop's name from the early thirteenth century onwards,[55] and often it was a Doctor or Licentiate of Canon Law who was appointed, or at least a Bachelor (though there are two interesting cases in the 1360s when two mere Scholars of Law held office in Glasgow and Brechin[56] — we may well wonder how they managed to cope).

Bishops employed their graduate clerks also in a miscellany of tasks, both within the boundaries of the diocese and on missions to the royal court or the Roman court.[57] There were certainly many job opportunities for university men here; and bishops even more than secular magnates had a wide range of patronage available to help them at various stages of their careers.

The existence of church courts at deanery, archdeaconry, diocese and provincial council levels (not to mention the Roman court) gave university men with law degrees opportunities for professional practice as lawyers. Again it is from the early thirteenth century that we find some retained by monasteries or cathedral chapters, or by individuals, to act as their proctors in the church courts.[58] Some also practised as notaries, offering services which today we associate with solicitors as general men of business.[59] Some acted on occasion as arbiters to settle disputes or as assessors sitting with episcopal officials and commissaries to advise them in making judgments.[60] And in the thirteenth century at least it was common for papal justice to be exercised within the realm by trios of papal judges-delegate chosen from local men with suitable qualifications to recommend solutions to problems to the pope or even to act formally and finally in his name.[61] The university-trained lawyer found therefore a wide range of professional employment in a country where there was no organisation for training secular lawyers in the common law of the country other than apprenticeship on the job.

If we now consider how frequently we find university men holding the more profitable benefices of the church in Scotland from parsonages and archdeaconries to cathedral canonries and dignities up to bishoprics, this is not to identify a group who were following wholly different careers from those already discussed.[62] It is true that in some cases the evidence does suggest that some benefice-holders did devote their lives to fulfilling the offices to which their benefices were attached. But this appears to have become less and less common during the two centuries in question here so far as university men were concerned. By the fourteenth century it was usual for the more ambitious holders of benefices to serve them by vicars or other deputies while following professional careers elsewhere. By then too pluralism had become common whereby a man might easily accumulate several benefices where no cure of souls was involved (particularly cathedral prebends), or by dispensation might hold more than one cure (provided that he paid vicars out of the revenues). It is a familar fact of later mediaeval church life that benefices were often treated just as sources of income for professional men, who visited them seldom or not at all. Ironically this situation can be found even among holders of benefices with educational functions, such as the mastership or rectorship of the local schools in places like Aberdeen, St Andrews, Cupar, Perth, Edinburgh or Roxburgh, where the university men who held these benefices appear on record only when performing some function which had taken them away from home, or at any rate out of the classroom.[63] Whatever the pros and cons of this attitude (let alone the rights and wrongs), it was one which enabled Scots to support themselves whether at university or during the course of their careers thereafter. And it is fairly certain that most Scottish university men who lived long enough to have a career worth the name received an income from benefices that contemporaries considered to be their due.[64]

There must surely have been some whose main interest was in acting as pastors of souls. This is an activity which leaves little trace in the records. At this time there were some 1100 parish cures in Scotland, and over two hundred years there is evidence that nearly three hundred of them had university men as incumbents at least once, while a few of the richer ones were held by a succession of them.[65] This leaves 800 parish benefices which may very well never have had so highly qualified an incumbent — which is surely typical of the general level of education among the parish clergy of Western Christendom in this period. And it is very much an open question how far the parishes which did at times have university-trained incumbents ever saw them in person. It could sometimes happen (as in the case of Eustace de Inverness, Licentiate of Civil Law and Bachelor of Canon Law, who served as a vigorous resident vicar in the church of what was presumably his home town of Inverness c.1361–83), but it can seldom be shown to have happened for any length of time. We come across similar problems when considering the many university men who were beneficed in the nine secular cathedrals of the mainland dioceses,[66] which in the course of two centuries acquired up to about 120 dignities and ordinary canonries, to which a total of fourteen archdeaconries throughout the country should be added.[67] Cure of souls was attached to only a very few of these 134 benefices: this presumably made them particularly attractive just as sources of income for career-minded clergy. Furthermore even in the mid-thirteenth century when the cathedral chapters were being carefully reformed by their bishops it was assumed that residence for much of the year would be expected of only a minority of dignitaries and canons;[68] and by the fourteenth century in Scotland as elsewhere two-thirds or more of them were customarily absent on their various career pursuits at any one time, though there might be a better attendance for special chapter meetings called to deal with matters like property deals, or the revision of statutes for the community, or the election of a bishop. Archdeaconries were particularly attractive to many university men, not only because of the good income most of them provided, but also because cure of souls was not attached to these offices and residence was not required. At least in Glasgow and St Andrews dioceses archdeacons could employ their own officials, apparently to perform their jurisdictional duties for them while they furthered their careers elsewhere.[69] Despite all this, in the period after 1340 some forty cases among 400 university men can be traced where they chose to reside at a cathedral centre for at least a few years and sometimes for very much longer, especially at Glasgow, Aberdeen and Elgin.[70] Some university men must surely have been found resident in nearly all the cathedral communities most of the time.

We can find firmer ground for being sure that the bishoprics of the country came in time to be all-but the preserve of university men. No figures can be produced for the thirteenth century, when quite a number of bishops are known to us only from very scrappy evidence. But we can observe a notable group of graduates in the principal sees at the time of crisis with Edward I at the turn of that century (Fraser and Lamberton at St Andrews; Wischard at Glasgow; Moravia at

Moray; Dundee at Ross; Crambeth and Sinclair at Dunkeld): they stand out as a highly qualified bunch. Then in the seventy-five years between 1350 and 1425 we can be more certain of our ground: at least four-fifths of episcopal appointments in this period are known to have gone to university men and perhaps more.[71] In England the proportion was rather smaller.[72] It is pretty certain that in Scotland by the end of our period it was highly unusual for any episcopal appointment not to go to a university man. Here presumably is a key reason for the customary return of most of such men from abroad to make their careers at home. There were top jobs to be had.

The place of the regular clergy in the general picture needs to be considered separately. Dominican friars at any rate are likely to have included university study as a normal part of their training; but most Dominicans who occur in Scottish records are mere names, even if it is quite likely that, following a common custom of the order, Scots were sent back to their home country after training abroad. A few attract notice because they became bishops, always of poor sees — Clement at Dunblane as early as the 1230s, William Comyn at Brechin in 1275, three successive bishops of Argyll in 1264, 1300 and 1342[73] (two of them apparently belonging to the local magnate family of Macdougall, lords of Lorn), and Adam de Lanark, king's confessor, appointed to Galloway in 1364. These were, of course, not typical Dominicans. Nor among the Franciscans was John Duns Scotus, the scholar of international reputation at the end of the thirteenth century at Oxford, Cambridge and Paris, nor Thomas de Rossy, who studied theology to doctorate level in England and Paris, and served his order in Scotland before employment as a penitentiary at the Roman court, whence he was sent home by Pope Clement VII in 1379 to be Bishop of Galloway. The later-fourteenth-century English kings came to look with suspicion at foreign friars at Oxford: in 1373 the Dominicans there had to obtain a licence from the king's council in each case before admitting foreigners;[74] and in 1388 the Franciscans were ordered to admit only those for whose loyalty to the king they were prepared to vouch.[75] It does not sound very welcoming.

There is not much sign that any Scottish monks or regular canons went near universities in the thirteenth century, though one Augustinian canon of St Andrews is found as a Master in the 1270s (Hervey de Dundee). In the early fourteenth century a Tironensian abbot of Kilwinning (William de Deyn) is found as a Licentiate of Canon Law, making good use of his skills as a litigant for his community; but he may well have studied before he became a monk. A much more positive approach followed the reforming decrees of Pope Benedict XII in the 1330s, under which it was mandatory for the larger Benedictine, Cistercian and Augustinian houses to maintain about one in twenty of their number in university towns.[76] Not many Scottish monasteries are likely to have been so large; but there is evidence for at least twelve houses arranging for some of their number to go to universities to study theology or canon law (the only permitted subjects) in the later fourteenth century.[77] Sometimes a papal licence was obtained by individual monks to cover the use of conventual revenues for this purpose.[78] The implication of these licences seems to be that some monastic superiors were failing in their duty to send the correct proportion of their communities to universities; but perhaps in some cases at least it was more a matter of securing formal papal backing to ensure that favoured monks were provided with a regular income whilst away at university.[79] Clearly as a result of this policy the intellectual level of at least some of the Scottish monasteries rose appreciably towards the end of our period. This was particularly true of St Andrews, where the Augustinian prior of the cathedral, James Bisset (a canon lawyer), was especially active in encouraging members of his community to seek university degrees, and then became much involved with Bishop Wardlaw in 1410 in founding a university. The cathedral priory was most hospitable to the masters and students of the new institution, in which the next prior, James de Haldeston, was to play a dominant part as Dean of Theology. By the early fifteenth century, then, monks and canons were a regular part of the university scene, as friars had been since the thirteenth century.

Trevor Aston and his fellow-authors conclude a study of Oxford and Cambridge thus: 'What strikes us most forcefully in the assembled evidence is the burgeoning importance of university men going back almost as far as the record will take us'.[80] This is the impression north of the Border also; but what kinds of importance can be identified so far as Scotland is concerned? Clearly some students died young and others have left little record of their activities because they did not have striking success in their careers. And the numbers of university men in Scotland were in the nature of things in our period never very large. But they can be observed as a class with distinctive characteristics in Scottish society. For one thing they had all been abroad. Of course they were not the only social group to travel — some merchants, a few soldiers, some crusaders, some pilgrims had the same experience; but all university men had this added dimension. With men of this kind in so many diverse occupations, whether behind the scenes or taking full responsibility in public life, Scotland was kept up with changing ideas and contemporary events in other countries. The reduced movement of these men, however, to just France and Avignon for much of the fourteenth century must surely have brought a period of narrower horizons. Perhaps a consolidation of the Franco-Scottish alliance was one result; but for Scotland to be cut off from fourteenth-century Italy was a serious cultural loss.

Learning for its own sake attracted few students for long then as now. University qualifications were for most people a means to an end;[81] they could lead to careers that must have been as attractive in job-variety for the ambitious as they were in material rewards. It is true that there were few, if any, professions in which university men established a closed shop in our period; but their educational qualifications did help many to rise high, and it has been particularly interesting to note how some undertook further study in middle life in order to rise even higher. At least in the eyes of the bureaucrats at the Roman court who controlled the rules regarding accumulation of profitable benefices, these qualifications had a market value.[82] University men were a privileged group who were thought to deserve successful careers. There is also some evidence that young masters who in their university days were elected to high administrative office (such as the rectorship at Paris) attracted attention which might lead to early promotion in professional life, rather like modern presidents of the Oxbridge Unions.[83] Everyone had to gain the attention of patrons, whether for jobs or benefices. University men were certainly helped regularly as a favoured group by successive popes; but they needed local patronage also, and so ties with lay and ecclesiastical patrons back home had to be maintained during years of study abroad. If this was irksome, there was compensation in the form of one great advantage demonstrably shared by university men, and this was the network of contacts (perhaps even friendships) which they established in their days of study and teaching between student and master and between fellow-students. We find people having parallel careers, meeting again in the royal service, on judicial business, in parliament, at meetings of cathedral chapters and of bishops.[84] And ecclesiastical patrons at home sometimes took the chance to help the careers of fellow university men whom they had known previously, besides university men in general.[85] There must have been a consciousness of shared experience, which probably led to clannishness. The common academic type of training must surely have provided the whole class of university men with a common cast of mind which enabled them to communicate efficiently with each other. This is most obviously demonstrable in the case of lawyers, who regularly chose to fill gaps in the national system of law with what they calmly asserted to be authoritative rules from Roman Civil and Canon Law.[86] University men had acquired wisdom from the study of revered set texts from the ancient and early Christian worlds; they had learned to evaluate these texts in accordance with the methods of the schools; they were prepared to apply this method to new problems that came their way, and were receptive to similar efforts by colleagues and superiors whose technique they appreciated. Thus was a sophisticated and civilised system of human relations in Scotland governed for two hundred years by attitudes imported by home-coming university men after their studies in other parts of Europe.

NOTES

1. For details see D. E. R. Watt, *A Biographical Dictionary of Scottish Graduates to A.D.1410* (Oxford, 1977), from which various figures mentioned here have been calculated (excluding the twelfth century). This book should be consulted regarding all graduates named in this study for the sources which support the text here.

2. See graduation lists in *Acta Facultatis Artium Universitatis Sancti Andree 1413–1588*, ed. A. I. Dunlop (Edinburgh, 1964).

3. E.g. Alexander de Brothy, (2) William Brown, Columba de Dunbar, William Fayrhar, William de Fores, Laurence Kant, William de Kynbethoc, Laurence Laverok, Hugh Raa.

4. T. H. Aston, G. D. Duncan and T. A. R. Evans, 'The medieval alumni of the university of Cambridge', *Past and Present*, no. 86 (1980), 27. See also R. N. Swanson, 'Universities, graduates and benefices in later medieval England', *ibid.*, no. 106 (1985), 35, n.31.

5. See lists in Watt, *Dictionary*, 386–7, 450.

6. *Auctarium Chartularii Universitatis Parisiensis*, vols. i–ii, ed. H. Denifle and E. Chatelain (Paris, 1894–7).

7. *Calendar of Entries in the Papal Registers relating to Great Britain and Ireland, Petitions to the Pope*, vol. i only, ed. W. H. Bliss (London, 1896); continued as *Calendar of*

Scottish Supplications to Rome, vols. i–iii, *1418–1432* (Scottish History Society, 1934–70), vol. iv, *1433–1447* (University of Glasgow Press, 1983).

8. *Calendar of Entries . . . Ireland, Papal Letters*, ed. W. H. Bliss and others (London, 1894–).

9. A bolder approach has been attempted for medieval alumni of Oxford and Cambridge, where the available biographical information has with computer help been 'encoded by twenty-year periods or 'generations' ' and then many kinds of conclusion are drawn (T. H. Aston, 'Oxford's medieval alumni', *Past and Present*, no. 74 (1977), 3–40; Aston, Duncan and Evans [as above, n.4], 9). But this method is open to serious challenge (e.g. see Swanson, 'Universities', 35), and should not even be attempted for Scottish university men, about whom comparatively little is known.

10. Aston, Duncan and Evans (as cited), 50–51.

11. A. B. Cobban, *The Medieval Universities: Their Development and Organization* (London, 1975), 198.

12. D. E. R. Watt, 'Scottish student life abroad in the fourteenth century', *Scottish Historical Review*, lix (1980), 17–19.

13. E. F. Jacob, 'English university clerks in the later middle ages', in *Essays in the Conciliar Epoch*, 3rd edn. (Manchester, 1963), 207–39, especially 234, n.3; cf. L. E. Boyle, *Pastoral Care, Clerical Education and Canon Law, 1200–1400* (London, 1981), Chapters 8–9.

14. E.g. William de Blackburn, William de Cheshelm, Richard de Creych, (1) John Dugaldi, (1) John Forrester, Walter Forrester, David de Mar, John de Peblis, William de Spyny.

15. (1) John Stewart, Thomas Stewart, Walter de Ross, Columba de Dunbar; (1) and (2) William Comyn, Alexander de Bruce, Hugh, James, (1) and (2) John de Douglas, Alexander, Ingram, James, (1) and (2) John, (1), (2) and (3) William de Lindsay; Robert, (1) and (2) William Cunyngham, James, (1) and (2) John, Robert, Thomas, (1) and (2) William Wischard, Donald Macnachtan, David de Hamilton, Walter de Danielston.

16. E.g. Alexander Barber, (2) William de Camera, Patrick de Spalding, (2) John Stewart, John Were.

17. E.g. W. de Bernham, William de Glendonwyn, Ingram de Ketenis, Donald Macnachtan, Simon de Mandeville, Robert de Moffat, Alexander, Henry and (2) Walter de Wardlaw.

18. Other examples are Thomas de Edenham, Andrew de Hawyk, Alexander de Lillesclif. See discussion in Watt, *Dictionary*, xii–xiii.

19. E.g. William Malveisin, John and Roger de Derby, Robert de Prebenda, Augustine de Nottingham, Ranulf de Wat, John de Mellento, Hugh de Meleburne, Thomas de Tynemue, Peter de Alinton, John de Cheam.

20. The Cambridge group was an aristocratic one, including Alexander de Bruce, (2) William Comyn, Walter de Ross.

21. M. Sarti and M. Fattorini, *De claris Archigymnasii Bononiensis professoribus*, ed. C. Malagola (Bologna, 1888–96), ii, 307–32.

22. See Watt, *Dictionary* under Baldred Biset, William de Eglisham and William Frere.

23. Cf. Watt, 'Scottish student life', especially 3–7; only one Scot (William de Lawedre) is known to have studied at Angers.

24. The first Scottish names in German university records appear to be those found at Cologne from 1419 onwards (*Die Matrikel der Universität Köln*, ed. H. Keussen [Bonn, 1919–31], i, 212 ff.), at Heidelberg from late 1423 onwards (*Die Matrikel der Universität Heidelberg von 1386 bis 1662*, vol. i, ed. G. Toepke [Heidelberg, 1884], 161), and at Louvain from 1426 onwards (E. Reussens, *Matricule de l'Université de Louvain* [Brussels, 1903]; J. H. Baxter, 'Scottish students at Louvain university', *SHR*, xxv [1928], 327–34).

25. The enrolled copies are printed in *Rotuli Scotiae* (London, 1816).

26. With Scotland in 1358 (*Chronicon Henrici Knighton*, ed. J. R. Lumby [Rolls Series,

1889-95], ii, 101; with France in 1360 (*Foedera*, ed. T. Rymer [London, 1704-35], vi, 292; *Chronicon Anglie*, ed. E. M. Thompson [Rolls Series, 1874], 48).

27. Thomas de Rossy OFM. As a friar he may have gone to England under a general protection issued to members of religious orders. See also Columba de Dunbar, Murdach Macalpin, Andrew MacGillance and Robert de Tyningham who were students in England after 1400, presumably under different arrangements.

28. Cf. G. Leff, *Paris and Oxford Universities in the Thirteenth and Fourteenth Centuries* (New York, 1968), 157, 160, 177, 180.

29. John Derling, David de Hamilton, Henry de Lychton, Robert de Merton, William de Narn; Walter de Dun, John Elwald, John de Crannach; Alexander de Caron, (1) John Forrester, Walter Forrester, (1) Matthew de Glendonwyn, Nicholas de Grenlaw, James de Lindsay; Malcolm de Dumbrek, William de Brenueth, Henry de Rane, Thomas de Lyn.

30. See list of eight teachers of theology, canon law and arts in *Joannis de Fordun Scotichronicon cum supplementis et continuatione Walteri Boweri [Chron. Bower]*, ed. W. Goodall (Edinburgh, 1759), ii, 445. Not all of these began to teach as early as 1410. William Fowles, for example, did not graduate in arts in Paris until 1411 (*Auctarium*[see n.6 above], ii, 100, 105-6).

31. More than thirty graduates of other universities can be traced in association with the new university. See for example the list of witnesses to Bishop Wardlaw's foundation charter of February 1412 (*Evidence . . . taken and received by the Commissioners . . . for visiting the Universities of Scotland* [London, 1837], iii, 173-4; cf. *Registrum Magni Sigilli Regum Scottorum* [Edinburgh, 1882-1914], ii, 46, no. 200).

32. E.g. David de Mar from 1350s to 1370s, (1) Walter de Wardlaw in 1370s, Alexander Trayl and Henry de Wardlaw in 1390s, Richard Hunter c.1403-8. For an example of this common phrase see *Cal.Scot.Supp.* [see n.7 above], ii, 68.

33. E.g. Gilbert Fleming, (1) Robert de Den, (2) Adam de Tyningham, Hugh de Dalmahoy, William de Narn.

34. E.g. (3) Radulf de Bosco, Thomas de Dundee, William de Fores, Alexander Trayl, John de Spyny, (2) Adam de Tyningham; cf. Hugh de Dalmahoy, who served in a cardinal's household before becoming a student.

35. Walter Trayl, Simon de Mandeville, Thomas de Butil and Richard de Creych were judges of the Rota. Trayl also held the high chancery office of referendary 1383-5 (cf. William Stephani and Patrick Spalding who held this office after the Schism in 1420s). Others in papal service were Thomas de Rossy OFM (a penitentiary), (2) Adam de Tyningham, (1) John Forrester, (2) William de Camera, Alexander Barber (though some of these may possibly have been honorary rather than working members of the papal household).

36. *Regesta Regum Scottorum*, ed. G. W. S. Barrow and others (Edinburgh, 1960-), *passim*.

37. See David de Bernham, Richard de Inverkeithing, Stephen de Donydouer, (3) William de Lindsay. The list of Chamberlains in *Handbook of British Chronology*, 2nd edn., ed. F. M. Powicke and E. B. Fryde (London, 1961), 177-9, requires amendment.

38. List *ibid.*, 173-5 requires corrections.

39. List *ibid.*, 185-6 requires amendment.

40. E.g. (1) Matthew de Aberdeen, Alan and William de Dunfres, Abel de Golin, William de Cramond, John de Keth, John de Musselburgh, Walter Forrester, John de Scheves, (1) John de Carrick, (1) John de Bothwell, (1) John Barber, David de Strivelyn, Andrew de Hawyk; cf. John de Tonirgayth.

41. *The Exchequer Rolls of Scotland* (Edinburgh, 1878-1908). *passim*.

42. E.g. Adam de Kirkcudbright, Gilbert Armstrong, Andrew de Trebrun, David de Mar, Ingram and John de Ketenis, Robert de Lany, David de Strivelyn, Richard de Cheshelm, Thomas Mercer, Andrew Ox, Stephen de Malcarston OSA, William de Blackburn, Donald Bannerman.

43. E.g. Peter de Alinton, (1) Reginald de Irewyn, Adam de Malcarston, Abel de Golin,

Master Godfrey, John de Keth, Roger de Inverness; cf. William Frere, William de Eglisham, James Ben, Adam de Moravia, Walter de Twynham, (1) Alexander de Kininmund, (1) William Bell.

44. Wardlaw was sent also to France and to parleys on the English Border; other notable envoys among the late-fourteenth-century university men were John de Peblis, Walter Forrester and John de Crannach.

45. Individual councillors can occasionally be identifed, e.g. Gilbert Fleming, John de Caron, John de Scheves.

46. Clerical proctors at the 1367 parliament included Andrew Umfray, David de Mar, Alexander de Kylwos, Alexander de Caron, Gilbert Armstrong, (1) John de Carrick.

47. *The Acts of the Parliaments of Scotland* (Edinburgh, 1814–75), i, 506, 508, 534.

48. Walter Trayl, (1) Matthew de Glendonwyn, Gilbert de Grenlaw, James Borthwick, Walter Forrester.

49. E.g. Master Alan, Hugh de Carrick, Nigel Cambel (Carrick); Adam de Thorenton (Galloway); John de Hadington (Atholl); Adam and Thomas de Kircudbright (Annandale); Robert de Tyndale (Badenoch); Richard de Strivelyn (Strathearn); John Lyon and (2) Bean Johannis (Isles); William de Cheshelm (Moray); John de Tonirgayth (March); John de Gamery (Ross); Gilbert Armstrong (Mar); (2) John Fleming (Crawford); Dugal de Lorn and Finlay Colini (Fife/Albany); Simon de Creych (Caithness/Atholl).

50. E.g. (2) Adam de Tyningham, Richard de Fogow, (1) Matthew de Glendonwyn, Alexander de Carnis, Gilbert Cavan, Matthew de Geddes.

51. (2) William Brown in Angus family c.1408; Gilbert Cavan in Douglas family c.1419.

52. E.g. William de Blackburn, Richard Knight, (1) Matthew de Glendonwyn, (2) John de Bothwell, (2) Bean Johannis, Richard Hunter.

53. E.g. William de Dunfres, William de Lamberton, William de Spyny, Michael de Monymusk, Thomas Trayl, John de Vaus, David de Malcarston.

54. E.g. Hugh de Meleburne, Adam de Malcarston, Radulf de Brade, Thomas de Carnoto, Henry de Culnehach, Simon de Carale, Malcolm de Innerpeffry, Alexander de Caron, John de Glasgow, (1) John de Hawyk, William de Strabrok; cf. Gilbert de Grenlaw (bishop's chamberlain), Thomas de Barry (bishop's chaplain).

55. S. D. Ollivant, *The Court of the Official in Pre-Reformation Scotland* (Stair Society, 1982), Chapters 3–4; for lists of holders of this office in each diocese see D. E. R. Watt, *Fasti Ecclesiae Scoticanae Medii Aevi ad annum 1638*, 2nd draft (Scottish Record Society, 1969).

56. John de Peblis and John de Drum.

57. Among uncommon commissions were those given to Peter de Campania and William de Kyngorn as vicars-general in the absence of a bishop of St Andrews in 1290s, and to James de Borthwick to same office in 1401 during the last months of life of another bishop of same see.

58. E.g. (1) William de Cunyngham, William de Eckford, Roger de Ballinbreth, William de Eglisham, Robert de Garvald, Malcolm de Gatmilk, Robert de Kidlau, William de Yetham, Andrew Ox, William de Spyny, Thomas de Stramiglot, Andrew de Trebrun.

59. E.g. Robert de Garvald, David de Strivelyn, Thomas de Kilconkar, Thomas de Edenham, William Boyle, (2) Thomas de Tyningham. No doubt the great majority of notaries practised without university qualifications.

60. E.g. (1) William de Cunyngham, Malcolm de Gatmilk, (1) William de Grenlaw, Robert de Merley, Thomas de Ayton, Walter Herok, Nicholas de Lochmaben, John de Scalpy, William de Dalgarnoch, Patrick de Spalding, John de Scheves, Richard de Cornell, John Laverok, John de Glasgow, Richard Knight, John Litstar OSA.

61. For this procedure see Ollivant, *Court of the Official*, 39–40, and Lord Cooper, *Select Scottish Cases of the Thirteenth Century* (Edinburgh, 1944). The judges involved can in many cases be traced in Watt, *Fasti* and Watt, *Dictionary*.

62. See discussion in D. E. R. Watt, 'University graduates in Scottish benefices before 1410', *Records of Scottish Church History Society*, xv (1964), 77–88.

63. E.g. Thomas de Bennum, John and Patrick de St Andrews, (3) John Scot, (3) Nicholas, Adam de Perth, Adam de Camis, (4) Thomas.

64. Watt, 'University graduates', 83–85.

65. *Ibid.*, 82–83.

66. Dornoch, Fortrose, Elgin, Aberdeen, Brechin, Lismore, Dunkeld, Dunblane, Glasgow.

67. For dignities and archdeaconries, see Watt, *Fasti;* for other canonries, whose date of foundation is often uncertain, see I. B. Cowan, 'The organisation of Scottish secular cathedral chapters', *Records of the Scottish Church History Society*, xiv (1960), 41–47.

68. J. Dowden, *The Medieval Church in Scotland* (Glasgow, 1910), 74–75.

69. Watt, *Fasti*, 190–1, 326–7.

70. E.g. John Penny, Hugh Raa, (2) John Stewart, William de Govan, (1) John de Hawyk, (2) John Wischard at Glasgow; (2) Duncan Petit, John de Dumbrek, (2) John Barber, Thomas de Edenham, Reginald de Ogston at Aberdeen; John de Ard, William Boyle, William de Cheshelm, William Gerland, (2) William de Pilmor, Alexander de Urchard at Elgin.

71. See names in Watt, *Fasti* and Watt, *Dictionary.* The succession in the diocese of the Isles is too confused to be included in these calculations. Galloway was the only mainland diocese where the appointment of apparent non-graduates was anything other than very exceptional.

72. Graduates made up just over 50% of Henry III's bishops, and nearly 70% of Edward III's (J. R. L. Highfield, 'The English hierarchy in the reign of Edward III', *Transactions of the Royal Historical Society*, 5th series, vi [1956], 126, n.1). Oxford and Cambridge together supplied the successful candidates for 36% of appointments 1216–1307, 65% of appointments 1307–99, 91% of appointments 1399–1499 (Aston, Duncan and Evans, 'Medieval Alumni', 69).

73. Laurence de Ergadia, (3) Andrew, Martin de Ergaill.

74. *Calendar of Close Rolls, Edward III* (London, 1896–1913), *1369–74*, 517.

75. *Ibid., Richard II* (London, 1914–27), *1385–9*, 519.

76. Relevant extracts of this legislation are printed in *Chartularium Universitatis Parisiensis,* ed. H. Denifle and E. Chatelain (Paris, 1889–97), ii, 448–50, 463–5, 480–1. See discussion in D. Knowles, *The Religious Orders in England,* ii (Cambridge, 1955), 3, 15, 24–25.

77. Arbroath, Kelso, Lindores; Dunfermline; Cambuskenneth, Holyrood, Jedburgh, St Andrews, Scone; Whithorn; Melrose, Sweetheart.

78. E.g. (2) William de Angus (Lindores), John de Dersy (Cambuskenneth), (2) Thomas de Kirkcudbright (Sweetheart), Alan de Auchtergaven (Dunfermline), John Cuthbertson (Arbroath).

79. John Bouer, a monk of Arbroath, was in 1403 in receipt of a pension of 20 marks from his abbey to support him as a student.

80. Aston, Duncan and Evans, 'Medieval alumni', 86.

81. Walter Bower, writing in 1440s, lamented the speed with which by then students were leaving the University of St Andrews as soon as they had obtained degrees 'and thus demean the learning which ought to distinguish them' (*Chron. Bower.* [see n.30 above], ii, 446).

82. Watt, 'University graduates', 83–84.

83. E.g. Philip Wilde (rector in 1339), (2) William de Grenlaw and (1) Walter de Wardlaw (1345), Simon de Ketenis (1359), (1) Matthew de Glendonwyn (1378–9), Robert de Cardeny (1390), Walter Forrester (1395), John de Crannach (1414–15).

84. E.g. a meeting of the Aberdeen cathedral chapter in 1392 was attended by seven university men, all of whom had been connected with Paris — two in early 1360s, two probably in late 1360s, and three in mid-1370s (*Registrum Episcopatus Aberdonensis* [Spalding Club, 1845], i, 179–82); a committee elected in parliament in 1367 contained nine known university men, four of whom had been law students together at Orléans in late

1340s, and two of whom had been master and pupil in arts at Paris in 1350s (*Acts Parl. Scot.*, i, 506).

85. Three pupils at Paris of Walter de Wardlaw (Thomas de Duns, Simon de Ketenis and John de Peblis) held prebends of Glasgow when he was bishop there 1367–87; two Paris pupils of Gilbert de Grenlaw (John and Walter Forrester) held prebends of Aberdeen when he was bishop there 1390–1421; Bishop Alexander Bur of Moray (1362–97) employed two Paris contemporaries (William de Cheshelm and William de Spyny) on diocesan business; Bishop Henry de Wardlaw of St Andrews (1403–40) employed at least three contemporaries from his student days at Avignon University (William de Strabrok, Patrick de Huyston and Richard Knight) in his household and on official business. Cf. Swanson, 'Universities', 53 for English parallels.

86. 'Fourteenth-century lawyers in Scotland . . . needed a quarry from which they could extract authoritative rules which could be used to fill gaps in the national system. The only available sources of such rules were the two bodies of law taught in the universities' (P. Stein, *Roman Law in Scotland* [Milan, 1968], 40).

2

THE FRENCH CONNECTION IN THE SIXTEENTH AND EARLY SEVENTEENTH CENTURIES

John Durkan

France suffered a huge military defeat in Scotland in 1559-60: did this also constitute a cultural defeat? Was the programme from then on to be Scottish conformity with England? Was it becoming commonplace for Scotsmen of ability to seek, at least in the higher echelons, a professional formation across the border rather than across the sea? Was the assertion of Scottish difference pushed into the background because of hostility to Catholic France, only to be taken up again some years after the foundation of Leiden university in the Low Countries? Nobody quite holds these views in these terms, but they persist as an undercurrent for lack of a definite picture as to how things were as between Scotland and France in cultural matters. Here there will be room only to examine some few facets of the continuing French impact on the Scots mind in the major fields of learning, an enquiry that will be far from exhausting the subject.

Some statistics were collected by the late W. A. McNeill, but they extend over periods that do not quite overlap. He, for instance, calculated 800 Scots names at Paris from between 1492 and 1633, 258 at Louvain in the period 1424-1527, 132 at Cambridge from 1546-1655, 70 at Geneva from 1559-1659, 31 at Heidelberg from 1570-1614.[1] He had no figures for the French provincial universities, partly because of the destruction or neglect of their records during the French Revolution and partly because of the discontinuities and disparities to be found in such records as we have. This essay likewise suffers from the absence in France of matriculation records on the German scale, yet nevertheless hopes to remedy the defect in part.

The motives of adolescents leaving Scotland in the first place were varied. With many, the attraction of higher studies under famous teachers was a potent factor, especially as no satisfactory teaching in law and medicine appears to have been available at home; and these may at least have had some initial financing from ambitious or rich relatives, one example being George Buchanan's uncle who first maintained him at Paris. Others left because of some family fall-out, in some instances for religious reasons. This religious concern was behind Thomas Smeaton's anxiety as principal of Glasgow University to win Sir Francis Walsingham's support for placing a student of divinity in Cambridge or Oxford. Scots students, he wrote, were well trained in Latin, Greek, Hebrew and all philosophy, but, once masters of arts, there were no provisions made for divinity, hence the majority were driven to France and there 'mak shipp wraik of conscience and religion'. The student for whom he appealed is found at neither English university, though he did go to live south.[2] But the danger could be just as acute in the other direction. We find John Petrie in 1608 described as having given up 'papistry' ten years earlier, solemnly embracing Protestantism at Bergerac in the Dordogne, where, after some further wanderings in France and Germany, he finally settled down.[3] Many travelled around from one academic post to another. In 1589 at Paris George Melvin was said, 'draining labour to the dregs', to have publicly taught 'in many camps of the Muses and Philosophy in France and Scotland' and so the German nation in the university accepted his entitlement to a regent's post there.[4] Robert Burnet, a youthful pedagogue at Castres in 1611, explained in a letter home to his elder brother why he needed to take up a teaching situation which provided him merely with board and 40 livres annually, a sum that in France would not even keep him in clothes, yet as much as a private post yielded in France. He found the work exhausting: 'The natur of it is (as of all uthirs in france) that I haue not half ane hour in the day to reid in ane priuat studie, and so I am compelled to tyne and spend the best of my age and most meit for study in teiching bairns, quhen I sould imploy it in studeing the Lawis'. Burnet was first regent at Nérac at 300 livres in 1613, resigning in 1615 before returning home, where, despite early hardships, he qualified as advocate in 1617.[5] Rewards for teaching were indeed unequal. John Brown of Edinburgh found his services in tiny Carpentras just as well recompensed as in Toulouse, though the appointment itself was less honourable.[6] In the end funds could only come from parents, and so contact with home had to be maintained, if possible through some official 'post,' if not, through visiting Scots traders or by way of bearers whose reliability varied. Other sources included provision for 'poor scholars'.

There is a letter of James, younger brother of John Lindsay, future Lord Menmuir, written from Paris in 1579 shortly before leaving for Geneva, where his death there the following year is commemorated in verses of Andrew Melville. His destination was Geneva, 'being pressit thereto baith be sundry writings of the ministry in Scotland, and also be an infinity of Scotsmen here, wha ye knaw, are mony ways fashious'.[7] Religious difference and poverty were two such ways.

The myth of a Scots college supporting several bursars in Paris persists. What we have are Grisy scholars, that is scholars of the bishop of Moray's foundation and revenues drawn from a farm of that name outside Paris.[8] Often even these had to supplement their incomes from other sources. There is mention in September 1519 of Mr John Williamson of Dunblane diocese, 'bursar of Grisy in Comte-Robert, Paris diocese', holder for the time of the post of porter in the College of Navarre.[9] The bursars were no more than four and are found in higher faculties than arts. For instance, on 17 December, 1537, there was a legal wrangle between John Douglas, bursar of Grisy and three fellow bursars, Archibald Hay, Mark Ker and Robert Crichton, provost of St Giles: both Douglas and Hay would later become future provosts of St Mary's College, St Andrews.[10] Four are again recorded in June 1548, led by William Cranston, 'formed' bachelor in theology, later provost of St Salvator's. Some revenues from Grisy were alienated to archers of the king's guard from 1509 and not recovered for half a century. About 1570 a petition was addressed to Queen Mary for financial help,[11] a request not immediately responded to, since in September 1571, her agent in France, Archbishop Beaton, complained that if the imprisoned Queen insisted on paying her servant, Ninian Winzet, out of the fund during his absence from the university, there would soon only be enough for three instead of four. By 1575 Mary had obliged with aid and six poor scholars were named.[12] James Cheyne at first hoped to set up his seminary for priests in Paris in 1576, a sort of new model cathedral school, inspired by the Council of Trent, but here a mission school abetted by bishops, but by bishops in exile. To this it was hoped to annexe the Grisy revenues, while lectures would be heard in the Jesuit College of Clermont, inclusive of three years' philosophy and Greek and Hebrew, followed by theology, especially controversies.[13] This was the sort of model Melville had in mind in Scotland of the university as 'anti-seminary'. Whatever temporary arrangement existed did not last, though Queen Mary's pension to scholars continued to be paid till her death, and the scholars of Grisy remained in Paris too. Although there is a mention of a hall of the Scots (*aula Scotorum*) in William Cranston's time, it would be wrong to interpret this body of Grisy scholars as a college except in terms of legal convenience, as when it is entitled 'Collegium Grysiacum' in a petition to the bishop of Moray: no more than the Royal College did the Scots College have a building till the seventeenth century.[14] Archbishop Beaton's will of 1603 made over to the poor scholars a house in the rue des Amandiers, its first principal, a doctor of law, being himself a scholar of Grisy, the overall director being the Carthusian prior in Paris.[15] Yet though there is a 'Collegium Scotorum Parisiense' mentioned in 1619, Grisy bursars were only fully amalgamated by royal decree in 1639.[16]

This seemed worth going into at length in view of prevailing misconceptions. Subsequent pages will deal more briefly with the educational situation in France for Scots, since 1560 opened wider the gap between Catholic and Reformed Scottish professionals in all learning spheres, especially in divinity, a gap so wide that it necessitated fresh centres of instruction. It seemed most convenient to take the modern map of France as the criterion for inclusion at the risk of excluding centres of French culture such as Louvain and Geneva, while making room for Douai at that time in Flanders.

To take the Catholics first, it must be said that little extra light can be thrown on their Paris college: towards 1620, it was in charge of Robert Philp and Alexander Pendrick with one more priest and five theological students.[17] But the history of the Scots college at Douai is even more unclear, bewildering because of constant flittings imposed by unsettled conditions. A new aspect is the evidence that there were Scots students at the town's university before the seminary existed. The earliest of these appears to have been James Cheyne of Arnage, a graduate of King's College, Aberdeen, in 1566.[18] Two others can now be traced there, John and George Durie, sons of the abbot of Dunfermline. They had previously been in Louvain, where they became bachelors in divinity. Letters survive written to their brother, Henry, and to the abbot. George, the elder, born in 1547, was boarded in the university college d'Anchin, while John stayed two miles away. The Duries preferred Douai as being nearer points where Scots ships arrived, and for not being predominantly Flemish. 'We may easelie,' they argued, 'recouer in duay owr franche tunge (quhilk in louan we had almost forzeit) becaus it is our common langage.'[19] George later became prefect of studies at the Jesuit college of Verdun, while John lectured in the Jesuit college of Clermont in Paris.[20] There in 1582 he issued a printed response to the polemic of the Cambridge Puritan, William Whitaker, against Edmund Campion,[21] an English Jesuit, polemic that undoubtedly circulated in Scotland. In 1588 it was reported, 'I heir that puir Mr Jhon Dury is tisic, quhilk ye knaw is incurabill diseiss, zit it is reportit that he hes guid couraige'.[22] One interesting titbit about a well-known controversialist occurs in a Durie letter of 1575: 'M. nyniane wynzett is passit licentiat heir schort quhyle syne and now is passit to rome with the byschop of Ross'.[23] Before his early death John Durie disturbed the Protestant neighbourhood with three Christmas masses at Sweetheart abbey in 1585.[24] It was not till 1580 that the first Scots college opened and that was in Lorraine at Pont-à-Mousson, but that was in temporary exile at Trier in 1585, and lacking the support of the papal alms discontinued by Sixtus V, it was extinct by 1590. Reopening in 1593 at Douai and two years later at Louvain, it again sought Douai in 1608 and was refounded there in 1612.[25]

Besides these quasi-permanent student retreats, there were Scots Catholics at the Jesuit novitiate at Tournai in Belgium on the French border, but especially at Paris university, where for the next half-century from 1560, they practically monopolised the German 'nation' there, not being replaced till after 1615 by an Irish monopoly. Few seem to have returned home except for some missionaries and crypto-Catholics. The Scots bishops abroad acted as a focus: Beaton in exile in Paris, Chisholm in Vaison, and the itinerant John Leslie. Their studies were mixed with underground activities on behalf of their imprisoned Queen, and one such exhibitioner of Mary's is worth more than a passing mention. He is George Douglas, son of an Edinburgh burgess, a graduate in St Andrews under his uncle the provost of St Mary's College, John Douglas, returning thence to Edinburgh as a Franciscan novice, ordained priest in Paris in Notre Dame, and when driven home by the attacks of the Prince de Condé on that city, taking up schoolmastering as a cover, it would seem, for missionary work in several places in England before his final capture. Passionately devoted to Queen Mary's cause, he was repeatedly interrogated and eventually sent to his death in York in 1587 as a Catholic recusant.[26]

Some post-1560 Scots taught in schools where Buchanan's friend, Florence Wilson, had formerly taught, at Carpentras and at the Collège de la Trinité at Lyons. Many were proud of their Scots teachers: Mersenne, the famous French mathematician, recalled his early training under George Crichton, royal reader in rhetoric, and John Brown, the Scots Minim.[27] Information on such Scots friars in France is, of course, very scattered, but even for Jesuit personnel sources are not always to hand. As time went on the work of such Scots in permanent exile in France must have become less relevant to conditions at home. Some did attempt to address themselves to the Scottish situation like the Jesuit, George Turnbull, who took on the prominent Aberdeen 'doctor', Robert Baron, a former St Andrews man;[28] but in the minds of foreign superiors the needs of Scotland took second place to papal concerns in central Europe. Moving away from such establishments to universities, we often find, as at Cahors, institutions where likewise the yield of information is minimal. Records exist merely of a Scots doctor of laws and one of theology, and an occasional Scots student surfaces to view.[29] One notable fact, true both sides of the religious frontier, was the almost total absence of highlanders in France.

The Scots Protestants have been more closely, if not always accurately, studied. The main distinction is that they had no pressing need of specifically Scots colleges. At Paris, at least after the foundation of the Royal public lectureships, there was no compulsion on students to matriculate, hence their situation is hard to picture, and it is easy to underestimate Protestant numbers. A letter of a first-year student written in 1564 will clarify the position in which they found themselves. The writer was hardly a typical student, though impecunious and confined in cramped quarters like most. He was George Bellenden, brother to Sir Lewis Bellenden of Auchnoull, lord justice clerk, able therefore to forward his letter by official post rather than await a merchant passing to Scotland as happened with previous correspondence. He and his room-mate, David Cunningham, had graduated two years earlier at St Andrews. In Paris, in company with a French student, they were able to share a room in the rue St Jacques, evidently one used before by other Scots searching for cheap lodgings. Bellenden was taking no chances on loss in transit, as he had been advised ever to 'wrytt the sammyn think', to ensure, as a necessary precaution that at least one of these identical newsletters got through to anxious relatives fearful always of a cataclysmic rise in the local political temperature. One reassuring item was that cousin William had secured an appointment in Rouen. Pairing off with Cunningham meant that both could compare notes in Greek and Latin, and as for the French tongue 'thair is na uthir spokin in our chalmir'. Both also attended public lectures in Greek as 'thair is na Latin at this present teachit by ony of the Kinges lectoris'. For a small monthly fee they also heard lessons from Guillon (mistranscribed in the printed version as Suittonius), not a royal lecturer, but giving a course on the epistles of Guillaume Budé. But their cash was limited. 'Thair is na thing sa deir in this toun as bukes', and where, until the session opened, Greek books had cost a mere 'lyard', now the price was 'hichted to four denners'. Books would be the most expensive item henceforward, for Bellenden had already sent home a bill for the cost of winter clothing and of the journey from Scotland.[30] Young Bellenden was lucky in his relations. Others would find studying abroad more taxing on their purses. While abroad one could keep a friendly or a wary eye on other tutors and their charges. Thus Thomas Hamilton of Priestfield, father of the first earl of Haddington, having sent to one of his kinsmen, James McCartney, a report on two scholars who were in Paris with him, was asked 'that my maister may knaw the samyn', while not forgetting the scholars next time, also to 'tak panis to knaw quhow James Makgill and his maister prosperis in thair letteres and thair conversatioun'. The pedagogue in question was Patrick Adamson, future archbishop.[31]

It was not till after the Edict of Nantes (1598), granting the French Protestants about 200 fortified towns, that their academies became important. Saumur, the greatest of these, was a useful counterbalance to Catholic Angers; Die to Lyons; Orange to Avignon and Carpentras; Nimes to the Jesuits at Tournon; Sedan to Pont-à-Mousson; Castres and Montauban to Cahors and Toulouse. There was no counterpoise to Paris, and when Walter Donaldson projected an academy at nearby Charenton he was circumvented. After the assassination of Henri IV the situation of Protestants declined steadily, though the final hammer-blows at their educational system had to await the Revocation of the Edict of Nantes in 1685. However, before the Edict, Scots Protestants had free access, as far as law and medicine went, to universities anywhere in France. Indeed when it was proposed to add a law faculty to Pont-à-Mousson in 1579, the Jesuits complained to the duke of Guise that members of such faculties would never subject themselves to Jesuit college discipline, that there were many famous law universities with which they could not hope to compete and that Protestants — Germans in particular — already superabounded in places like Bourges and Poitiers.[32] In the new Protestant academies, Scots were often professors of philosophy rather than of Greek and Hebrew, and thus philosophy deserves a mention, however brief.

In philosophy, as in much else, the growing significance of the Paris colleges is often overlooked. In some, like those of Cambrai or Ave Maria, the royal readers occasionally taught, so that pedagogues might look for rooms for their charges thereabouts. Others, like Montaigu at the beginning of the century, were considered reactionary by humanists, as they specialised in the language games of logic, anathema to most of them. Others held the attraction of famous figures like Buchanan's college of Cardinal Lemoine, 'at the sign of the cardinal's hat', where Thomas Randolph, the English ambassador, found the only token of holiness in his fellow-student, William Kirkcaldy of Grange.[33] Much ink has been spilled concerning the influence on Scots university teaching of Pierre de la Ramée (Petrus Ramus), but there are other French influences of a less discernible kind. At the college of Sainte Barbe, where both John Mair and Buchanan had been, there was a constant trickle of Scots, all thinkers independent of Ramus. Some of these had taught in St Andrews or Aberdeen, where presumably the doctrine they dispensed was not very different, and the trend at Sainte Barbe was certainly not Ramist. The massacre of St Bartholomew in which Ramus was a victim helped his reputation among the Reformed, and it may be, with his stress on praxis or 'use', his name meant more to Scottish divines than to professional logicians or grammarians who mostly continued to follow Jean Pellisson or similar disciples of Johannes Despauterius, the acknowledged model chosen by Scots grammar compilers of the Renaissance. A disputed question is how soon Ramism entered Scots universities. Certainly John Rutherford was not favourable, preferring the Aristotle in Ciceronian Latin of his master, Nicolas de Grouchy.[34] But what are we to make of Roland McIlmaine, a graduate of St Mary's College in 1570? Must we ascribe his Ramism to his St Mary's regents, one of whom was, we know, Alexander Hamilton, or was Ramism part of Andrew Melville's revolution in university training? Hamilton was certainly in Paris both as tutor to Mark Kerr of Newbattle and as Queen Mary's pensioner, but that was momentarily and after his teaching days at St Andrews were over.[35] The title of McIlmaine's 1574 version of

Ramus's logic, published in London, referred to 'P. Ramus Martyr' as its author, but also as corrected after 'the mynde of the author'. How was such correction possible if McIlmaine did not know Ramus personally before the assassination of 1572? The answer is that it is highly probable he did, for McIlmaine himself studied in Paris in 1571, that is, a year after he had already left St Andrews behind him.[36]

It was a fortunate thing that most academically qualified Scots lawyers went to study their specialism in France. A brief review cannot do justice to the French movement, but it is enough here to indicate that it largely grew out of the application of new linguistic techniques to venerable texts. Finally these concerted achievements were shaped into organised form by Hugues Doneau and the great Jacques Cujas. Though philosophy was not absent from all this rethinking, a new impetus towards a less philological and more rational approach was to come in time from Holland, but there was no sign of its arrival till after 1600. Protestant influences may have been paramount in Scots theology, but as yet they were no more paramount in law than they were in philosophy, at least not in any simple sense of a rewriting of the law. Yet it was recognised early that a new canon law was a *desideratum* as a counter to the secular concerns of the civilists, though in fact Scots lawyers continued to equip themselves in both laws in their university studies. The problem is highlighted by Sir Thomas Craig employing canonist theory while simultaneously denouncing it as a papal invention.[37] Pierre Pithou among others tried to come to grips with the sources of canon law, he by editing a manuscript containing a comparison of the law of Moses and the Code,[38] and one of William Welwood's books produced parallel citations from divine and human law to demonstrate their congruence in essentials, a mere skeleton outline, however.[39] Welwood also turned his talents to maritime law, whose sources were largely French.[40] Here he had a rival who invoked the same wayward patron, Francis Stewart, earl of Bothwell, a former student at Angers. The author was Alexander Regius or King (not Roy, as Lord Clyde rendered it), deputy judge-admiral whose father also had worked in the Admiralty Court. King's background was very French, having studied at Louvain, Douai, Paris and Angers, Craig himself paying tribute to him as one of learned legists of the time.[41] He was brother to Adam Regius or King, who also inherited maritime interests, though confined to printing a table of tides as an addendum to his translation of a Jesuit catechism.[42]

Of Scots students in law before 1560, aside from those at Orléans, our information is patchy.[43] Two bishops, Gordon of Aberdeen and Dunbar of Glasgow, were students at Angers. Bishop John Leslie, who spanned the Reformation divide, trained at Paris, Poitiers and Toulouse. Two notable jurists were products of Bourges, Henry Scrimgeour and Edward Henryson.[44] About William Skene, first the canonist, then the commissary, at St Andrews, we have no direct information, but it is likely that he too studied there, for he owned a rare little oration delivered in its law schools but unknown to bibliographers, *Oratiuncula in schola Biturigum*, listed in his inventory, but also, more significantly, manuscript notes of Hugues Doneau, 'Annotationes hugonis duelli' (*sic* for 'donelli'), as the scribe carelessly wrote, describing it as a paper book, 'liber chartaceus.'[45] At the risk too of superimposing more years on the already venerable Robert Howie who died in the 1640s, having been successively principal of Marischal College, Aberdeen, and of St Mary's at St Andrews, we have to add two further items to his biography: for we find him at two law universities, in 1571 at Poitiers and at Toulouse in 1574, and that before he even began his theological pilgrimage to the German centres of learning.[46]

The prospective student's ideal was to proceed wherever famous teachers could be found. Alexander Sym, junior, admitted advocate in 1588, declared that since his first youth he had studied 'guid letteris' before passing to France 'quhair be the space of thre zeris I completit my resort ordinar to the lawis, sumytyme extraordinarlie resorting to the maist lernit and cunning men, bissenis and conferences', but, alas, his student days were broken off by the death of his parents.[47] Hercules Rollock was probably one of those who paid for his studies by teaching on the side. In September 1578 a plea was made in the town hall of St Maixent in Poitou that the regents in the schools were unfit persons since they spoke no French. The principal responded by presenting a Scots regent who had been in France for seven and a half years. It is doubtful that Rollock was away from Aberdeen for as long as that, but some link with the town is needed to explain verses he prefaced to a booklet printed in honour of a native of St Maixent achieving his doctorate in medicine.[48] Some of these 'maist lernit' men to whom Scots addressed themselves may have been Scots also. A French lawyer, Etienne Baluze, paid a flattering tribute in his life of Petrus de Marca to the latter's former preceptor, James Kidd of Dundee, Latinised as 'Cadanus', professor of canon law at Toulouse from 1591 till 1614, manuscript notes of whose lectures are preserved at Paris: 'Thereafter for three continuous years he heard civil and canon law at Toulouse which at that time was easily ahead of others in Europe in juristic learning, attending great doctors like Guillaume Maran, William (*sic*) Kidd, Scot, Vincent Chabot and Jean de La Coste, who then professed both laws publicly in that city. But above all he followed Kidd commenting then on Novellae 123 of the emperor Justinian; a man, as he would relate, expert in both laws, but a wonderful canon lawyer, and one who added humane letters to his knowledge of civil and canon law. He deplored the backwardness of those who would find Kidd obscure. I remember well how he used to expound the excellent method of studying canon law taught him by that man, and how he would extol the stimulus Kidd gave to spur on the young mind, proceeding to praise too his industry and shrewdness combined in him with an inborn literary flair'.[49]

Of those who entered as advocates before the Court of Session in the period 1560 to 1600, several do not specify academic qualifications, but of those who do the vast majority qualified in France. The first post-Reformation applicant noted, John Logie, a student at Bourges, asked for admission as a licentiate in both laws, 'and the lordis obseruand his admission be the doctoris in burges of berry and his qualifications', granted his request.[50] It is noteworthy that with a single exception all such applicants were qualified in canon as well as civil law. Of special St Andrews interest is William Skene's successor as law professor, John Arthur, kinsman of Archbishop Adamson. On his admission as advocate Arthur stated, 'I heifing completit my burss of philosophie and techit the samin publiclie diuers zeirs in the uniuersitie of Sanctandrois theireafter I past to the partis of france and thair in the uniuersiteis of poitiers and tulloyis and uthers I appleit my self to the studie of gud lettres and namelie of the lawis and profession tharof be the space of sevin zeiris'.[51] Other distinguished luminaries of the Scottish legal scene were likewise in France, James Elphinstone, future Lord Balmerino, and, on the evidence of a note on his father's copy of *Regiam Majestatem,* Sir Thomas Henryson of Chesters, both of them students at Poitiers.[52] After 1600 influences other than French began to make themselves felt, though slowly. Nathaniel Udwart from Leiden, son of an Edinburgh merchant burgess, was admitted advocate in 1600, but he was, it seems, too interested in trade experiments to influence the legal trend.[53] A more serious candidate might be another Edinburgh man, John Murdison, schoolmaster once in Middelburg, whom the Dutch historians tend to kill off in 1605, but who, having studied law concurrently with his arts teaching at Leiden, came home as advocate in 1607 and was still alive in 1618. He might be a more serious candidate for the reversal of the pro-French trend in Scots law since his whole training hitherto, in Helmstedt and Wittenberg, had been German.[54]

The study of medicine in France did not make the strides that it made in Italy or later in Holland. Basically it meant a slavish reading of texts. The French had reason to glory in the work of Guillaume Cop in producing versions of Galen and Hippocrates from the Greek, and such Scots academics as read some medicine, John Douglas and John Rutherford for instance, were well read in such established texts.[55] In France the accepted medical wisdom was based on purging and bleeding. Good health depended on the correct blend of the four humours. The liver, heart and brain had their parts to play: the liver to make blood and pump it all over the body; the heart to supply the arteries; and the brain to turn the blood into nervous juices. Any tear or blockage threw this equilibrium out, and so the Paris physicians responded with a technique of bleeding, while those of Montpellier turned to purging to restore the body's lost balance. But Joseph Duchesne or Quercetanus, a Huguenot and Paracelsian, who preferred the new metallic drugs like mercury and antimony, was favoured by some academics including Robert Boyd of Trochrague, though Boyd was not himself by profession a physician.[56]

Of Paris we are imperfectly informed and likewise of Orange, where students often went to finish their doctorates at less expense to their purses. At Montpellier there were several Scots students of medicine even before 1600, but between then and 1638 at least twenty-six, including George Sharp, professor afterwards at Bologna.[57] They were not all Protestants. Patrick Hepburn, who subsequently practised in Edinburgh, was from the Scots College, Rome, and Edward Scott had been in the Scots College, Douai.[58] David Echlin later took his doctorate in Caen and some years after that, along with George Eglisham in 1618, his bachelorship in Paris. Eglisham met with some opposition from the Paris faculty censor who challenged his certificate of study from Louvain, affirming that he had acted towards his colleagues less than modestly.[59] However, the official was overruled by the presentation of letters of the university in Eglisham's favour. There was some tension between the two great universities in the north and south. Paris was unswervingly pro-Galen and thus put up a stormy resistance to William Harvey's theory of the circulation of the blood. In the three Montpellier Scots medical theses of George Sibbald, Abernethy and Sharp there is no evidence of medical novelty, and one suspects that this unexampled devotion to medicine was a new one, not unconnected with the fact that the new king of Great Britain liked to have Scottish medicos in his entourage.[60]

The move south had been a blow to whatever endowed medicine existed in Scotland, in Aberdeen at the Court's expense, or at the Court, in the person of Gilbert Skene, at Aberdeen's expense.[61] Even so, by accident, Scottish medicine benefited from the plethora of would-be royal physicians in London, a queue of expectants for appointment as extraordinary doctors to James, and thereafter as physicians in ordinary, the summit of medical ambition. Abernethy wrote to John Craig, whom James VI would take south with him, with news of his condition and noting the superabundance of physicians in England; this was while Craig was still in Scotland and Abernethy still at Bordeaux, perhaps as yet undecided about medical studies, although, when he was thinking about becoming a divine and still in Scotland attached to the household of the young earl of Glencairn, it was Craig who counselled him to turn his mind to medicine.[62] Yet Abernethy never managed to insinuate himself into the royal service. Around the king's deathbed some years later were some Scots, including James Chalmers, a one-time colleague of Abernethy at Nimes, one of those testifying that the king died naturally.[63] Another, whom a contemporary characterised as 'a mad Scottish poet and physician', Dr George Eglisham, in a fiery pamphlet printed at Frankfurt accused the duke of Buckingham of having poisoned James. He also professed to have seen a roll of names due for the same treatment, among them the marquess of Hamilton and himself.[64] Eglisham was royal physician for a decade, and as such had turned a critical eye on the scholarship of Buchanan's psalm paraphrases, but his secret marriage by a priest in the Clink, secret to keep it from James's ears, does not seem to have helped his career either as personal physician or as member of the London Royal College.[65] Arthur Johnston, who broke into the royal magic circle enough to be physician extraordinary to Charles I, complained in acid verses about the hearty condition and consequent slowness to oblige by dying of the physicians in ordinary, a thoughtlessness on their part that retarded the movement up the ladder of Court promotion. The alternative was not to take up practice in Edinburgh, a bad medical patch in which to settle on account of the obstinately rude health of its robust inhabitants.[66] All in all, the plethora of expectants augmented the number of practitioners in Scotland, and that in time had a civilising influence.

The catchpenny titles of most medical works from the Edinburgh presses concerned either the virtues of tobacco or the therapeutic advantage of taking the waters. Gilbert Skene, James VI's second-order physician (Gilbert Moncrieff being house physician), had drawn attention to the well of Womanhill, Aberdeen, and he was French-trained.[67] The theme was taken up by Dr William Barclay and again by Patrick Anderson who was with Barclay in Paris in 1603. Well aware that in Scotland water was not exactly the national drink, Anderson prefaced his *Colde Spring of Kinghorne Craig* with the admission that water was 'but a warish and taistles subject, whereof manie lyke litle to heare, far less to taist ... ' Among diseases curable by taking the waters were those brought on by over-indulgence, by 'superfluous drying of Cuppes'. The metallic qualities in the water produced these benefits, but not as 'my verie lerned frend and old Parisien acquentance, Dr William Barclay', claimed, along with the Paracelsians, merely because of their tin content.[68] Anderson also made pills that he called 'angel grains', a chemical concoction that he first found in the Martinelli brothers' shop in Venice near the Rialto. These he put up for sale in Paris in 1603, and then, on his return, at the head of the West Bow in Edinburgh, where they sold merrily for three centuries. His booklet, *Grana Angelica*, did not appear until 1635, heralded by the verses of two Edinburgh University principals commending the pills to those with the painful obstructions he so feelingly depicted. One might think it a mercy that the poor were spared the quirky attentions of such high-class quackery through inability to afford the fees that his patrons, the Earl and Countess of Mar, provided. He had his solemn side as editor of his minister's meditations, though he saw the Rev. James Caldwell as a spiritual Sir Philip Sidney, coining for his book the title *The Countesse of Marres Arcadia*, and he shows an urbane jocularity absent from many of his contemporaries. He claimed he too was a poor man, wryly confessing that the doctor had three faces: the face of an angel when his counsel was sought, next of a god when offering his help, and finally having effected a cure and requesting his fee, a face every bit as horrid as that of Satan himself.[69]

In theology, the watershed on the Protestant side was the Synod of Dordrecht of 1618 condemning Arminianism: it may be that comments by participants after that date obscure their role before it. It has been claimed that Ramism led to ecclesiastical turmoil as Beza thought it would, and it is not easy to judge from Scottish theses where Scottish theology stood in these matters. But there was certainly sympathy at St Andrews for the German theologian, Johannes Piscator, stemming from Johnston, Howie and Melville, for his Ramist doctrine, and his dichotomy between Christ's life and his death, so that only his saving death and not his whole sacrificial human existence was the basis of man's salvation. There was also a feeling generally that certain questions were still open among the Reformed. Hence the tolerance shown by Melville and other Scots to Daniel Tilenus at Sedan; in 1613 John Welsh, Knox's son-in-law, shows himself sympathetic to Tilenus, and the St Andrews professors had attempted to mediate through Philippe Duplessis Mornay, governor of Saumur, the theological school, in which John Cameron, another Ramist, was a notable defender of semi-Arminian views.[70] At the age of 28, as pastor of Verteuil and Ruffec, Robert Boyd of Trochrague produced a list of theologians he favoured, a list excluding Perkins, Rollock and Gomarus, but including Piscator and the doctrinal poet, Du Bartas; while his favoured philosophers included Ramus, somewhat cancelled by the presence of the Jesuits Fonseca and Toletus, and the anti-Ramist, Isaac Casaubon.[71] In 1611, Pierre du Moulin, minister in Paris, met the newly exiled

Andrew Melville on his way to join Tilenus at the academy of Sedan. Though disapproving of Tilenus and Piscator, the Frenchman was unwilling to press Melville on the point, as he had heard the Scot was rather choleric, and this although convinced that by such views 'the foundations of our faith are like to be shaken'.[72] In 1606 Arthur Johnston was on such good terms with Tilenus that he called his son Daniel after him and had Tilenus as godfather. Tilenus grew more and more Arminian, yet verse exchanges between him and the two Scots continued. As late as 1617 a Sedan thesis appeared with versified felicitations by both Tilenus and Melville, the latter even praising Tilenus as an avenger of God's justice in his theory of justification.[73] Boyd's later position was affected by his Leiden correspondent, André Rivet, who did his utmost to win him to what became the majority view. An embittered Tilenus, sacked by Sedan, did not help his position with the Scots after Dordrecht by attacking them in general as zealots for Geneva.[74]

Too little account has been taken of development under French and other influences, except in purely literary spheres, where the impact of Ronsard, Saluste du Bartas and Desportes has long been appreciated. In an unpublished eclogue to his cousin, Mark Alexander Boyd, Robert, the future divine, describes the cosmological poem, 'La Semaine', of Du Bartas in these words:
'Soitque dedans nos vers, de la ronde machine
Descrire nous voudrons la source et l'origine
En tallonant les pas de ce divin Saluste
Qui entre les Gaulois, par jugement très juste
Seul emporte le prix, filz aisné d'Uranie'.

Surprisingly he had also some high-flown Latin lines of praise of the Catholic principal of Bordeaux' college de Guienne as a new year offering for 1599, and also to the future Court poet, Sir Robert Ayton, evidently with him in that town.[75] Boyd also sets out his proposals for the teaching of rhetoric, which could be relevant to procedures at Glasgow of which he became principal.[76] Even in those days doubts were cast on the value of rhetoric, but public orations were the order of the day, and those of the Protestant principal of the academy at Nérac, John Matheson, highly savoured at the time. Some who offered their services at home were neglected. Adam Abernethy had cared for the Viscount Cranborne, son of Cecil, while at Montpellier, and duly wrote to a fellow Scot at the court of Prince Charles on 2 January 1614. He told Sir Robert Ker that he would be worth taking on as the prince's physician in view of his other qualifications entitling him to become royal librarian or successor to William Camden in his heraldic and historical duties:[77] 'If auld Salisbury had leiffit, he gaue me assurance of his fauours for sum seruice done to his sone in Montpelier. Sundry of my Frends both Inglische and scottis a few zears sence told me that auld Camden his place in Ingland is evir gevin to ane literat man versit in Genealogies, antiquiteis, medailles, and armes with ther coulours, blasons, escussons, emblemes and deuises etc to qhiche gentilesses and recreations having tyme and lasur fra my ernistir studeis of theologie and medecine, I haue giffen my salf. I mycht haue the office and tytill coniunctly of the prince his Historien and Medecinir. (*In*

margin:-Princes lykuyse hes bibliothecairs the quhilk cassaubon had in france).'
King James took the hint by appointing Thomas Dempster as his historiographer
royal![78]

Dempster's name is a reminder that there is a good seam of Scottish biography
to be mined in local French records. His life, as we know, was lived in the middle of
a whirlwind, and the hitherto unknown French slice of it was no less colourful.
Because he is usually presented as a perfervid Scot who was also a perfervid
Catholic, it has been doubted that he could have been author of a recantation now
lost but printed formerly at La Rochelle in 1604, *Déclaration et Confession de foy
de M Thomas Dempster par laquelle it renonce au papisme*. Clues can be found in
several places, however. First of all he was in that neighbourhood producing a
Latin play, *Stilicho*, for the school at St Maixent.[79] Secondly we find from an
Edinburgh publication of his in 1608 that a friend was 'Johannes Rosa', that is
John Ross. Ross, from Glasgow diocese, is first mentioned in 1588 in a work of
Thomas Bicarton, and he was then at Poitiers, maintaining that Bicarton's
eloquence had persuaded him to abandon his studies in divinity.[80] André Rivet
was Ross's student, a Scot, he claims 'who at the time professed publicly in the
academy of La Rochelle', before, that is, 1590 when Rivet moved to Béarn. There
are some manuscript lectures Ross delivered at La Rochelle as commentator on the
logic and physics of the Franciscan Frans Titelmans, an author favoured in
pre-Melville days at Glasgow University. Later in 1598 Ross may have moved to
Saintes where he was teaching the French minor poet, Pierre Arquesson. Thus we
can hardly doubt that Ross met Dempster in the vicinity of La Rochelle.[81]

From there he went briefly to Catholic Toulouse. Soon he accepted the
invitation of Abernethy and Andrew Currior to go to Protestant Nimes (not to
Montpellier, which has misled biographers).[82] At Nimes he was appointed to the
royal chair of eloquence in November, 1604. There is a thesis of early 1605
presided over by Abernethy to which Dempster contributed some lines of verse,
lines addressed to the magistrates of présidial of the town. Soon he would have
need of their help. His appointment had not met with general approval and in
March he was set on by some Germans. At first he got support, but later a cabal
against him was formed, and at six one morning in the town hall a decision was
taken to deprive him without giving the Scot a hearing. An anonymous pamphlet,
Veneris monumentum nefandae, produced by the local printer, accused him of
pederasty; its authors are said to have been the college principal, Isaac Cheiron,
and a municipal luminary, Chalas. A letter from Nimes to Casaubon, dated 26
April, 1605, shows him still in prison. The 'consistoire' was consulted and three
ministers testified: Dempster had attended the Lord's supper, a fact that told in
his favour. His crime seems to have been to comment rather freely on the poet,
Martial. The affair was referred back to the college by the court of the parliament
of Toulouse and the chamber of the court of the edict (of Nantes) sitting at Castres.
From there it went to the présidial at Nimes where he was cleverly defended by a
former regent turned lawyer, masculine despite his name, Anne Rulman. Thus
technically readmitted to the college, and though a nearby town was interested in
his services, Dempster decided to move on to other quarrels in other places, now

mostly Catholic places. Yet the affair simmered on. The remaining Scots produced an anonymous pamphlet, *Epidepnides*, at the same printers. They made a united front consisting of Abernethy, Alexander Inglis, James Chalmers and Hugh Lawtie. Naturally the principal was not pleased, especially as it had been financed by the town council, and soon there was a new staff of Scotsmen at Nimes.[83]

Scots indeed were to be found not only as students and teachers, but as benefice-holders and ministers in all parts of France. Some important works of theirs issued from French presses: one thinks of John Cameron at Saumur and John Sharp at Die, of philosophers like Robert Balfour and Walter Donaldson and of a talented mathematician like Alexander Anderson. Moreover, there was no department of Scottish thinking immune from French influences, and for half a century after the Reformation and beyond, at least for the Scottish elite, a policy of conformity with France was as notable as increased conformity with England. Partly this was due to favourable treaty arrangements for Scottish nationals, partly because England was not as yet hospitable to Scots scholars wishing to take up places in its universities, but most of all it was because Scots professionals became vigorous propagandists for French culture when once they returned home.

NOTES

1. Glasgow University, Ross fund collections, papers of the late W. A. McNeill, for access to which I am grateful to Professor I. B. Cowan. The standard work on Scots-French relations remains Francisque Michel, *Les Ecossais en France: Les Français en Ecosse*, 2 vols. (London, 1862).

2. *Calendar of State Papers relating to Scotland and Mary, Queen of Scots 1547-1603*, ed. J. Bain *et al* (Edinburgh, 1898-1969), henceforward *CSP*, vi, 635. He seems to be present in London in 1584, *Miscellany of the Wodrow Society* (Wodrow Soc., 1844), i, ed. D. Laing, 452. If he did enter Cambridge, it was not till seven years later.

3. Oxford, Bodleian Library, Smith MS 77 fo 101; also in Appendix to this essay, s.v. Bergerac.

4. Paris, Archives Nationales, H^3 2589, fo 203v.

5. *The Family of Burnett of Leys*, ed. J. Allardyce (New Spalding Club, 1901), 130-1; Appendix, s.v. Nérac; *The Faculty of Advocates in Scotland*, ed. Sir F. J. Grant (Scottish Record Society, 1944), 25.

6. Papers of James Brown, merchant, Edinburgh in Scottish Record Office (SRO), RH9/2/28.

7. A. W. C. Lindsay, *Lives of the Lindsays* (London, 1849), i, 328.

8. D. E. R. Watt, 'Scottish masters and students at Paris in the fourteenth century', *Aberdeen University Review*, xxxvi (1955), esp. 178-9; my note in *Innes Review* (*IR*), ii (1951), 112-3.

9. Paris, Bibliothèque de l'Université, Archives de la Sorbonne, Liber Receptoris, Registre 91, fo 185.

10. SRO, Notaries' Protocol Books, NP1/5B, Protocol Book of Edward Dickson, paged, 11-13.

11. Edinburgh, Columba House, Scottish Catholic Archives, The Book of Grisy, fos 10, 28, the large petition folded inside volume.

12. N. Winzet, *Certain Tractates*, ed. J. K. Hewison (Scottish Text Soc., 1888), i, page liii; *CSP*, v, 125.

13. H. Chadwick, 'The Scots College, Douai', *English Historical Review*, lvi (1941), 573; A. Theiner, *Annales Ecclesiastici* (Rome, 1856), iii, 112–3.

14. Paris, Bibliothèque Nationale, Liber Rectoris, MS Latin 9954, fo 77v; Book of Grisy, i; W. A. McNeill, 'Documents illustrative of the history of the Scots College, Paris', *IR*, xv (1964), 66–85.

15. *Liber Protocollorum M. Cuthberti Simonis*, ed. J. Bain and C. Rogers (Grampian Club, 1875), i, 229–238; J. Durkan, 'Grisy burses at the Scots College, Paris', *IR*, xxii (1971), 50–52.

16. *Records of the Scots Colleges at Douai, Rome, Madrid, Valladolid and Rome* (New Spalding Club, 1906), 105; McNeill, 'Documents', 67.

17. Rome, Vatican, Barberini Lat. 8614, fo 123.

18. W. P. D. Wightman, 'James Cheyne of Arnage', *Aberdeen University Review*, xxxv (1954), 369–383.

19. SRO, Durie and Pitcairn Writs, GD1/299/2 and 3; *Calendar of State Papers Foreign Series Elizabeth 1569-71*, ed. A. J. Crosby (London, 1874), nos 2005–6.

20. Appendix, s.v. Verdun; see preface to book cited below for Paris reference.

21. J. Duraeus, *Confutatio responsionis Gulielmi Whitakeri in Academia Cantabrigiensi* (Paris, 1582).

22. *Miscellaneous papers principally illustrative of events in the reigns of Queen Mary and James VI* (Maitland Club, 1834), 52.

23. SRO, Durie and Pitcairn Writs, GD1/299/3.

24. W. Forbes-Leith, *Narratives of Scottish Catholics under Mary Stuart and James VI* (London, 1889), 205.

25. Chadwick, 'The Scots College, Douai', 571–585; for the Trier period, *CSP*, xi, 611, 613.

26. *CSP*, iii, 460–1; *Unpublished documents relating to the English Martyrs 1584-1603*, ed. J. H. Pollen (Catholic Record Soc., 1908), i, 88–90, 192.

27. Hilarion de Coste, *La Vie du R. P. Mersenne* (Paris, 1649), 9, 14.

28. *Imaginarii Circuli Quadratura Catholica* (Rheims, 1628).

29. Appendix, s.v. Cahors.

30. *Acta Facultatis Artium Universitatis Sanctiandree* (Scottish History Soc., 1964), ed. A. I. Dunlop, 415 note; Historical Manuscripts Commission, *Calendar of the Laing Manuscripts in the University of Edinburgh* (London, 1914), i, 20–1.

31. Sir W. Fraser, *Memorials of the Earls of Haddington* (Edinburgh, 1889), ii, 115.

32. C. Collet, *L'Ecole doctrinale de droit publique de Pont-à-Mousson* (Paris, 1965), 7.

33. *CSP*, iii, 147.

34. J. Durkan, 'John Rutherford and Montaigne: An early influence?', *Bibliothèque d'Humanisme et Renaissance*, xli (1979), 115–122, esp. 120.

35. *CSP*, iv, 672; *Ibid.*, v, 131.

36. W. A. McNeill, 'Scottish entries in the *Acta Rectoria Universitatis Parisiensis* 1519 to c. 1633', *Scottish Historical Review* (*SHR*), xliii (1964), 78.

37. Sir T. Craig, *Jus Feudale*, ed. James A. Lord Clyde (Edinburgh, 1934), 31–48.

38. *Mosaycarum et Romanarum legum collatio ex bibliotheca Petri Pithoei I.C.* (Basle, 1574).

39. *Iuris divini Iudaeorum ac Iuris Civilis Romanorum Parallela* (Leiden, 1594).

40. Welwood dedicated his *De Aqua* (Edinburgh, 1582) to Francis Stewart, earl of Bothwell and his *The Sea Law of Scotland* (Edinburgh, 1590) to King James; the latter is reprinted in *Miscellany Volume* (Scottish Text Soc., 1933), 25–79.

41. *Acta Curiae Admirallatus Scotiae*, ed. T. C. Wade (Stair Soc., 1937), 41; SRO Dalhousie Muniments, GD45/26/50, fo 3; Craig, *Jus Feudale*, 695.

42. *Ane catechisme or schort instruction of Christian religion* (Paris, 1588).

43. J. Kirkpatrick, 'The Scottish nation in the University of Orléans 1336-1538',

Miscellany of the Scottish History Society, ii, 47–102. We have no details, but between 1550 and 1793 there were 243 Scots at Rheims medical school, R. Bénard, 'Le centre medical universitaire de Reims', *Histoire de la Médecine*, i (1951), 41.

44. Appendix, s.v. Bourges, Paris, Poitiers, Toulouse.

45. Testament-inventory, St Andrews University Archives, SS110 AP2.

46. Contrary to the accepted view, Howie was already graduate in 1575, *Registrum Magni Sigilli Regum Scotorum*, ed. J. M. Thomson *et al* (Edinburgh, 1882–1912), v, 2360, but he clearly graduated before 1571 when he was at Poitiers, contributing two Latin epigrams to Caye Iule de Guersens, *Panthée*, a tragedy 'from the Greek of Xenophon', and at Toulouse as evidenced by his signature dated 1574 in Pliny Secundus, *Epistolarum libri x* (Paris, 1533), copy in the National Library of Scotland, SRO Commissariot of St Andrews, Testaments, CC20/4/10. unfoliated says he died in 1626, but he survived for another 20 years.

47. SRO, Books of Sederunt of the Lords of Council and Session, CS1/4/1/ fo lv.

48. *Journal de Guillaume et de Michel le Riche*, ed. A. D. de la Fontenelle de Vaudoré (St Maixent, 1846), 297–8, 303.

49. *Stephani Baluzii tutelensis canonici Remensis Epistola ad ... Samuelem Sorberium ... de vita ... Petri de Marca* (Paris, 1663), 10.

50. SRO, Books of Sederunt, CS1/2/1. fo 79.

51. Ibid., CS1/3/1. fo 115.

52. J. Plattard, 'Scottish masters and students at Poitiers', *SHR*, xxi (1924), 85 and s.v. Poitiers.

53. *Album Studiosorum Academiae Lugduno Batavae*, ed. G. du Rieu (The Hague, 1875), column 30 ('Edouardus'); *Register of the Privy Council of Scotland*, ed. J. H. Burton *et al* (Edinburgh, 1877–98), ix, 592, where Udward was campaigning for new methods of making 'Holland' cloth.

54. R. W. Innes Smith, *English-speaking medical students at Leyden* (Edinburgh, 1932), 163, gives brief biography; *Advocates*, ed. Grant, 158.

55. J. Durkan and A. Ross, *Early Scottish Libraries* (Glasgow, 1961), 91, show Douglas's interest in Galen and Fernel; Durkan, 'Rutherford and Montaigne,' *Bibliothéque d'Humanisme et Renaissance* (later *BHR*), xli (1979), 116.

56. L. W. B. Brockliss, 'Medical teaching at the University of Paris, 1600–1720', *Annals of Science*, xxxv (1978), 221–251; Edinburgh University Library, Laing MS II, 228, item 2, Boyd's 'Apodyterium' of 1 Sep. 1608, when aged 28.

57. *Institutionum medicarum pars prima* (Bologna, 1638).

58. *Scots Colleges Records* (henceforward *SCR*), 4, 102.

59. Innes Smith, *Students at Leyden*, xvi; excerpts from MS commentaries of the Paris medical faculty, vol. xi, fos 284, 302, 303 (Glasgow University Library (GUL), Ross fund collections, McNeill).

60. Sibbald, *Quaestio medica* (1613), Abernethy, *Quaestiones IV Cardinales* (1609) and Sharp, *Quaestiones medicae* (1617), all Montpellier theses, as is also William Gray's *Utrum in febre exquisita pestilenti venae sectio conveniat?*, which I have not seen.

61. *Memorials of the family of Skene of Skene*, ed. W. F. Skene (New Spalding Club, 1887), 95–6; St Andrews University, Skene of Hallyards Papers, nos 40, 41, 44. He did not dispose of the mediciner's manse in Aberdeen till 1587, though he had an Edinburgh residence earlier.

62. Inscribed note by Abernethy in the British Library copy of his *Daphne Montispeliaca* (Montpelier, 1609), dedicated to Dr Craig.

63. Hist. MSS Commission, *13th Report, Manuscripts of the Earl of Lonsdale* (London, 1893), 2,5,9.

64. *Calendar of State Papers Domestic of the reign of Charles I 1625–26*, ed. J. Bruce (London, 1858), 337; *Prodromus vindictae in ducem Buckinghamiae, pro virulenta caede Magnae Britanniae regis Jacobi ...* (Frankfurt, 1626).

65. I. D. McFarlane, *Buchanan* (London, 1981), 278, 282; *Cal. S.P. Dom. Charles I*

1629-31 (London, 1860), 168; Sir G. Clark, *A History of the Royal College of Physicians of London* (Oxford, 1964), i, 246n.

66. *Musa Latina Aberdonensis*, ed. Sir W. D. Geddes (New Spalding Club, 1892), i, 32, 260.

67. *Ane breif descriptioun of the qualiteis and effectis of the well of woman-hill besyde Abirdene* (Edinburgh, 1580; reprint, Bannatyne Club, 1860).

68. *The Colde Spring* (Edinburgh, 1618), preface to John, earl of Mar, sig. C3v. Sig. D3 has an advertisement for his pills, advising 8 or 9 in a poached egg.

69. *Grana Angelica* (Edinburgh, 1635), preface to earl of Mar, sig. B8v; Anderson is an 'empiric' and his advice, according to the title page of *The Colde Spring*, was 'found true by Experience', J. Caldwell's book with Anderson's preface was reprinted in Edinburgh in 1852.

70. Robert Wodrow, *(Biographical) Collections upon the lives of the most eminent Reformers and Ministers* (Maitland Club, 1845), ii, 327-8, later cited as *BC. Letters of John Johnstone and Robert Howie*, ed. J. K. Cameron (Edinburgh/London, 1963), 195.

71. EUL, Laing MS II, 228, item 2.

72. *BC*, ii, 102-3.

73. P. Mellon, *L'Académie de Sedan, centre d'influence française* (Paris, 1913), 192-209.

74. *BC*, ii, 351; Tilenus, *Paraenesis ad Scotos, Geneuensis Disciplinae Zelotas* (London, 1620), to which Sir James Semple of Beltrees replied two years later.

75. GUL, R. Boyd's Latin poems, MS General 1282, fos 8 (Ayton), 13 (M. A. Boyd), 14v (Balfour). The principal in question was Robert Balfour.

76. An early rhetorical scheme of Boyd's is in GUL, MS General, 1483/119, fo lv.

77. *Chronique d'Isaac de Pérès*, ed. M. A. Lesueur de Pérès (Agen, 1879), 112-3, 132, 151, 187.

78. SRO, Lothian Papers, GD40/Portfolio XIII/6; *Issues of the Exchequer: Pell Records, James I*, ed. F. Devon (London, 1836), 181.

79. The lost recantation is listed in *Catalogus Librorum Cl. D. Phil. de la Coste* (Paris, 1722), 182; *Stilicho* is listed as a tragedy in Dempster, *Historia Ecclesiastica*, ii, 678.

80. *Epithalamion in Nuptiis Generosissimorum Comitis Perthani et Isabellae, Comitis Wintonii filiae* (Edinburgh, 1608), lv, verses by 'Ioan. Rosa.' For a note on Ross at Poitiers, see Durkan, 'The Bickertons', *IR*, xxiii (1972), 80, where, however, no mention is made of Ross describing himself as 'of Glasgow diocese'.

81. J. Meursius, *Athenae Batavae* (Leiden, 1625), 315; J. R. Scott and N. D. White, *Catalogue of the Manuscripts remaining in Marsh's Library, Dublin* (Dublin, 1913), 16; *Musa Latina Petri Arquessonis Santonis* (Saintes, 1598), 17.

82. Dempster, *Historia Ecclesiastica*, ii, 676.

83. Note by A. Puech contributed to *Académie du Gard: Mémoires* (1876), 841-6; *Harangues prononcées aux entrées de plusieurs princes ... avec quelques plaidoiers* (Paris, 1612), no. II, by 'maistre Anne Rulman'.

APPENDIX

These lists are confined to professors and students, as far as they can be identified. They cover the period 1500–1625, and, while still not professing completeness, they correct previous lists such as those in J. Pannier, 'Scots in Saumur in the Seventeenth Century', *Records of the Scottish Church History Society*, v (1935), 140–3; P. Bourchenin, *Etude sur les Académies protestantes en France au XVIe et au XVIIe siècle* (Paris 1882); and P. Delattre, *Les Etablissements des Jésuites en France* (Enghien 1939–55). The manuscript of Strachan's album has been checked for doubtful readings; it is now National Library of Scotland MS, Dep. 217, no. 12.

The following abbreviations are used:

AC = Archives Communales

AD = Archives Départementales

AN = Archives Nationales

AHSJ = *Archivum Historicum Societatis Jesu*

Alba = *Alba Amicorum of George Strachan, Thomas Cumming and George Craig*, ed. J. F. Kellas Johnstone (Aberdeen 1924).

BC = *(Biographical) Collections on the Lives of the Reformers and the Most Eminent Ministers of the Church of Scotland*, by R. Wodrow (Maitland Club, 1834–48).

Carrez = L. Carrez, *Catalogi Sociorum et Officiroum Provinciae Campaniae Societatis Jesu* (Chalons, 1897–1903).

Con = George Con(aeus), *Praemetiae* (Rome, 1621).

D = Thomas Dempster, *Historia Ecclesiastica Gentis Scotorum* (reprint, Bannatyne Club, 1829). Its entries are roughly in alphabetical order.

D and K = J. Durkan and J. Kirk, *The University of Glasgow 1451–1577* (Glasgow, 1977).

Delattre = as above.

DuB = C.E. Du Boulay (Bulaeus), *Historia Universitatis Parisiensis*, 6 vols. (Paris, 1665–73).

FM = Francisque Michel, *Les Ecossais en France: Les Français en Ecosse* (London, 1892).

Foley = *Records of the English Province of the Society of Jesus* (London, 1877–84).

IR = *Innes Review.*

McF = I. D. McFarlane, *Buchanan* (London, 1981).

SCR = *Records of the Scots Colleges Abroad*, i. (New Spalding Club 1906).

SHR = *Scottish Historical Review.*

Swinne = A. H. Swinne, *John Cameron, Philosoph und Theolog 1579–1625* (Marburg, 1968).

1. Provincial Centres

AGEN: Andrew Nevay n.d. (D). AIX: Joseph Drummond c. 1612 (D). ALBI: —
Gordon 1609 (M. J. Baudel, *Les écoles d'Albi*, Cahors 1879, 17). AMIENS: John
Tailliour 1598 (*SCR*, 2). ANGERS: Gavin Dunbar c. 1516 (D and K, 207);
William Gordon c. 1530 (*Aberdeen University Review*, xlviii, 270); Alexander
King c. 1580 (SRO Sea Laws, GD 45/26/50 p. 3); Francis Stewart, earl of
Bothwell c. 1580 (*Ibid.*, p. 19); James Elphinstone 1582 (Foley, vii, 1283); John
Durie 1585 (*AHSJ*, vi, 67); William Barclay 1604 (*Revue de l'Anjou*, xx, 401);
Andrew Stewart of Ochiltree 1609 (BC, ii(1), 77); James Baillie (A. á Wood,
Athenae Oxonienses (*Fasti* appendix), London 1813–20, ii, 405); Walter Heard
n.d. (D). ARRAS: David Lowis 1503 (*Edinburgh Bibliographical Society
Transactions*, iii, 78). AVIGNON: William Crichton 1571 (*AHSJ*, vi, 77); George
Turnbull 1598 (*SCR*, 3); John Brown 1603 (*IR*, xx, 20); David Colville c. 1606
(*IR*, xx, 50); Alexander Macbreck 1620 (A. Hamy, *Chronologie biographique de la
Compagnie de Jésus, ser. 1: Lyon*, Paris 1900, 124). BERGERAC: John Cameron
1600 (Swinne, 15); John Petrie 1608 (Oxford, Bodleian, Smith MS 77, fo 101).
BILLOM: Thomas Smeaton 1571 (J. M. Prat, *Maldonat et l'Université de Paris*,
Paris 1856, 615); William Crichton 1605 (W. Forbes-Leith, *Narratives of Scottish
Catholics*, Edinburgh, 1885, 283). BORDEAUX: unnamed Scots regent 1521 (E.
Gaullieur, *Histoire du Collège de Guyenne*, Paris 1874, 11); George Buchanan
1539 (McF, 78); William Ramsay 1550 (*SHR*, lxii, 75); John Rutherford 1555
(*BHR* xli, 117); James Martin 1561 (Gaullieur, 258); Andrew McGruder 1573
(*Ibid.*, 350); Henry Wardlaw 1581 (McF, 463); two Scots regents 1581 (*Ibid.*);
Robert Balfour 1587 (NLS MS 2236); Mark Alexander Boyd 1590 (Book); John
Hegate 1590 (Boyd's book above); William Douglas –1595 (SRO, CS1/4/2, fo
284); Arthur Gordon 1596 (*SCR*, 2); David Echlin 1597 (British Library, MS
Harley 1670, printed theses); Robert Boyd of Trochrague 1599 (GUL, MS Gen
1282); Robert Ayton 1599 (*Ibid.*, fo 8); Adam Abernethy 1600 (*Alba*, 5); W.
Balfour 1600 (*Alba*, 4, checked with MS); John Campbell of Calder 1600 (*Alba*, 5);
James Echlin 1600 (*Ibid.*); Theodore Hay 1600 (*Ibid.*); David Strachan 1600
(*Ibid.*); William Wood, 1600 (*Ibid.*, MS reads 'Vedeus' not 'Hegatus'); James
Robertson n.d. (D); James Drummond 1604 (*Miscellany of the Spalding Club*, ii,
393); William Hegate 1606 (date in his *De Lampade*, 1607); James Gordon of
Huntly 1608 (Delattre, i, 759); Thomas Melville 1607 (*BC*, ii (1), 287); Robert
Lindsay 1614 (FM, ii, 269); James Gordon of Lesmoir 1615 (J. Forbes, *Jean
Ogilvie*, Paris, 1901, 174); Patrick Anderson (*Ibid.*, 176); James Coldin 1616 (in R.
Balfour book, verses); John Petrie (*Ibid.*, verses); John Sharp 1620 (SRO, Shairp
of Houstoun Muniments, GD30/1696). BOURGES: Henry Scrimgeour c. 1538
(Edinburgh *Bibliographical Soc. Transactions*, v (1978), 2); Edward Henryson
1547 (*Ibid.*); John Logie –1563 (SRO, CS1/2/1, fo 79); Alexander Arbuthnot
1561 (Spottiswoode, *History of the Church of Scotland*, Spottiswoode Soc.,
1851–5, ii, 319); James Boyd –1604 (*BC*, i, 206); Patrick Adamson 1567 (*The
Bibliotheck*, iv, 1964, 66–72); James McGill 1567 (Adamson was his tutor);
William Barclay 1575 (Collet, cited in text); Nicol Dalgleish c. 1578 (*The

Autobiography and Diary of Mr James Melvill, ed. R. Pitcairn, Wodrow Soc.,
1842, 76n); David McGill 1579 (SRO, Stair Muniments, GD135 Box 121);
Alexander Scott n.d. (uncertain, but was student under Cujas); Mark Alexander
Boyd -1585 (NLS, Adv. MS 15.11.7, fo 192); William Drummond of
Hawthornden 1607 (inscribed book, R. H. McDonald, *Library of D. of H.*,
Edinburgh 1971, 152); 15 Scots 1619-24, uncertain if all are students (FM, ii,
263); Arthur Stuart 1625 (*SCR*, 20). CAEN: William 'Bass' 1547, medicine
(*L'Université de Caen 1432-1932*, ed. A. Bigot, Caen 1932, 82); William Bruce
1587, law (*Archives Départementales, Calvados sér. D*, i, 107); George Wauchope
1595 (H. Prentout in *Mémoires de L'Acad. Nat. des Sciences, Arts et Belles-
Lettres de Caen* (1907, 88); Adam Stuart 1612 (*Catalogue des manuscrits des
Départements de France*, xliv, MSS de la Collection Mancel no. 19 fo 39); David
Echlin 1613 (Innes Smith, cited text). CAHORS: William Bruce -1586
(*Edinburgh University and Poland*, ed. W. Tomaszewki, Edinburgh 1968, 21);
Alexander Meldrum 1597 (*SCR*, 2); unknown student from St Andrews 1624
(*Bulletin de la Société française d'Histoire de la Médecine* (1924), 55. CAR-
PENTRAS: Florence Wilson 1535 (R. Douglas, *Jacopo Sadoleto, humanist and
reformer*, Cambridge Mass., USA, 1959, 65); John Brown 1595 (SRO,
RH9/2/28); William Crichton 1609 (Forbes *Jean Ogilvie*, 102); Alexander Scott
1615 (D). CASTELJALOUX: George Hegate 1624 (*IR*, xxi, 153). CASTRES:
Adam Abernethy 1601 (*Veritatis Testimonium*, 1611); Robert Burnett 1611 (cited
in text); Alexander More, senr. 1611, principal (A. Poux, *Histoire du Collège de
Castres des origines à 1840*, Paris/Toulouse, 1902, 122); Alex. More, junr. born
Castres, 1616 (*DNB*); Robert 'Mourab' 1623 (Paris, Archives Nationales,
Exposition France-Ecosse). CHALONS-SUR-MARNE: William Chalmers
1625 (Carrez, ii, 118). CHAMBERY: William Crichton 1582 (*AHSJ*, vi, 77);
Alexander Hume 1597 (S. François de Sales, *Oeuvres: Lettres*, i, Annecy 1900,
304). DIE: John McCollo 1604 (E. Arnaud, *Histoire de l'Acad. protestante de
Die*, 113); — Anderson 1605 (J. Chevalier, *Essai historique sur Die*, 1909, iii, 338);
John Sharp 1607 (came from La Rochelle, Arnaud, 38); John Leslie 1611 (came
from Uzès, Arnaud, 58); William McGill 1615 (Arnaud, 63). DIJON: William
Hegate -1606 (D); Thomas Melville 1607 (*BC*, ii (1), 287); William Barclay 1617
(Carrez, ii, 7). DOLE: Robert 'Mambre' (Macbreck?) (London, Public Rec.
Office, State Papters, SP78/53, fo 213). DOUAI: see text of paper above, and
SCR, passim. FLECHE (LA): Thomas Dempster 1607 (Book); John Seton 1625
(*SCR*, 21). FONTENAY: Mark Alexander Boyd (NLS, Adv. MS 15.1.7).
LAMOTHE: R. Williamson 1605 (FM, ii, 214); John Leech 1619 (Adv MS
17.1.9, fo 178). LESCAR (later ORTHEZ): John Dalziel *c.* 1587 (D); Alexander
Blair (*Alba*, 4); James Fleming (*Alba*, 3); Gilbert Burnet (*Alba*, 3); John Blair laird
of Blair 1599 (*Alba*, 4); (Samuel?) Kilpatrick 1599 (*Alba*, 4); John Wallace younger
of Dundonald (*Alba*, 4). LYONS: Florence Wilson 1537 (Douglas, *Sadoleto*,
182); William Crichton 1565 (Delattre, ii, col. 1561); Andrew Baird 1595 (*AC
Lyon*, iv, 1949, 9); Edward Scott (*Ibid.*); John Hay 1607 (*AHSJ*, vi). MANS (LE):
William Heard n.d. (D). MANTES: David Echlin *c.* 1620 (Con). MILLAU:
Robert 'Mourab' 1623 (see s.v. Castres). MONTAUBAN: Robert Boyd of

Trochrague 1599 (GUL, MS Gen. 1483/119); Robert Wemyss 1600 (GUL, MS Gen. 1282); Thomas Ross (*Alba*, 5); Patrick Kinnear 1603 (Book); Patrick Ramsay 1604 (*BC*, ii (1), 36); William Duncan -1606 (M. Nicolas, *Histoire de l'Acad. protestante de Montauban*, Montauban, 1885, 252); Gilbert Burnet 1610 (Nicolas, 249); Robert McGill 1614 (Nicolas, 280); John Maxwell 1616 (Nicolas, 242); Thomas Galbraith 1619 (Nicolas, 396); John Cameron 1624 (Swinne, 15). MONTPELLIER: the following are from M. Gouron, *Matricule de l'Université de Médecine de Montpellier 1503-1599* (Travaux d'Humanisme et de Renaissance no. 25, Geneva 1957): Thomas 'Hycotor' of Aberdeen 1509; Archibald Richardson 1515; Andrew Durie 1519; John Gray 1528; John Cunningham 1538; Patrick Tod 1548; Thomas Anderson 1581; David Kinloch 1583; Thomas Morrison 1586; Thomas Landels 1590; John de Cars 1595; John Haeduus (Haddowie?) 1597; Edward Scott 1598; Clement King ('Regius') 1599; Alexander Morison 'Sterlinensis' (?Dunblane) 1599; Robert Ross 'Coylensis' (=Kyle) 1599. To these add two law students from L. Guiraud, 'Un registre inconnu de l'Univ. de Droit de Montpellier,' *Comité des Travaux historiques et scientifiques: Bulletin philologique et historique* (Paris, 1913), 111: John Cunningham 1538; David Mill 1538. Robert Hill *c.* 1600 (D); John McCollo 1600 (*Alba*, 6). The following names are in Montpellier, Faculté de Médecine, Archives, registre S20: William Dunbar 1601 (fo 117v); George Sharp 1603 (fo 122v); Patrick Kinnear (*Ibid.*); David Echlin 1605 (fo 130); Alexander Kincaid (fo 136); Robert Whitelaw 1608 (fo 140); Thomas Maule 1608 (*Ibid.*); Adam Abernethy 1609 (*Ibid.*, though his *Veritatis testimonium* shows that he came to Montpellier in 1607); William Gray 1609 (fo 142); John Kinnear 1610 (fo 146v); Patrick Hepburn, from Rome 1611 (fo 148); Robert Bruce 1613 (fo 158); George Sibbald 1613 (fo 160v); Mark Duncan 1614 (fo 162); Frederick Wauchope 1615 (fo 166); James Primrose 'of Bordeaux' 1615 (fo 167v); Patrick Blair 1618 (fo 179v); John Vair 1620 (fo 185v); John Myrton 1624 (fo 194v). Reg. S7 adds the following: Alexander Inglis 1606 (fo 130v); Alexander Tait (fo 149); Peter Goldman 1607 (fo 133v). *AC*, ix, 24 gives William McGill 1618; James Hay 1624. J. Barbot, *Les chroniques de la Faculté de Médecine de Toulouse* (Toulouse, 1905), i, 120, gives: Walter Reid *c.* 1620. SRO, Shairp of Houstoun Muniments, GD30/1696: John Sharp 1620. NANCY: John Hay 1607 (*AHSJ*, vi); Alexander Ogilvie 1622 (*SCR*, 15). NANTES: William Hegate 1603 (his book, *Paralogia*, so dated); William Barclay, M.D. *c.* 1610 (D). NARBONNE: *Bulletin de la Commission archéologique de Narbonne pour l'Année 1892*, 93: John Cunningham 1538. NERAC: John Mathison 1600 (G. de Lagrange Ferregues, 'Le collège royal de Nérac', *Revue de L'Agenais* (1959), 81-105); William Duncan 1612 (*Ibid.*); William Fletcher 1613 (*Ibid.*); Robert Burnet 1613 (*Ibid.*); — Lockhart 1615 (*Ibid.*); Thomas Foster 1615 (*Ibid.*); David Peirson *c.* 1620(D). NIMES: Patrick Todd 1549 (A. Puech, *La Renaissance et la Réforme à Nimes*, Nimes 1893, clxv); John Todd 1578 (SRO, Brown papers, RH9/2/29); Adam Abernethy 1601 (his *Veritatis Testimonium*); Andrew Curror 1603 (*AC* ser. RR, RR55); Thomas Dempster 1604 (above, in text); Alexander Inglis 1607 (*Ibid.*); Patrick Dun 1607 (*AC*. ser. E, E572); Hugh Lawtie 1607 (E573); James Chalmers (E573); Patrick Kinnear ('d'Enere') 1609 (*AC* RR39);

Alexander Kincaid 1610 (E575); William Johnstone 1619 (E584). NIORT: George Hegate 1617 (Delattre, iii, col. 694). ORANGE: Thomas Skene 1583 (*Registres de la Compagnie des Pasteurs de Genève*, ed. O. Labarthe *et al*, Geneva 1976, 227); William Gray 1614 (Innes Smith, preface); William Johnstone 1622 (*Ibid.*). ORLEANS: for students 1501–1537 see *Miscellany of the Scottish History Society*, ii. Robert Stewart 1551 (NLS Wigtown Papers, Acc. 3142, vol. ii, no. 240); John Gordon 1567 (Archives du Loiret D214, fo 255); David Cunningham 1567 (*Ibid.*); Thomas Maitland 1567 (*Ibid.*); David Guthrie 1567 (*Ibid.*); Andrew Ayton 1567 (*Ibid.*). POITIERS: Robert Ireland, professor 1502 (Dreux du Radier, *Bibliothèque historique et critique de Poitou*, 1849, ii, 143); John Leslie 1549 (Paris, Bibliothèque Nationale, MS Anglais (paged), 22; Gavin Hamilton 1554 (McF, 540); Patrick Hamilton 1554 (*Ibid.*, tutor to preceding); Duncan Macruder 1562 (D and K, 268); Andrew Melville 1566 (*Ibid.*, 266, 268); Gilbert Moncrieff 1566 (*Ibid.*); Robert Howie 1571 (verses, see text above); John Carnegie 1576 (SHR, xxi, 85); Hercules Rollock 1576 (Book); John Moncrieff 'Strathearn diocese'(!)1579 (Poitiers, Archives de la Ville, Registre de l'Université 1, 47v); John Arthur –1580 (SRO, CS1/3/1, fo 115); Richard Lawson –1583 (D and K, 268); James Elphinstone 1584 (*SHR*, xxi, 85); Thomas Bicarton 1588 (*Ibid*, 84); John Ross (in Bicarton book); George Melvin 1588 (*Ibid.*); Thomas Henryson 1590 (British Library, MS Harley 4700); William Douglas –1595 (SRO, CS1/4/2, fo 284); — Dunbar 1597 (*BC*, ii (1), 12); — 'Legat' 1597 (*Ibid.*, probably Hegate); Thomas Barclay 1596 or 1614 (P. Boissonade, *Histoire de l'Univ. de Poitiers*, Poitiers 1932); William Hegate 1598 (Book); John Mathison 1598 (Verses in Hegate's *Gallia Victrix*); Robert Hamilton –1600 (CS1/4/2, fo 288); Lewis Craig (*Ibid.*, fo 289; (John?) Sharp 1603 (SRO, Shairp of Houstoun Muniments, GD30/1672); John Haliday of Tulibole –1605 (CSI/4/2, fo 349); R(obert?) Wedderburn 1613 (NLS, Adv MS 33.5.7). PONT-A-MOUSSON: Edmund Hay 1574 (L. Carrez, *Catalogi Sociorum et Officiorum Provinciae Campaniae Societatis Jesu*, Chalons-sur-Marne, 1897–1903, i, 166); John Hay 1576 (*Ibid.*, i, 32); William Barclay, civil law (*Diarium Universitatis Mussipontanae 1572–1764*, Nancy 1911, ed. G. Gavet, col. 7); Walter Hay 1578 (Carrez, i, 32); William Murdoch 1578 (*Ibid.*, i, 34); Thomas Oswald 1578 (*Ibid.*, i, 178); George Durie 1579 (*Ibid.*, i, 158); James Gordon 1582 (*Ibid.*, i, 37); James Shaw 1583 (Gavet, xxi); John 'Currerius' (not certain if Scots, but prefect of Scots seminary) 1584 (Carrez, i, 38); John Myrton 1584 (*Ibid.*, i, 192); John Scot 1586 (Gavet, xxi); James Tyrie 1588 (Carrez, i, 44); Alexander McQuhirrie (*Ibid.*, i, 172); Alexander Hume 1592 (*Ibid.*, i, 110; Alexander Hay 1599 (*Ibid.*, i, 166); Patrick Anderson 1600 (*Ibid.*, i, 48); George Turnbull 1605 (*Ibid.*, i, 172; John George Mortimer 1614 (*Ibid.*, i, 97); George Hegate 1621 (*Ibid.*, ii, 52); Alexander Ogilvie 1624 (*Ibid.*, ii, 97). RENNES: Gilbert Skene 1563 (*BHR*, xii, 113); David Kinloch –1597 (*Reliquiae antiquae Scoticae*, ed. G. R. Kinloch, Edinburgh 1848, 77); Walter Heard, M.D. 1626 (*Inquisitionum ad Capellam Domini Regis Retornatarum Abbreviatio*, ed. T. Thomson, 3 vols., Edinburgh 1811–16, Inquisitiones Speciales, Fife, no. 370). ROCHELLE, LA: John Ross –1593 (Dublin, Marsh Library, MS Z2.2.5); George Thomson –1603, prof. philosophy

(*BC*, ii (1), 34); John Douglas of Musselburgh 1603 (Book of G. Thomson); John Scott 1604 (*BC*, ii (1), 34); Thomas Dempster 1604 (Book, cited above in text); John Gellie 1605 (Book); Thomas Melville 1607 (*BC*, ii (1), 290; Andrew Duncan 1607 (*Ibid.*); John Sharp –1607 (s.v. Die); William Hart 1608 (*BC*, ii (1), 59); John Dunbar of Enterkin 1610 (SRO, Montrose Writs, GD220/6/1882(2)); Andrew Stewart of Ochiltree 1609 (*BC*, ii (1), 319; John Macdowell of Garthland (*Ibid.*); George Sibbald *c.* 1612 (NLS, Adv. MS 33.7.18). ROUEN: Thomas Motto 1586 (W. M. Bryce, *The Scottish Grey Friars*, ii, (Edinburgh, 1909), 193); George Eglisham n.d. (D); Patrick Anderson 1609 (Forbes, *Jean Ogilvie*, 102); Colin Campbell 1600 (*The Clan Campbell*, ed. H. Paton, Edinburgh 1918, vi, 73). SAINTES: Thomas Bicarton n.d. (D). ST. MAIXENT: Hercules Rollock 1578 (Verses in Book); Adam Newton First regent, Greek *c.* 1585 (A. Rivet, *Opera omnia*, Rotterdam 1660, iii, prefatory funeral oration by Daubers); Robert Boyd (not Trochrague) 1595 (NLS, MS Adv. 15.7.11); Thomas Dempster 1603 (D). ST. MAXIMIN: George Thomson *c.* 1581, principal (*SCR*, 2); John Macollo 1603 (Book). ST OMER: William Hardie 1623 (*SCR*, 16). SALINS: Alexander Chalmer 1597 (*SCR*, 2). SAUMUR: Andrew Ramsay 1600 (Book); William Craig 1602 (*BC*, ii (1), 48); Mark Duncan 1606 (J. Pannier, 'Scots in Saumur in the Seventeenth Century', *Records of the Scottish Church History Society* (*R.S.C.H.S.*), v, 140-3); Robert Boyd of Trochrague 1606 (*BC*, ii (1), 46); — Murison, doctor of laws *c.* 1606 (*The Bannatyne Miscellany*, Bannatyne Club 1827, i, 289; John Glassfurd 1608 (*Scottish Notes and Queries* (*SNQ*), 3rd series, xi (1933), 75); — Lockhart 1609 (*BC*, ii (1), 554); Adam Henrison 1611 (*SNQ*, 3rd ser., xi, 89); Zachary Boyd 1611 (*BC*, ii (1), 93); Patrick Kinloch 1613 (*BC*, ii (1), 112; William Geddie 1615 (*SNQ*, 3rd ser. xi, 75); John Cameron 1618 (Swinne, 15); Philip Grayson 1621 (doubtful, *SNQ*, 3rd ser., xi, 76); Alexander Hunter 1622 (*Ibid.*, 90); — Newton ('Nuton') 1625 (*Ibid.*, 90). SEDAN: John Cameron 1602 (Swinne, 15); Arthur Johnston 1603 (*Musa Latina Aberdonensis*, ii, p. xxix); Walter Donaldson 1603 (*Ibid.*); John Smith 1604 (T. McCrie, *Life of Andrew Melville*, Edinburgh 1819, ii, 420); Andrew Melville 1611 (*Ibid.*, ii, 411); John Drummond 1607 (*Spalding Club Miscellany*, ii, 394-5); John Forbes 1613 (D. T. Bird, *Catalogue of 16th Century Medical Books in Edinburgh Libraries*, Edinburgh 1982, 216); Alexander Colville 1619 (*Musa Latina Aberdonensis*, ii, p. xxxiv); John Hume 1620 (McCrie, *Melville*, ii, 457); George Craig 1622 (Book). THOUARS: Robert Boyd of Trochrague 1597 (*BC*, ii (1), 12); John Hay, 'sieur du Poirier' 1613 (*SNQ*, 3rd ser. xi, 75); John Leech 1618 (NLS, Adv. MS 17.1.9, fo 213). TOULOUSE: John Leslie *c.* 1552-3 (Paris, BN MS Anglais (paged), 23); Adam Blackwood *c.* 1570 (*Opera omnia*, Paris 1644, in 'elogium' by G. Naudé); Robert Howie 1574 (dated inscription in his copy of Pliny, NLS RBm37); George Crichton 1579 (mentioned in his *Oratio habita in Collegio Harcuriano*, 1584); William Bruce *c.* 1586 (s.v. Cahors); Robert Balfour –1587 (SRO, RH9/2/27); Mark Alexander Boyd *c.* 1590 (NLS, Adv. MS 15.11.7, fo 192); James Kidd 1591 (Paris, BN MS Lat. 4402, flyleaf note); David Reid 1593 (J. Barbot, *Les chroniques de la Faculté de Médecine de Toulouse*, Toulouse, 1905, i, 120); James Gordon 1593 (Foley, vii, 879); John Brown 1594 (SRO, RH9/2/25);

Thomas Barclay 1596 (*AC*, i, 322); Robert Ayton 1599 (*Alba*, 4); Thomas Dempster 1604 (D); — Spital n.d. (Con; Andrew?); Walter Heard n.d. (Con); Andrew Nevay –1604 (D); James Drummond 1608 (*Spalding Club Miscellany*, ii, 393); Walter Reid c. 1620 (Barbot, i, 120). TOURNON: John Hay 1581 (*Revue du Vivarais*, lix (1959)); Alexander Scott 1584 (Book). TOURS: Thomas Bicarton 1583 (Book). UZES: John Leslie 1604 (s.v. Die). VERDUN: George Durie 1593 (Foley, vii, 879).

2. Paris Colleges

Ave Maria: Patrick Buchanan, as tutor 1553 (McF, 39); *Beauvais*: John Dempster 1553 (*SHR*, xliii, 73); William Davidson, his student 1553 (Bibliothèque National BN MS Lat. 9954, fo 202v); Thomas Winterhope 1562 (Scottish Catholic Archives, Book of Grisy, fo 36); George Crichton 1586 (Book); Thomas Dempster c. 1613 (*Dictionary of National Biography*). *Boncourt*: Robert Gray 1522 (verses in John Vaus Book); William Cranston 1543 (SRO, Acts and Decreets of Court of Session, C7/1, fo 194v; Patrick Buchanan c. 1549 (*IR*, xv, 187); George Buchanan 1553 (McF, 164); John Stewart, president 1560 (DuB, vi, 538); James Martin 1566 (DuB, vi, 653); Henry Blackwood 1568 (Paris, Archives Nationales, AN H³2589, fo 132v); John Hamilton c. 1580 (DuB, vi, Index); George Crichton 1586 (J. Hamilton, *In Amplissimum Senatum*, verses); James Leith 1603 (*SHR*, xliii, 77); Robert Philp n.d. (Con); George Sibbald 1612 (*IR*, xx, 147). *Bons Enfants*: William Bog 1536 (Paris, Univ., Reg. 15, fo 391v); Henry Blackwood 1557 (DuB, vi, Index). *Bourgogne*: Gilbert Crab 1509 (Paris, Univ., Reg. 90, Certificats, fo 5); Robert Heriot 1538 (*SHR*, xliii, 76); Adam Elder 1558 (Book). *Calvy*: William Bog 1544 (E. Coyecque, *Recueil des actes notariés relatifs à l'histoire de Paris*, Paris, 1905, nos. 2328–9); William Cranston 1540 (*SHR*, lxiii, 72); John Stuart 1550 (*Ibid.* 81). *Cambrai*: Alexander, David and James Beaton 1550 (*Religion and Humanism*, ed. K. Robbins, Oxford 1981, 191 and *IR*, xv, 187); John Davidson 1603 (Public Record Office, SP78/50, fo 35). *Clermont*: Edmund Hay 1564 (*Papal Negotiations with Queen Mary*, ed. J. H. Pollen, Scottish Hist. Soc., 1901, 483); James Tyrie 1573 (Forbes-Leith, *Narratives*, 72); John Hay 1580 (Book); John Durie 1582 (Forbes-Leith, 85); George Christie 1593 (Foley, vii, 879); Alexander Hay 1593 (G. Dupont-Ferrier, *Du Collège de Clermont au Lycée Louis le Grand*, iii, 49). *Coqueret*: Robert Galbraith 1509 (Paris, Univ., Reg. 89, fo 175v). *Fortet*: William Fowler 1581 (Book). *Grassins*: George Crichton n.d. (C. Jourdain, *Histoire de l'Université de Paris*, Paris 1888, 54); William Barclay n.d. (BN, MS Lat. 8746); Thomas Dempster 1611 (Paris, AN, H³2589, fo 258). *Harcourt*: Adam Blackwood 1563 (Book); Henry Blackwood 1568 (DuB, vi, 670); John Christie 1574 (*SHR*, xliii, 85); George Crichton 1583 (Jourdain, *loc. cit.*); John Hamilton 1586 (*SHR*, xliii, 85); John Fraser, principal 1602 (Jourdain, *loc. cit.*); *La Marche*: Thomas Levyntoun 1511 (Paris, Univ., Reg. 90, fo 6); George Lockhart 1516 (Book); Robert Fergushill 1528 (Reg. 15, fo 161v). *Lateran*: James Curle 1575 (*State Papers, Rome*, London 1926, ii, 219); Thomas Winterhope 1580 (Scottish Catholic Archives, Book of Grisy, fo 60v). *Lemoine*: George Buchanan 1543

(McF, 92); William Davidson 1557 (AN, H³2589, fo 42); William Barclay 1598 (BN, MS Lat. 8746). *Lisieux*: John Williamson 1508 (Paris, Univ., Reg. 89, fo 153); David Paniter 1530 (Reg. 15, fo 305v); John Dempster 1557 (BN. MS Nouv. Acquisitions Latines 535); John Hamilton 1560 (*Ibid.*, fo 170); Adam King 1588 (AN, H³2589, fo lv); George Crichton *c.* 1600 (BN, MS Lat. 6677); William Hegate 1601 (AN, H³2589, fo 222v); Thomas Dempster 1610 (H³2589, fo 254v). *Mans, Le: Robert Wauchope 1524 (Paris, Univ., Reg. 15, fo 68); Alexander Hamilton 1528 (Ibid.*, fo 134v); George Strachan *c.* 1615 (D). *Montaigu*: Hector Boece 1493 (Boece, *Vitae Episcoporum*, 1522); Patrick Paniter (*Ibid.*); John Mair 1495 (A. Broadie, *George Lokert, Late-Scholastic Logician*, Edinburgh 1983, 5); Robert Walterston 1499 (*Ibid.*, 8); David Cranston 1499 (*Ibid.*); George Lockhart 1504 (*Ibid.*); John Annand 1506 (Paris, Univ., Reg. 90, fo 21v); Thomas Levyntoun 1508 (Paris, Univ., Reg. 89, fo 6); William Manderston 1508 (Reg. 90, fo 34v); Archibald Richardson 1513 (Reg. 90, fo 23); John Douglas 1533 (Reg. 15, fo 348); Archibald Hay 1540 (Book); John Dempster 1554 (Book); John Stewart, John Scot, John Matheson 1562 (Book of Grisy, fo 36); Thomas Dempster 1601 (A. Rulman, *Harangues*, 272). *Navarre*: John Mair 1506 (Broadie, 6); John Williamson died there, 1522 (Paris, Univ., Reg. 91, fo 207); Thomas McLellan *c.* 1543 (SRO, CS7/1, fo 490v); David Henderson 1543 (*Ibid.*); John Hamilton 1584 (DuB, vi, 785). *Plessis, Du*: Robert Heriot 1533 (Paris, Univ., Reg. 15, fo 346v); Archibald Hay 1543 (Book); John Dempster 1564 (mention in his Book, 1569); Adam King ('Le Roy') 1581 (DuB, vi, Index); Simon Simson 1584 (AN, H³2589, fo 181); David Echlin 1602 (Book). *Presles*: John Douglas 1528 (Paris, Univ., Reg. 15, fo 147); William Cranston 1534 (Ibid., fo 374); Andrew Lockhart 1539 (*SHR*, xliii, 78); John Stewart 1549 (Book); James Stewart, later earl of Moray 1550 (*Historical MSS Commission, 6th Report*, London 1877, 647). *Reims*: George Lockhart 1506 (Paris, Univ., Reg. 90, fo 2); William Davidson 1560 (Book; see also *BHR*, xii (1950), 100). *Royal*: George Crichton 1595 (A. Lefrance, ed., *Le Collège de France 1530–1930: Livre Jubilaire*, Paris 1932, 22); David Sinclair 1599 (*Ibid.*); James Leith 1605 (*Ibid.*). *Sainte Barbe*: John Mair 1493 (Broadie, 4); William Manderston 1528 (McF, 28); Simon Simson 1537 (Paris, Univ., Reg. 15, fo 409); Alexander Thornton 1553 (Quicherat, *Hist. de Ste Barbe*, ii, 307); John Rutherford 1553 (*SHR*, xliii, 82); Adam Blackwood 1560 (BN, N. Acq. Latines 535, fo 170); William Davidson 1568 (Quicherat, ii, 92); John Dempster 1569 (Book); John Hamilton 1579 (Paris, AN, H³2589, fo 169); James Cheyne 1580 (Book); George Crichton 1582 (Quicherat, ii, 92). *Sorbonne*: John Mair 1506 (Broadie, 5); George Lockhart 1512 ('hospes', Broadie, 20); Simon Simson 1540 (BN, MS Lat. 15441, paged, 3); William Cranston 1547 (*Ibid.*, 73); William Davidson 1560 (*Ibid.*, 184); James Laing 1576 (*Ibid.*, 269).

3. Other Paris Students

— Forman –1563 (*Protocol Book of Mr Gilbert Grote*, Scottish Record Soc., 1914, no. 255); — Stewart –1563 (*Ibid.*); William Lumsden 1566 (SRO,

Edinburgh Testaments: John Greenlaw, i, fo 95); Richard Lawson 1566 (*Ibid.*); Thomas Hamilton 1568 (see text above); John Melville S.T.B. 1573 (*State Papers, Rome*, ii, 227); Nicol Dalgleish *c.* 1578 (*The Works of William Fowler*, ed. H. W. Meikle, Scottish Text Soc., 1933, ii, 27); James Borthwick (of Lochhill) 1579 (SRO, Henderson of Fordell Writs, GD172/218); Nicol Burne 1581 (Book); Robert Gordon (of Straloch) 1599 (*The House of Gordon*, ed. J. Bulloch, New Spalding Club 1910, ii, 32); Thomas Annand 1601 (*The Miscellany of the Third Spalding Club*, 1940, ii, 55); Henry Wemyss 1603 (*Alba*, 10); Robert (?) Arbuthnot 1603 (*Ibid.*); Alexander Livingstone (of Dunipace) 1603 (*Ibid.*); Alexander Morisius 1603 (*Ibid.*); Walter Scot of Buccleuch 1603 (*Ibid.*); T. Scot 1603 (G. Strachan Album MS); John Erskine 1606 (*Alba*, 13); John Chisholm 1606 (*Ibid.*); William Drummond of Hawthornden (R. H. McDonald, *Library of Drummond of Hawthornden*, Edinburgh 1971, 158); Peter Hay 1609 (*Alba*, 14); John Drummond 1610 (*Miscellany*, Spalding Club 1842, ii, 395); George Eglisham 1610 (In T. Dempster's *Musca*); Alexander Inglis, 'mathematician' 1610 (*Ibid.*); Edward Little 1613 (SRO, Calendar of Craigmillar Writs, no. 820); William Ker 1624 (*Correspondence of Sir Robert, first earl of Ancram and his son, William*, Edinburgh 1875, i, page xlvi).

4. Advocates Who Studied in France

Thomas Craig is not given in the Books of Sederunt. Robert Lumsden, 'professor' –1577 (Books of Sederunt of Lords of Council, SRO, CS1/3/1, fo 36v); William Hervy –1577 (fo 40); William Oliphant (of Newton) –1577 (fo 52); Robert Lyntoun (of Reivarfield) –1577 (fo 52v, in Italy also); John McGill –1580 (son of Clerk Register, fo 137); Alexander Sym younger (later commissary Edinburgh) –1585 (CS1/4/1. fo 1); William Barclay –1600 (*Ibid.*, fo 297); Robert Johnston –1601 (fo 298); James Skene (of Curriehill) –1603 (CS1/4/2, fo 335); Alexander, master of Elphinstone –1605 (fo 347); Robert Foulis –1606 (fo 354v, also in England); Oliver Colt –1606 (fo 360); James Haliday (commissary Dumfries) –1607 (fo 372v); Thomas Hamilton –1587 (younger of Priestfield, Sir William Fraser, *Memorials of the Earls of Haddington*, ii, 280). Another student of law in France was Alexander Hume, minister of Logie, *Wodrow Miscellany*, i, 567–8, Robert Burnet, regent in humanity, Edinburgh, who went to France in 1616, seems to have become an advocate in 1622 (M. Wood, ed., *Extracts from the Records of the Burgh of Edinburgh 1604–1626*, Edinburgh, 1927, 69).

3

SOME CONTINENTAL VISITORS TO SCOTLAND IN THE LATE SIXTEENTH AND EARLY SEVENTEENTH CENTURIES

James K. Cameron

Nearly one hundred years ago Hume Brown published his well-known book *Early Travellers in Scotland*. In the years that have followed no comparable study has replaced it and within the last decade or so it has been reprinted unaltered.[1] It contains accounts of Scotland written by those who visited the country prior to 1700 and comprises, apart from Hume Brown's brief introductions, material that was already in print. For the sixteenth and seventeenth centuries seventeen accounts are reproduced; six are by visitors from the continent, the others are all by Englishmen. The accounts by continentals are for the most part exceedingly brief: in total fewer than forty printed pages, and every single one far shorter than any of those of their contemporary English observers. Four years after the appearance of Hume Brown's book this source material was considerably augmented by the publication of the journal of Lupold von Wedel (1546–1615), a Pomeranian nobleman who visited England and Scotland in 1584–85.[2] This diary contains a detailed description of Wedel's tour of Scotland. Since the appearance of this account nothing comparable had come to light until the discovery of the itinerary of a tour undertaken in 1591 by Johan Peter Hainzel von Degerstein of Augsburg, drawn up in Latin and German versions by Caspar Waser, the young scholar who accompanied his rich pupil on his travels.[3] Regrettably this document is precisely what its title indicates and nothing more, an itinerary, which Waser no doubt intended to publish for the help of others. It contains very little by way of recorded impressions of the country or of the people whom the visitors met.

The paucity of source material of the kind that interested Hume Brown has resulted in the drawing of a number of unwarranted conclusions by those who have written on this topic. We are told, for example, by E. S. Bates in that generally informative and entertaining classic, *Touring in 1600*, published in 1910, that very few visitors came to Scotland. He wrote: 'of Scotland and Wales it can only be said that the former was practically ignored except by a few Frenchmen as a result of the ancient alliance, while to Wales they [foreign travellers] paid as little attention as the semi-Welsh Queen did — none at all'.[4] More recently W. D. Robson-Scott, in his most interesting study *German Travellers in England 1400–1800*, published in 1953, has singled out von Wedel's account as 'one of the very few German travel diaries down to the end of the eighteenth century which include Scotland in their itinerary'.[5]

Unfortunately those who have written on this general topic have ignored one of the most valuable collections of source material, material that will not perhaps directly increase our knowledge of the visitors' impressions of Scotland or of the Scots but which will put an end to the frequently held opinion that in the sixteenth and seventeenth centuries Scotland was from the point of view of the educated traveller remote, barbarous, and unwelcoming, and consequently was ignored or went largely unvisited. Hume Brown had this to say: 'Even to the close of the seventeenth century Scotland was still a kind of *terra incognita*, which men thought of as a half mythical country where strange things might exist which it was irrational to look for in any place nearer home . . . it still remained a country regarding which travellers' tales were received with a foregone feeling of their intrinsic probability'.[6] The material largely unstudied is the extensive collection of autograph albums that were the treasured possessions of virtually all travellers of this period, the precursors of those gentlemen who at a later date went on the Grand Tour.

The practice of keeping an autograph album, *album amicorum* or Stammbuch began in Germany among students toward the middle of the sixteenth century, possibly in Wittenberg. As students usually visited more than one university, the custom of keeping such albums in which friends and acquaintances entered their names for rememberance sake developed. These little pocket volumes with the inscriptions of professors and other eminent people served also as a kind of passport into university and aristocratic circles. They usually contained a motto in Latin or Greek or Hebrew or even in all three languages. There are also in several albums entries in German, English, French, Italian, Spanish, even Welsh, Irish and Arabic, and of course, details of the place of entry and of the date. Such albums often contain richly illuminated coats of arms, miniature paintings (usually of excellent quality) of Kings and Princes, local dignitaries, sketches of everyday life, and often drawings of important buildings, for example London Bridge, Windsor Castle, the tombs in Westminster Abbey and the like. There are hundreds of these albums in libraries on the continent and probably many more in private collections. The collection in the British Library, now some five hundred volumes in all, is the largest single collection outside Germany. There are very few in Scotland's libraries, but those that are, are of exceptionally high quality.[7]

The collection in the British Library produces ample evidence that London was one of the most frequently visited cities, but most tourists extended their visit to include the royal palaces and the universities. Those who went farther afield are less numerous; nevertheless, taken along with albums that are in continental libraries, they provide more than ample evidence that Scotland was far from ignored.

The group of travellers represented by Hume Brown consists mainly of those who visited the country with political interest uppermost in their minds. They are for the most part best described as emissaries of other political powers. Those whose visits are discussed here formed a quite distinctive type of traveller in the sixteenth and early seventeenth centuries. They were for the most part young men of noble or patrician or merchant class, sent on their travels by their parents or guardians to acquire a knowledge of the world. In the second half of the century, a large number of such travellers began to visit England and not infrequently Scotland. Between 1566 and 1619 well over a dozen of these travellers (or rather groups of travellers) who came to Scotland have left albums or other records, but there were undoubtedly many more visitors than those whose albums have survived. We learn, for example, from Lupold von Wedel that the Earl of Morton, who was executed in 1581, had shown more friendship and honour to foreigners, especially to Germans, than had ever been done since.[8] The geographical representation among the travellers whose albums or itineraries are known is extensive, and the countries of origin include France, Bohemia, the Low Countries, Denmark and Germany. Some paid only brief visits of a week or two and seem not to have gone far beyond Edinburgh, but others made extensive tours lasting most of the summer. Lupold von Wedel went as far north as Perth, Hainzel von Degerstein included Aberdeen and the West of Scotland before crossing over to Ireland, and both Thomas Cuming and Jacob Fetzer included much of the north-east and the far north before crossing to Stirling and Glasgow.

Lupold von Wedel came primarily to acquire some knowledge of the Scottish Court, and the high point of his tour was undoubtedly the opportunity of seeing the King at worship in St John's Church, Perth, one Sunday morning.[9] Others such as Hainzel and his tutor, Caspar Waser, were intent, among other things, on visiting their Scottish friends, John Johnston and Robert Howie, whom they had known on the continent and with whom they had studied at German and Swiss universities,[10] and there were others, such as Johannes Haan,[11] and Otto Heinrich von Herberstein,[12] who were primarily interested in the universities, and Thomas Cuming,[13] the Belgian Scott, who was visiting his relations and family friends, and there were still others such as Jacob Fetzer,[14] who were out to see as much as they could and obtain as broad a knowledge of the country as was possible. The autograph albums of neither Lupold nor Hainzel appear to have survived, although we do know that Hainzel had one and that it had been subscribed in Scotland,[15] but we have Lupold's diary, Hainzel's itinerary and Fetzer's album. These three sources are in a fortunate way complementary.

Lupold, a younger son, was initially expected to follow a learned profession; having no liking for that life, but rather a keen desire to travel, he left home in the early thirties for an extensive tour first in Egypt and the Holy Land, then in Spain and Portugal. Thereafter, in 1584–85 he visited England and Scotland, but only after he had spent some time in military service on the Protestant side in France. His journal is full of interest, not least in that part which covers his weeks in Scotland, despite the fact that it is much less full than his record of his English tour. He was the leading member of a group of seven Germans of like quality, including an interpreter from the Hanse Merchants in London.[16] Furnished with a royal passport, they set out from London on 29th August and within a week, travelling by post horses, arrived at Berwick. This method seems to have proved expensive, for on the return they bought their horses in Scotland and took them south. Hainzel and Waser followed the same route north, but we are not sure how large their party was. They left on 2nd March 1592 and when they reached York made a detour to Keswick to visit the German miners, whom Queen Elizabeth had brought over from Hainzel's native Augsburg to work the rich copper mines. From there, they travelled through the Lake District to Carlisle, back to Keswick, and then via Hexham to Newcastle and thence to Berwick, where they arrived on the 3rd of May. Lupold, following Camden, the usual authority for travellers, described Berwick as 'the last town in England', but Waser, following Boece, commented that it was 'the first city [*urbs*] of Scotland, although presently occupied by the English'.[17] Both writers mentioned their warm reception and the provision of a band of soldiers from the Governor to see them safely across the border regions and into Scotland.

Lupold spent from 12th September to 2nd October in Scotland. Hainzel's visit was from 2nd May to 2nd July 1592. Following the coastal route to Edinburgh, Lupold's group visited Dunbar, and like Hainzel soon after him, was rowed out from Tantallon Castle to the Bass Rock. The visitors showed considerable interest in this fortress island, and in the solan geese, of which Lupold gives a detailed description, including some of the unusual tales that were told to travellers about them; for example, that they were not able to fly if they did not see water, but the moment they saw it, they could fly. Waser, much less credulous, merely records they were good to eat.[18] He may well have been familiar with Conrad Gesner's detailed description and drawing of the solan goose in his *Historiae Animalium,* published in Zürich in 1555. The description and the drawing had been sent to Gesner by Bishop Reid.[19] On the way to Edinburgh, Lupold and his party were shown where the Battle of Pinkie had been fought, and where, so they were told, some thirty thousand Scots had fallen.

At Edinburgh, among the sights to be seen was the house in which Darnley was killed, according to their informers, at the instigation of the Queen by her lover, and there, of course, the travellers picked up a lot of gossip. Five days later they moved to Perth, crossing from Leith to Kinghorn, and finally obtained permission to see the King in church on the following Sunday. There is an interesting account of the service, described as 'Zwinglian as in England', at which Bishop Adamson dressed in a long red taffeta coat delivered the sermon. The next day they returned to Edinburgh, and in the course of the week, attended yet another service in St Giles, and Adamson was again the preacher. Earlier, in the previous year, 1584, the leaders of the Presbyterian faction had fled to England as had some of the leading members of the nobility. Something of the unpopularity of Adamson, who had taken the place of the minister, James Lawson, in Edinburgh is reflected in Lupold's account of what appears to have been a forerunner of the more famous Jenny Geddes 'incident'. The women, we are told, would have stoned him to death had he not saved himself by flight. The King, Lupold recorded, wanted to make himself head of the church and the Bishop, who was on his side, was suspected of reintroducing popery. This belief had in part enraged the Edinburgh ladies.[20] There is also a gruesome description of the early Scottish form of the guillotine used in 1581 for beheading the Earl of Morton.[21]

During the days the German wayfarers spent in Edinburgh, their host was the father of William Fowler, a scholar who was well-connected with the court and later became secretary to Queen Anne.[22] William Stewart, the captain of the King's Guard whose wife was a German Countess, entertained them, and later on we find him making it possible for Hainzel and Waser to meet the King at Dalkeith Palace.[23] Another generous benefactor of the visitors was Robert, sixth Lord Seton, and later first Earl of Winton, who was reported to have kept at Seton Palace 'a very hospitable house where the King and Queen, as well as French and other Ambassadors and strangers of quality, were nobly and frequently entertained'. Waser described him as 'ein sehr gelehrter Edelman, uund ein liebhaber frömbde nationen'. Unfortunately, he was not in residence when Lupold arrived but he does mention the palace and its gardens, which Groome, in his *Gazetteer*, tells us 'excelled in taste and elegance any other mansion of the sixteenth and seventeenth century, and was esteemed much the most magnificent castle in Scotland. Its gardens and terraced walks, as well as its splendid interior, were the delight of Kings'.[24]

Hainzel's visit, as well as being longer in duration, was also much more extensive than that of Wedel. He and his tutor had come to visit friends and had brought letters from leading authorities on the continent. It was probably the fact that they had letters to King James from Theodore Beza, the renowned theologian and Calvin's successor in Geneva, that secured for them an audience and the royal entries in Hainzel's album.[25] They also were welcomed by the leading members of Edinburgh University, and in particular by the Dutch humanist, Adrian Damman, who was engaged in turning into Latin Du Bartas' *Septimania*. He gave Waser a copy for him to comment upon which he later returned.[26] They were also entertained by Thomas Seget, one of the early graduates of Edinburgh University, the tutor to the Seton family, who in the following years had a distinguished career on the continent as the friend of Lipsius, Kepler and many others. Seget's album is preserved in Rome, and is one of the few kept by Scotsmen that has survived. It records that Hainzel and Seget met up again in Venice in October 1597.[27]

At St Andrews, where they stayed for five days, the travellers were entertained by Andrew Melville, Rector of the University, and others to whom they were commended no doubt by letters from Beza and other distinguished scholars on the continent, and also by William Dundas of Fingask, who was later to become a friend of Karl von Zerotin, the Bohemian nobleman, who at one time intended a visit to Scotland.[28] Among those mentioned as having entertained the visitors in St Andrews, apart from the Melvilles in St Mary's College, were David Moneypenny, Dean of the Faculty of Arts, and John Kennedy, Earl of Cassillis, a student resident at that time in St Mary's. To all of them Waser wrote letters of thanks which have not survived, but letters from Cassillis and Moneypenny to Waser, written in 1594, have been preserved.[29] They also met the ministers and the newly elected Provost, William Murray.[30] From St Andrews, the journey northward was broken to meet at his home at Easter Seatown in Angus Peter Young, one of Beza's first students in Geneva, and later along with George Buchanan one of James VI's tutors. Thereafter they proceeded to Aberdeen to meet Robert Howie, the recently appointed Principal of the newly erected Marischal College. Unfortunately, we know little of the visit apart from Howie's pleasure in meeting his old friends. He seized the opportunity to give to Waser letters for his friends on the continent.[31] On their return to Edinburgh they moved westwards to Linlithgow, Stirling and Glasgow, where they were also entertained by members of the university. On the Sunday they went to visit Dumbarton Castle, a popular excursion for tourists, as was Dunnottar Castle in the east. At first they intended crossing to Ireland from Ayr, but thwarted by the weather they made their way to Kirkcudbright and crossed in a boat manned by 'two wild sailors from Knockfergus'.[32] It is a matter of regret that only the itinerary and a number of letters have survived and that that album that would undoubtedly have added greatly to our information has not come to light. Its loss is in part made up by the preservation of the album of Jacob Fetzer who, following a similar itinerary, visited Scotland in 1619.

Fetzer, like Hainzel the son of a patrician family, came from the prosperous German city Nurenberg. Born towards the end of the sixteenth century, he died in 1637 in his native city in which he had become a lawyer and a magistrate.[33] His education began in Wittenberg in 1611 and was continued at Jena, Altdorf, and Basel. He came to England for the first time in July 1618 and then again in 1619. From every point of view, his album is undoubtedly the finest of any visitor to Scotland, the second of two in which he kept the record of his European tours. The earlier one covers the period 1610–1620 and the latter 1617–1627.[34] On his second visit to Britain he made an extensive tour of the British Isles. Leaving London about 23rd June 1619, he took the usual route north and about three weeks later arrived in Berwick,[35] where he obtained the signature of William Boyer, the Captain of the garrison. Crossing into Scotland, he made his way along the coastal route to Edinburgh where he arrived on 18th July.[36] The following day he made the usual excursion to the Bass Rock, then crossed over from Leith to Fife, visited St Andrews and Dundee, and made his way to Aberdeen, where he arrived on 29th August.[37] Two days later he progressed along the north-east coast and visited the far north. By 10th October he had returned to Edinburgh[38] and about a month later he was back in London.[39] His tour of Scotland is both the longest in duration and the most extensive so far known of any German traveller.

The visit is well represented in the numerous inscriptions he obtained. One of the earliest entries is that of Robert Wilkie, a member of a well-known Edinburgh family and a relative of the St Leonard's College professor. The entry is the only one made in Scotland which has a family coat of arms. There is also a motto in French.[40] The professors of Edinburgh figure prominently, George Sibbald,[41] Andrew Young[42] and Patrick Sands;[43] but most interesting for us is the fact that he obtained the entries of many of those of highest rank, Alexander Seton, Earl of Dunfermline and Chancellor of Scotland,[44] Thomas Hamilton, Earl of Montrose,[45] John Hay of Yester,[46] William Scott of Elie,[47] Frederick Stewart of Pittenweem,[48] and many others. Among this number of notables is the signature of Archibald Napier, *Magni ilius Naperii filius*,[49] as he styled himself, and also Peter Young.[50] There is only one entry recorded at St Andrews, that of the Provost of the day by name John Knox.[51]

Of great interest to Fetzer seems to have been the visit to Scotstarvit near Cupar on 23rd August, where he was entertained by Sir John Scot,[52] Director of the Royal Chancery, a former student and later a generous benefactor of St Leonard's College. His wife, Anna Drummond, the sister of the poet William Drummond of Hawthornden, and one of the very small number of women to sign the album, entered her name under her family motto 'Go warlie'.[53] At Scotstarvit our young traveller obtained in addition the signature of a St Mary's College student from Middelburg, Abraham Sauchelle.[54] A literary party of scholars had in fact gathered at Scotstarvit at this time which included William Drummond[55] and William Alexander, first Earl of Stirling, the poet and dramatist.[56] On the way north Fetzer obtained at Dundee the signature of John Scrymgeour, First Viscount Dudhope,[57] and at Aberdeen the signatures of Andrew Edie, Principal of Marischal College,[58] and another professor, Patrick Johnstone.[59] The leading ecclesiastics and noblemen of the north are all well represented. The list includes Bishop Patrick Forbes,[60] Bishop Patrick Lindsay.[61] Sir Thomas Burnett of Leys,[62] and, as Fetzer went farther north, Colin Mackenzie of Kintail,[63] Sir Rory Mackenzie of Coigeach,[64] Gilbert Gray of Skibo,[65] and Robert Gordon of Sutherland.[66] All these entries indicate that Fetzer travelled farther north than any other known student visitor. He may well have returned south by the Great Glen, for we find him at the beginning of October in the area of Loch Lomond at the home of Sir William Livingstone of Kilsyth,[67] before returning to Edinburgh and making a visit to Thomas Foulis[68] at Leadhills, who was prospecting for gold on licence from the King. The album that records this most interesting tour is profusely illustrated for the periods spend in England and the continent; regrettably, there are no illustrations at all for the Scottish period. This list of Germans could be easily increased. Zeiller in his *Itinerarium magnae Britanniae* in 1634 published the itnerary of a journey to Scotland and Ireland by a 'Count of the Holy Roman Empire' who had visited this country in 1609. This I have not been seen.[69] Two years later there took place the visits of Frederick Gizköfler (1592–1653), the son of a wealthy merchant of Augsburg who got as far north as Perth.[70]

Of the more strictly academic visitors Jonas van Reigersberch, Johannes Haan, and Otto Heinrich von Herberstein are typical and representative. Jonas van Reigersberch (1578–1611)[71] visited Scotland in 1597. The second son of the burgomaster of Campvere, he was related to the great humanist scholar and legal and political writer, Hugo Grotius. Reigersberch came to Britain in August 1596, and visited the Universities of Cambridge, Edinburgh, St Andrews and Oxford, in that order, then returned to the continent to study at Heidelberg, Strasbourg and Basel. He spent almost a year at Cambridge before leaving for Scotland in July 1597.[72] After entering the country he made the regular visit to Seton Palace and obtained a dedication in his album from the Earl of Winton.[73] At Edinburgh he seems to have associated himself primarily with his fellow countryman, Adrian Damman, whom James VI had brought over from the Low Countries.[74] He also got to know Adam King, the Commissary and Clerk to the General Assembly,[75] and Robert Rollock, Principal of the University.[76] At St Andrews he was welcomed by the Rector, Andrew Melville, who had just seen the University put through a severe visitation by the King and several royal commissioners.[77] He also met Melville's nephew James and his colleague John Johnston. Johnston's entry is of interest — a quotation from Lucretius given a Christian dress by prefixing an additional line

> Sine Deo nihil!
> O parvas hominum mentes, o pectora caeca!
> Qualibus in tenebris vitae, quantisque periclis
> Degitur hoc quodcumque est aevi.[78]

A Danish nobleman, Andrew Schwendi[79] (whose album will be mentioned below), at that time a student in St Mary's, inserted his name on 3rd August. Before leaving Fife, the visitor went to Falkland Palace and secured from King James the usual royal inscription found in several later albums: 'Est nobilis ira leonis'. There is also the well-known quotation from Vergil *Aeneid* 6 which the King took as one of his mottos: 'Parcere subjectis et debellare superbos'.[80] This royal inscription occupies the position of honour in albums, being written on the front pages. Others who added their signature include John Erskine, Earl of Mar,[81] Alexander Dixon,[82] and William Fowler, the Scottish poet and secretary to Queen Anne,[83] and probably that of Archibald Harbertson. This album and that of Schwendi are, as far as is known, the earliest to include visits to Scotland.

Schwendi's album, now in the Royal Library, National Library of Sweden in Stockholm, is of special interest. It is an interleaved printed book, Nicolas Reusner's *Icones sive Imagines virorum literis illustrium*, the edition published at Strasbourg in 1590.[84] Before setting out from his homeland he secured the signature of the King of Denmark and in 1590 that of King James VI in his own hand, along with his usual inscription; unfortunately no precise days or places are given. The Scottish King was at that time seeking his Danish bride, the future Queen Anne. Schwendi's academic tour was in many ways similar to that of Robert Howie on the continent.[85] From 1591 to 1593 he studied at Herborn, left for the autumn Frankfurt Book Fair and made his way to Lausanne and then on to Geneva. On his return he visited Basel, Strasbourg and Heidelberg and again Frankfurt. When or where he entered Britain is not known. The earliest British signatures apart from that of King James are in 1595. That he had sailed across to Orkney may be tentatively deduced from the signature of Patrick, Earl of Orkney, on 5th January 1594 (1595 n.s.).[86] By mid-July he was in Aberdeen where he met the minister and recently appointed bishop, David Cunningham,[87] and the Commissary Clerk, George Abercrombie.[88] He seems to have stayed at least two to three weeks in the north and met professors at both of Aberdeen's universities including Peter Udney on 12th July[89] and four days later Professor William Forbes[90] and his namesake, the minister of Kintore,[91] another minister, David Robertson,[92] and Professor Alexander Scrogie of the newly founded Marischal College.[93] Gilbert Gray[94] and Peter Blackburn,[95] one of the Aberdeen ministers, added their names on 31st July and 1st August. The one for whom he would have had much news was however Robert Howie, the Principal of Marischal College. He entered his inscription and fulsome dedication on 1st August.[96] Twelve days later Schwendi was in St Andrews and matriculated in the university,[97] where he also met his fellow countryman, Johannes Ottensen.[98] Unlike those who have been mentioned earlier, Schwendi appears to have become a regular student at St Andrews where he remained until at least the end of the summer of 1597. Unfortunately many of the prominent members of the St Andrews community, for example Andrew Melville and John Johnston, are not represented in his album. There is however an entry from the pen of James Kennedy, the young Earl of Cassillis, at that time a student in St Mary's College;[99] for 1596 the name of James Clark is entered, and for 1597 the names of John Munro,[100] and David Black,[101] one of the ministers of St Andrews. Black records in his dedication the fact that he had that summer been deprived of his St Andrews charge. An added interest in this album is the fact that it records the names of three other continental visitors to St Andrews at this time whose presence is otherwise unknown: Demetrius Kleinfelt, 2nd August 1597,[102] Lauge Christensen (Lago Christianus), July 1597 whose entry includes a quotation in Arabic,[103] and Matthias Husgarterus from Zurich, 8th July 1597.[104] There is no record of Schwendi visiting other parts of Scotland or of England. On his return home he became a canon of Roskilde.[105]

Five years later another Dane, the 'rigrrad' Tage Thott (1580–1658),[106] a nephew of the astronomer Tycho Brahe, included Scotland in his educational tour that included the usual continental academic centres, Heidelberg, Strasbourg, Basel, Geneva, Orléans, Paris and London. Thott's brief visit to Scotland is recorded in his beautifully illustrated album.[107] He was at Falkland on 14th July 1602 where he obtained the signature of Sir James Ramsay.[108] The only other Scotsman to add his name in Scotland was William Fowler; it is dated at Edinburgh on 16th July.[109] He had earlier on the continent met Scots, including Alexander Arbuthnot in Heidelberg in 1600,[110] and a fellow-Dane Christopher Hansen Dalby who had been at St Andrews along with Schwendi and had graduated in 1595.[111]

To those predominently Scandinavian visitors should be added the names of Johannes Haan, a medical student from Würtzburg, and Otto Heinrich von Herberstein. Haan seems to have been constantly on the move between 1596 and 1608. His album[112] bears, alas, the marks of former careless or disrespectful owners, who allowed their children from time to time to use its blank pages as a scribbling or doodling pad. Nevertheless it has survived. Haan's tour of Scotland took place in the historic year 1603. Toward the end of July, along with some unknown German companions, he set out from London for Cambridge, where he made the acquaintance of the University's most distinguished members. Passing through Connington, he met on 12th September Sir Robert Cotton, the famous collector of the Cottonian Manuscripts in the British Library, along with William Camden on a visit to Huntingdonshire.[113] Exactly where and when he entered Scotland the album does not record. It is, however, probable that he came by the west route, for we find the first Scottish entry dated at Glasgow on 9th October.[114] His visit lasted about a month. On 5th November he was in Berwick[115] on his way to Oxford and London. Into this short period he put a considerable amount of travelling, visiting Glasgow, Perth, Banff, Dundee, St Andrews, Dunfermline and Edinburgh. His main interest was in the universities, but he did, like others, visit two of the most impressive sights of the day, the great western Scottish fortress, Dumbarton Castle, and Dunnottar Castle in the east.[116] At Edinburgh we find him in the company of some of the most prominent citizens — Adam King,[117] Adrian Damman[118] and a number of others, including John Napier of Merchiston.[119] Napier's entry is in an elegant hand and reads

> Sola salus servire deo, sunt caetera fraudes.

At Dundee he obtained the signature and an entry from the minister, Robert Howie, recently translated from Aberdeen,[120] and in St Andrews the signature of Robert Wilkie of St Leonard's College at that time rector of the University.[121] Andrew Melville's signature is also accompanied by a Greek inscription.[122] John Johnstone's entry which he also inserted in other albums is, as befitted a distinguished neo-Latin poet, particularly high minded!

> Sursum mens, suspecta
> Terrenaque despice cuncta.[123]

Travellers such as Haan were keen to meet not only leading academics, but also foreign students who like Schwendi and Reigersberch regularly inscribed each other's albums. We have in this album, as in Reigersberch's, the entry of another Danish student in St Andrews, Albert Löthöffell.[124] From St Andrews Haan visited Dunfermline, where he was entertained by Patrick Sands, the minister and one of the first graduates of the University of Edinburgh. Sands, who had also studied abroad, later became Principal at Edinburgh University.[125]

Otto Heinrich was born in 1590, the third son of Sigmund Fredrich von Herberstein, who was in the service of the Emperor, Rudolph II. The father was a Protestant, as were two of his sons. Other members of his family elected to be Catholic, one becoming a Provincial of the Dominicans. Otto had leanings toward learning and studied at a number of universities. His album shows a considerable interest in Protestantism and in Protestant theologians, but there are also representative entries from aristrocrats and diplomats.[126] His British itinerary began on 23rd October 1609, with visits to Oxford and Cambridge. In July of the following year he arrived in Edinburgh. The contribution to the album by Principal Henry Charteris in Hebrew, Greek and Latin is dated 25th July.[127] The next day Herberstein was in St Andrews, but secured only one inscription, that of John Johnston, who was recovering from a severe illness. Johnston was obviously delighted to meet the young German, whose visit brought back memories of his own student days in Germany. Johnston had been on the continent from 1584 to 1590. After his name he adds significantly 'affectu et educatione Germanus'.[128] The young Count does not appear, however, to have travelled farther north, but to have made his way westward to the home of James Hamilton, Earl of Abercorn.[129] In addition to the entry made by the Earl there are those of his physician Robert Hamilton, and Robert Kaus who signed as secretary to the Earl.[130] by 7th August he had reached Anglesey and secured an entry in Welsh.[131]

These aristocratic and student travellers whose albums have survived and which have been discussed here, it must be stressed, are merely representative of a considerable number of overseas students who included Scotland as part of their educational tour.

The final visitor selected for consideration, Thomas Cuming, was regarded by J. F. Kellas Johnstone in his unique study of Scottish student albums as a Scot.[132] He rightly singled out Cuming's album as one of the finest of a very small number of extant examples formerly belonging to Scotsmen. Cuming was born in Holland, where his father, a Scot, was a lieutenant in the Scottish company in the service of the States General of the Dutch republic. Thomas descibed himself as 'Belga Scotus', and apart from the summer of 1611 which he spent travelling in Scotland, the rest of his life was lived on the continent.[133] Like all those whose albums have formed the basis for this study, he was a visitor nevertheless with a particular incentive for his journey — the opportunity to meet relatives and to see the land of his fathers.

Cuming's academic career had begun in 1604 at the Scots College in Rome, but finding he had no vocation to the priesthood, he returned to Hardenwyk. The student travels recorded in his album, now in the British Library.[134] began in 1611 and ended in 1619. Rich in inscriptions, including those of members of British and continental royal families, of dukes, counts, barons, archbishops, bishops, professors and fellow students, it has also twenty-one fully coloured painted armorial bearings. The tour of Britain began in Aberdeen in 1612 from where he set out to visit relatives and a wide circle of prominent people in church and state. Peter Blackburn, formerly one of Andrew Melville's colleagues in Glasgow University and since 1600 Bishop of Aberdeen, met Cuming on 14th August 1612.[135] His clan chief, James Cuming of Altyre, dated his entry at his home in Moray.[136] There follow the entries of Alexander Douglas, Bishop of Moray,[137] David Lindsay, Bishop of Ross,[138] and Andrew Lamb, Bishop of Brechin.[139] The most celebrated of the later Aberdeen bishops and doctors, John Forbes of Corse, contributed an entry in Latin with a pleasing play on words 'Constat aeterna positumque lege est ut constat gentium nihil'.[140] At Perth he visited the minister, John Malcolm, a former St Leonard's College student and regent.[141] Archbishop George Gladstones of St Andrews,[142] John Wemyss, rector of the University,[143] and Robert Howie, since 1611 Andrew Melville's successor as Principal of St Mary's College, are all represented. Howie's quotation from Tertullian is typical of the vast majority of moral aphorisms in most albums: 'Si apud Deum deposueris injuriam, ille ultor erit. Si damnum ille restautator erit; si dolorem ille medicus erit; si mortem rescuscitator erit'.[144] By October Cuming had reached Edinburgh, where Patrick Sands, Principal of the University,[145] is the sole representative from the Scottish capital to record his name and give the album's owner his good wishes. Cuming's visit to his fatherland had lasted about ten weeks, from 14th August to 9th October. He was not to return. The greater part of his visit to Britain was spent in England.[146]

The Scot was in the sixteenth and seventeenth centuries as in many others a familiar figure at the universities and at the royal courts, in the centres of commerce and in the armies of almost every part of the continent. That students from foreign countries came to the Scottish universities at that time was one of the proud boasts of the diarist James Melville and a matter for which he loyally gave his uncle Andrew Melville full credit. [147] Detailed evidence for the attendance in significant numbers at the universities of Glasgow, St Andrews, and Edinburgh by students from most European countries was, however, first provided by Thomas McCrie in the second edition of his well-known biography of Andrew Melville as long ago as 1824.[148] Such lists have now been substantially increased, although details based on recent research have not yet all been published. That Scotland was included along with other countries in the travels of a wide variety of young men seeking experience of the world, when it has not been denied, has, nevertheless, been regarded by writers on the subject as virtually incredible, or at best as an excursion to be ventured upon only by a few courageous spirits. The evidence discussed here provides an entirely different picture. As well as young Scottish students and noblemen going to France, Germany, Switzerland, Italy and elsewhere, many of their counterparts, eager to enhance their experience, travelled throughout Scotland, visited its universities, its royal palaces, the houses of its nobility and of its learned gentlemen and there found a cordial reception within a cosmopolitan society with which they were already familiar throughout the continent.

NOTES

Throughout the research that had lead to this paper I have had most valued and unstinted help from Mr R. N. Smart, Keeper of the University Muniments, St Andrews.

1. P. Hume Brown, ed., *Early Travellers in Scotland* (Edinburgh, 1981).

2. 'Lupold von Wedels Beschreibung seiner Reisen und Kreigerlebnisse', ed. Max Bär, *Baltische Studien, herausgegeben von der Gesellschaft für Pommersche Geschichte und Altertumskunde* (45 Jahrgang, Stettin, 1895); 'Journey through England and Scotland made by Lupold von Wedel in the years 1584 and 1585', translated by Gottfried von Bülow, *Transactions of the Royal Historical Society*, New Series, Vol. 9, (1895), 223–270; Victor von Klarwill, *Queen Elizabeth and Some Foreigners*, translated by T. H. Nash (London, 1928), gives a good account of Wedel and a translation of the English section only of his itinerary.

3. J. K. Cameron, ed., 'The British Itinerary of Johann Peter Hainzel von Degerstein by Caspar Waser', *Zwingliana* Vol. 15 (Zürich, 1980), 259–295.

4. E. S. Bates, *Touring in 1600* (London, 1910), 127.

5. W. D. Robson-Scott, *German Travellers in England 1400–1800* (Oxford, 1953), 42f.

6. Hume Brown, *Early Travellers*, ix.

7. On the general subject of 'Alba amicorum' or 'Stammbücher' see further M. A. E. Nickson, *Early Autograph Albums in the British Museum* (London, 1970) and in particular the bibliography, 29–31; J.-U. Fechner, ed., *Stammbücher als kulturhistorische Quellen* (1981), 7ff., 111ff; J. F. Kellas Johnstone, *The Alba Amicorum of George Strachan, George Craig, Thomas Cuming*, 1ff., 32f.

8. Transactions of the Royal Historical Society (*T.R.H.S.*), Vol. 9, 246.

9. *Ibid.*, 245.

10. *Zwingliana*, 268, 284; J. K. Cameron, *Letters of John Johnston and Robert Howie* (Edinburgh, 1963), 5f., 63ff., xliiiff.

11. Haan was a medical student at Würtzburg. British Library, Additional MS 19828; Nickson, 18.

12. Erich Zöllner, 'Aus dem Stammbuch des Freiherrn Otto Heinrich von Herberstein',

Mitteilungen des Instituts für österreichische Geschichtsforschung, Vol. 63 (1955), 358ff.

13. J. F. K. Johnstone, *The Alba Amicorum,* 32ff.

14. Hans Butzmann, *Die Blankenburger Handschriften* (Frankfurt on Main), Vol. 11 (1966), 225, 238.

15. *Zwingliana,* 280ff.

16. *T.R.H.S.,* 223ff.

17. William Camden, *Britannia* (ed. E. Gibson, London 1722), 1009; *Zwingliana,* 278ff.

18. *T.R.H.S.,* 241f; *Zwingliana,* 286.

19. C. Gesner, *Historical Animalium* (Zurich, 1555), Vol. 3, 158.

20. *T.R.H.S.,* 245f.

21. *Ibid.,* 246.

22. *Ibid.,* 247; *Dictionary of National Biography (D.N.B.),* 20, 89; H. W. Meikle, ed., *The Works of William Fowler,* 3, ixff.

23. *T.R.H.S.,* 245f; *Zwingliana,* 280f; *D.N.B.,* Vol. 54, 362ff.

24. *T.R.H.S.,* 247; *Zwinglian,* 278f; F. H. Groome, *Ordnance Gazetteer of Scotland* (New edition, 1901), 1462.

25. *Zwingliana,* 280f.

26. *Zwingliana,* 282; Cameron, *Letters of John Johnston,* lxxii, 159ff., 169f.

27. O. Odlozilik, 'Thomas Seget: a Scottish Friend of Syzmon Szmonowicz', *Polish Review,* Vol. 11 (1966), 3-39; Baumgarten, *Ein schottisches Stammbuch, Zs f. vgl. Lit. Gesch.,* N.F.5., 1892, 94; James Kirk, *The Records of the Synod of Lothian and Tweeddale,* The Stair Society (Edinburgh, 1977), 82.

28. *Zwingliana,* 267, 282f; Cameron, *Letters of John Johnston,* 92ff.

29. Cameron, *Letters of John Johnston,* 360ff.

30. Murray had been elected provost in 1593, an election which occasioned disputes and litigation. Cameron, *Letters of John Johnston,* 92.

31. Cameron, *Letters of John Johnston,* 303ff.

32. *Zwingliana,* 288f.

33. H. Butzmann, *Die Blankenburger Handschriften, Kataloge der Herzog-August Bibliothek, Wolfenbüttel* (Frankfurt on Main, 1966), 225, 238; Mss 231 and 235; *Die Matrikel der Universität Basel* (ed. H. G. Wackernagel, Basel 1962), Vol. 3, 200 no. 75; H. E. Knesche, *Neues allgemeines Deutsches Adels Lexicon* (Leipzig, 1859), Vol. 3, 239; K. H. Schaible, *Geschichte der Deutschen in England* (Strassburg, 1885), 230.

34. Details of both albums are given by Butzmann, 225ff., 238ff.

35. Herzog-August-Bibliothek, Wolfenbüttel, Ms. Blankenburg, 235 fos. 182v, 184v, 103r.

36. *Ibid.,* fos. 63v, 68r, 43r.

37. *Ibid.,* fo. 59v.

38. *Ibid.,* fo. 46v.

39. Ms. 231, fo. 308v.

40. Ms. 235 fo. 198r.

41. Ms. 235 fo. 47r.

42. Ms. 235 fo. 68r; A. Dalziel, *History of the University of Edinburgh* (1862), Vol. 2, 40ff.

43. Ms. 235, fo. 63v; *Fasti Ecclesiae Scoticanae* (ed. Hew Scot, 1928), Vol. 1, 381; Dalziel, *History of the University of Edinburgh,* Vol. 2, 19ff; A. Grant, *The Story of the University of Edinburgh* (1884), 199ff.

44. Ms. 235, fo. 36r, 31 July 1619; *D.N.B.,* 51, 261ff; *The Scots Peerage,* Vol. 3, 369ff.

45. Ms. 235, fo. 37r, Thomas Hamilton (1563-1637), Earl of Melrose, described himself as King's Advocate; *D.N.B.,* Vol. 24, 209ff; *The Scots Peerage,* Vol. 4, 310.

46. Ms. 235, fo. 42r; subsequently first Earl of Tweeddale. *The Scots Peerage,* Vol. 8, 447ff.

47. Ms. 235, fo. 172r. *The Scots Peerage,* Vol. 3, 346.

48. Ms. 235, fo. 41v; subsequently Lord Pittenweem. *The Scots Peerage,* Vol. 7, 68f.

49. Ms. 235, fo. 51r. Archibald Napier (1576–1645), Baron of Merchiston, described as Treasurer-depute. *The Scots Peerage*, Vol. 6, 422ff; *D.N.B.*, Vol. 40, 35.

50. Ms. 235, fo. 43r; *D.N.B.*, Vol. 63, 386ff.

51. Ms. 235, fo. 81v. John Knox was provost of St Andrews from 1616 to 1618. D. H. Fleming, *Municipal Relics of St Andrews and some of its Early Provosts* (St Andrews, 1905), 11.

52. Ms. 235, fo. 57r. Sir John Scot or Scott of Scotstarvit, *D.N.B.*, Vol. 51, 39ff.

53. Ms. 235, fo. 57r.

54. Ms. 235, fo. 57v. 1619. Abraham Sauchelle was a student at St Mary's College, St Andrews, 1616–17, 1618–19. St Andrews University Muniments UY 152/2, 223 and UY 305/3, 163.

55. Ms. 235, fo. 61r. William Drummond (1585–1649). *D.N.B.*, Vol. 16, 45ff.

56. Ms. 235, fo. 58r. William Alexander (*c.*1567–1640), *D.N.B.*, Vol. 1, 275; *The Scots Peerage*, Vol. 8, 170ff; C. Rogers, *Memorials of the Earl of Stirling* (2 vols., 1877).

57. Ms. 235 fo. 36v; *D.N.B.*, Vol. 51, 152; *The Scots Peerage*, Vol. 3, 313ff.

58. Ms. 235, fo. 59v. Andrew Edie or Adie, was Principal from 1616 to 1620, *Fasti Ecclesiae Scoticanae*, Vol. 7, 357; Fetzer had met Edie when he was a professor in Danzig, Blankenberg Ms. 231, fo. 299r; P. J. Anderson, *Studies in the History and Development of the University of Aberdeen* (Aberdeen, 1906), 70f., 73.

59. Ms. 235 fo. 82v. Patrick Johnstone listed among *Laurea donati* at Marischal College on 27 July 1619; *Fasti Acad. Marisc.* Vol. 2, 195.

60. Ms. 235 fo. 54v. Patrick Forbes (1564–1635), Bishop of Aberdeen, *Fasti Ecclesiae Scoticinae*, Vol. 7, 330; *D.N.B.*, Vol. 19, 407f.

61. Ms. 235, fo. 56r; Patrick Lindsay, Bishop of Ross and subsequently Archbishop of Glasgow, *Fasti Ecclesiae Scoticinae*, Vol. 7, 330; *D.N.B.*, Vol. 33, 312.

62. Ms. 235, fo. 41r. Sir Thomas Burnett of Leys had in this year been created Baron. G. Burnett, *The Family of Burnett of Leys* (New Spalding Club, Aberdeen, 1901), 41–59.

63. Ms. 235, fo. 38r. Colin, second Lord Mackenzie of Kintail, *The Scots Peerage*, Vol. 7, 506f.

64. Ms. 235, fo. 38v. Sir Rory or Roderick Mackenzie, *The Scots Peerage*, Vol. 3, 69ff.

65. Ms. 235, fo. 50v. Gilbert Gray, one of the commissioners for the sheriffdom of Sutherland, *Reg. P. C. Scot.*, Vol. 12, 313.

66. Ms. 235, fo. 50r. Sir Robert Gordon 1580–1656, *The Scots Peerage*, Vol. 7, 345f; *D.N.B.*, Vol. 22, 224ff; W. Fraser, *Sutherland Book*, Vol. 1, 192ff.

67. Ms. 235 fo. 44r; *The Scots Peerage*, Vol. 7, 189f.

68. Ms. 235, fo. 56r; 'a wealthy goldsmith in Edinburgh'; cf. *The Scots Peerage*, Vol. 4, 492 and 8, 171; *D.N.B.*, Vol. 1, 275.

69. Robson-Scott, 83. It has not been possible to see Martin Zeiler, *Itinerarium Magnae Britanniae* (Strasbourg, 1634) (Second edition, 1674).

70. Robson-Scott, 89.

71. P. J. Meertens, 'Het Album Amicorum van Jonas van Reigersberch (1578–1611)', *Archief vroegere en Latere Mededelingen 1946–1947* (Middelburg, 1947), 1–39.

72. Meertens, 7.

73. Meertens, 7, 33. See above, note 24.

74. Meertens, 13; his entry in the album is dated 15 July 1597. *Nieuw Nederlandsch Biografisch Woordenboek*, Vol. 3, 273ff; Cameron, *Letters of John Johnston*, 161.

75. Meertens, 29, Adam King (1625), advocate and commissary of Edinburgh. F. J. Grant, *The Faculty of Advocates in Scotland* (Scottish Record Society, 1944), 45, 117.

76. Meertens, 29, 5 August 1597. Rollock was at this time at Falkland Palace, with the King as a member of a recently appointed commission of the General Assembly. *D.N.B.*, Vol. 49, 171ff. *Fasti Ecclesiae Scoticanae*, Vol. 1, 37.

77. Meertens, *op.cit.*, 25; the entry is dated 2 August 1597; *Evidence, oral and documentary taken and received by the Commissioners … for visiting the Universities of Scotland* (London, 1837), Vol. 3, 197ff.

78. Meertens, 7, 19; *Titi Lucreti Cari De Rerum Natura* (ed. C. Bailey, Oxford, 1963), II, 14–16:

> O miseras hominum mentis, o pectora caeca!
> qualibus in tenebris vitae quantisque periclis
> degitur hoc aevi quodcumquest!

79. Meertens, 32; H. Ilsøe, 'Danske Studerende ved St Andrews Skotland 1595-1610', *Personal historisk Tidsskrift*, Vol. 4 (1962), 23–26. The album of Schwendi (1576–c.1646) is in the Royal Library, National Library of Sweden, K.885. Schwendi was in St Andrews in 1595, '96 and '97. St Andrews University Muniments, UY 152/2. 200–202. Ilsøe (24f.) lists six Danish students at St Andrews between 1595 and 1609.

80. Meertens, 7, 19; Vergil, *Aeneid*, 6.853.

81. Meertens, 10. The Earl of Mar (1558-1634) had at this time charge of the infant Prince Henry, *The Scots Peerage*, Vol. 5, 615ff., *D.N.B.*, Vol. 17. 422-426.

82. Meertens, 14; Alexander Dickson (1558-1604), J. Durkan, 'Alexander Dickson and S.T.C. 6823', *The Bibliothek*, Vol. 3, 1962, 183–190.

83. Meertens, 15; William Fowler, see above, note 22.

84. A microfilm copy of the relevant portions of this manuscript was kindly provided for the University Library, St Andrews by the National Library of Sweden. It was not unusual for travellers to use an interleaved emblem book as an album or *stammbuch*.

85. Cameron, *Letters of John Johnson*, xviiff., xxiiiff., xliii.

86. National Library of Sweden Ms. K885.

87. *Ibid.* See further, *Fasti Ecclesiae Scoticanae*, Vol. 7, 328.

88. Ms. K885. Master George Abercrombie of Overcarden was Commissary of Aberdeen, *Extracts from the Council Register of the Burgh of Aberdeen, 1570-1625*, Vol. 2, 170.

89. Ms. K885, 290v. Peter Udney was Sub-principal at King's College, P. J. Anderson, *Officers and Graduates of King's College, Aberdeen* (New Spalding Club, 1893), 40.

90. Ms. K885, 292v. William Forbes was senior regent at King's College, Anderson *op.cit.*, 40, and succeeded Andrew Edie as principal of Marischal College in 1620. P. J. Anderson, *Studies in the History and Development of the University of Aberdeen* (1906), 41f.

91. Ms. K885. William Forbes, minister of Kintore, *Fasti Ecclesiae Scoticanae* Vol. 6, 168.

92. Ms. K885, 400v. David Robertson was later minister of Fetterangus, *Fasti Ecclesiae Scoticanae*, Vol. 6, 218.

93. Ms. K885, 402v; *Fasti Ecclesiae Scoticanae*, Vol. 6, 18f.

94. Ms. K885, 22v. Gilbert Gray subsequently was Principal of Marischal College from 1598 to 1616, Anderson, *Fasti Acad. Marisch.* 1. 60f; P. J. Anderson, *Studies in the History and Development of the University of Aberdeen* (Aberdeen, 1906), 40.

95. Ms. K885, 8v; *Fasti Ecclesiae Scoticanae*, Vol. 7, 329.

96. Ms. K885, 354. Cameron, *Letters of John Johnston*, lxiiiff.

97. St Andrews University Muniments UY 152/2. 200–202.

98. Ilsøe 23, Ms. K885, 408v. This name has not been identified in the University records.

99. See above, note 29, and Ms. K885. This is the first entry in the book.

100. Ms. K885, 297r. Clark has not been identified; John Munro had graduated in 1589 and became minister at Tain in 1599. *Fasti Ecclesiae Scoticanae*, 7, 70f.

101. Ms. K885; D. H. Fleming, ed., *The Minister, Elders and Deacons of the Christian Congregation of St Andrews*, Vol. 2, 828; Cameron, *Letters of John Johnston*, lx, 93, 131f.

102. Ms. K885, 410v. This name has not been identified in the St Andrews records.

103. Ms. K885. This name has not been identified in the St Andrews records.

104. Ms. K885 34v. Husgarterus has not been identified in St Andrews records; a

Johnnes Valesius Belga was in St Andrews in 1599–1600, St Andrews University muniments UY 152/2. 205.

105. Ilsøe, 24.

106. P. Engelstoft and Svend Dahl, *Dansk Biografisk Leksikon*, Vol. 24, 62ff.

107. Vello Helk, *Stambøger I det Kongelige Bibliotek før 1800* (1980), 43, No. 68. I am grateful to Dr Thomas Riis of Copenhagen for examining this album for me (N.K.S. 681 in 8°) and supplying the details.

108. Ms. N.K.S. 688 fo. 79v; *D.N.B.*, Vol. 47, 243f.

109. Ms. N.K.S. 688 fo. 79r. and above, note 22.

110. Ms. N.K.S. 688 fo. 140r.

111. Ms. N.K.S. 688 fo. 139; Ms. K885; Ilsøe, *op.cit.*, 25. Christophorus Johannides Danus responded to theses at which Andrew Melville was *praeses* in 1595. For details of the published theses, see R. G. Cant, 'The St Andrews University Theses 1579–1747', *Edinburgh Bibliographical Society Transactions* (Edinburgh, New Series, 1946), Vol. 2, 143.

112. London, British Library Additional Ms. 19828; Nickson, *op.cit.*, 18.

113. Fos. 33r and 34r. *D.N.B.*, Vol. 12, 308; Vol. 8, 277f.

114. Fo. 10; an entry made by Michael Wallace as Professor of Greek in the University of Glasgow, J. Durkan and J. Kirk, *The University of Glasgow* (1977), 272.

115. Fo. 11r.

116. Fos. 61v, 74r.

117. Fo. 6r; see above, note 74.

118. Fo. 78r; see above, note 73.

119. Fo. 66r; *D.N.B.*, Vol. 40, 59ff.; The Scots Peerage, Vol. 6, 417ff.

120. Fo. 14r; Cameron, *Letters of John Johnston*, lxvif.

121., Fo. 14r. He was also principal of St Leonard's College; R. G. Cant, *University of St Andrews* (2nd ed., 1970), 65n.

122. Fo. 50r.

123. Fo. 13v.

124. Fo. 30r; Albertus Löthöffell, Regiomontanus Borusus, St Andrews University Muniments UX 305/3. 135.

125. Fo. 51r; see above, note 42. He signed Thomas Seget's album in Padua on 14th March 1598: Baumgarten, *op.cit.*, 94.

126. Erich Zöllner, 'Aus den Stammbuch des Freiherrn Otto Heinrich von Herberstein', *Mitteilungen des Instituts für österreichische Geschichtsforschung*, Vol. 63 (1955), 358ff; London British Library, Egerton Ms. 1239; Nickson, *op.cit.*, 18.

127. Egerton Ms. 1239, fo. 82r; Zöllner, 366.

128. Egerton Ms. 1239, fo. 83r; Zöllner, 366; Cameron, *Letters of John Johnston*, xviiff., xxviiff., xlff.

129. Egerton Ms. 1239 fo. 4r; Zöllner, 366; *D.N.B.*, Vol. 24, 176; *The Scots Peerage*, Vol. 1, 46.

130. Egerton, Ms. 1239 4r, 4v; Zöllner, 366f.

131. Egerton, Ms. 1239 fo. 61; Zöllner, 367.

132. Johnstone, *op.cit.*, 32ff; see above, note 7.

133. Johnstone, *op.cit.*, 36, 40ff.

134. Additional Ms. 17083. See description by Johnstone, *op.cit.*, 31ff.

135. Fo. 46r; see above, note 94; Johnstone, *op.cit.*, 34.

136. Fo. 58r; Johnston, *op.cit.*, 34f.

137. Fo. 67r; he refers to Cuming as a blood relation; Johnstone, *op.cit.*, 35; *Fasti Ecclesiae Scoticanae*, Vol. 7, 351.

138. Fo. 67v; Johnstone, *op.cit.*, 35; *Fasti Ecclesiae Scoticanae*, Vol. 1, 160; Vol. 7, 355.

139. Fo. 68r; Johnstone, *op.cit.*, 35; *Fasti Ecclesiae Scoticanae*, Vol. 1, 165; Vol. 7, 334.

140. Fo. 68r; Johnstone, *op.cit.*, 35, plate XV; *Fasti Ecclesiae Scoticanae*, Vol. 7, 330.

141. Fo. 72r; Johnstone, *op.cit.*, 35f; *Fasti Ecclesiae Scoticanae*, Vol. 4, 230.

142. Fo. 143r; Johnstone, *op.cit.*, 35f; *Fasti Ecclesiae Scoticanae*, Vol. 7, 326.

143. Fo. 133r. John Wemyss of Craigton was elected rector on 1st March 1611. He was commissary of St Andrews and later a jurist, St Andrews University Muniments, UY305/2, 113; D. Dalrymple, *An Historical Account of the Senators of the College of Justice of Scotland* (Edinburgh, 1849), 262; see also Cant, 'The St Andrews University Theses', 149f.

144. Fo. 134r; Johnstone, *op.cit.*, 36 and plate XV; Cameron, *Letters of John Johnston*, lxxviiff. The entry is a quotation from Tertullian, *De Patientia*, 15.

145. Fo. 146r; Johnstone, *op.cit.*, 36; see above, note 42.

146. Johnstone, *op.cit.*, 36, 39f. He was in England from November 1612 to the beginning of October 1613.

147. *The Autobiography and Diary of Mr James Melvill*, ed. R. Pitcairn (Edinburgh, 1842), 418.

148. T. McCrie, *Life of Andrew Melville* (Edinburgh, 1824), 2. 496ff.

4

THE SCOTTISH EXPORT TRADE, 1460–1599

Isabel Guy

1. Introduction

The custumars' accounts which form part of the Exchequer Rolls of Scotland were used in this study as a data source to make a quantitative examination of the Scottish export trade, from 1460 to 1599. Other historians, notably Dr Athol Murray, have shown that information about the Scottish export trade and the state of the Scottish economy can be drawn from the custumars' accounts.[1] Despite the problems associated with using them for compiling quantitative records, they cover one of the few areas of the Scottish economy which is recorded quantitatively. Studying the volume and nature of the goods exported has supplied considerable information on Scottish trade and thereby on some areas of the early-modern Scottish economy. While the records give no particulars of the destination of the exports, it is beyond doubt from the work of other scholars that most of them were headed for Europe rather than for England or Ireland.

The accounts have many gaps and inconsistencies. For five years out of the period the Exchequer Rolls themselves are missing, and so no information is available. Also, there is a complete gap in the detailed records from 1583 to 1589 when the great customs were leased for £4000 Scots per year. There was also the problem of standardised units: the measures in use varied not only with different commodities, but also at times within the one commodity. Regular attendance by the custumar at the Exchequer audit was required, but not always enforceable. Some accounts were not rendered annually but covered three or four years, with the worst offenders the custumars of Wigton and Kirkcudbright, who in 1592 rendered an account which covered the previous twenty-seven years.[2]

In presenting the data the problem of incomplete coverage was dealt with by constructing a chart using a series of symbols indicating the state of the record for each burgh for each year. There are seven different categories of accounts: regular, short, long, irregular, averaged, tack, and missing. Of these, only the missing accounts are really of no use whatsoever, and in the chart they appear as blanks. For full details of the different categories, and how to use them in evaluating the data, readers are referred to my M.Phil. thesis.

The material is comprehensive enough to enable the viability of any burgh's account to be checked, but it also demonstrates that over 80 per cent of all customs revenue was generated by the top four burghs alone (Edinburgh, Aberdeen, Dundee were the top three, and Perth generally the fourth). The contributions of the burghs ranked fifth to eighth are not large enough to cover the next 10 per cent and the rest are smaller still. Thankfully, for the entire period the accounts of the custumars of Edinburgh are present for all but thirteen years, thus providing records for over 90 per cent of the period for the burgh, which alone covered 60 per cent of all the Scottish export trade.

All the custumars' accounts in the published volumes of the Exchequer Rolls covering the years 1460-1599 were gone through several times and complete data sets were compiled (all commodities, all burghs, all years). The information was entered into data files in the University of St Andrews main computer. Statistical manipulation of the data was unsophisticated: simple arithmetical calculations were made, percentages taken, burghs and commodities ranked. The primary advantage of using the computer was in organising the sheer quantity of data involved. Figures were produced from the data files by computer graphics programmes.[3] It is the trend rather than figures for individual years that is reliable.

2. Trends in the commodity composition of Exports

One thing that becomes clear from the Exchequer records is the degree to which the Scottish export trade — perhaps much of the market economy — was heavily dependent upon sheep. Wool, woollen cloth, and woolfells together over the period account for over 60 per cent of all customs revenue.

Raw wool was sold abroad in declining but still substantial amounts until the early 1540s (Fig. 1). After this date the record deteriorates for some years, but it is clear that by the end of the century the wool trade had contracted to a fraction of what it had been. A comparison of Scottish and English wool exports over the period for which both sets of figures are available, reveals no strong or sustained association between them (Fig. 2).[4] But the trend of the English figures was also downward, and the frequent coincidence of noticeable peaks and troughs suggests that Scotland was sensitive to the same forces of supply and demand within the European market as England.

For wool exports, the period can be split into four phases: 1460-1475, a period of unsteady prosperity; 1476-1533, a gradual decline; 1534-1542, an apparent upsurge; but from 1543 until the end of the century, a dramatic and irreversible slump. During this last phase the state of the record for perhaps half the time is either deficient or missing, and so the wool export figures are either imperfect or lost altogether. However, those years for which the record is good show consistently that the raw wool trade had suffered long-term contraction. Also, we know that Edinburgh's accounts were in good shape for most of the time, and Edinburgh dealt with over 75 per cent of the wool trade, virtually 100 per cent of it by the end.

Over the period the trade in woollen cloth (Fig. 3) followed a clear rise until the peak in 1541, then a dramatic slump followed by recovery. Again, the trade was dominated by Edinburgh. Seventy-six per cent of woollen cloth exports went out through the capital, followed by Dundee, Ayr, and Aberdeen, which together accounted for less than 7 per cent. Figures for the English cloth trade were compared to those for Scotland. They followed a fairly similar pattern: both countries went through a long period of growth, Scotland peaked a few years earlier than England, then both went through some upheaval and recovery. Certainly there are many years in which the figures for the two countries moved in opposite directions, but when the trends are compared overall the similarities are clear, and it seems possible that Scotland's cloth trade was subject to the same or similar influences, and affected by equivalent market forces, as was the cloth trade of England. On the other hand, the Scottish cloth trade was of trivial proportions compared to the English: whereas the wool trade from Scotland was generally 20 per cent of the English figure, and on occasion much more, the cloth trade was seldom more than 2 per cent of the English equivalent (Fig. 4).

The next most important group of exports were those of animal skins, which were unusually widespread throughout the burghs, especially during the first fifty years. They have been categorised into three main groups: 'fells', the skins of adult sheep, killed six months after sheering; 'hides', the skins of animals without wool or fur, i.e. mainly cattle; and 'skins'. This last group is a collection of many different animal skins, each type listed separately in the accounts, which together generated much less revenue than the other two groups, despite their large numbers. But they provide insight into the nice distinctions that the sixteenth-century Scots could make between seven different types of sheep or lambskins, and the wide range of animal furs that could be made available for export if need be.

The shape of the graph for woolfells (Fig. 5) is something like the reverse of that for wool. This may be evidence for attempts to get around repeated bans on wool exports, by taking it out of the country still attached to the sheep's skin, as a woolfell. This cannot be a complete explanation, however, as the wool trade had been declining long before it was nominally prohibited in 1581. The growth of trade in Scottish woolfells was more or less accounted for by Edinburgh alone, and this became increasingly the case over time. By the 1590s Edinburgh's share was over 80 per cent.

Fells were reckoned singly, and paid a constant rate of duty throughout the period of 13s 4d per long hundred. The quantities exported grew steadily, the only long breaks in the graph being where the record deteriorates. There is a peak in 1539 followed by the 1540s slump, but trade had recovered well by the mid-1550s and woolfells continued to do well, particularly in the late 1590s.

Hides (Fig. 6) were reckoned in lasts and dacres, ten hides to the dacre, and twenty dacres to a last. They paid a constant rate of duty, 2s 8d per dacre or £2 13s 4d per last. The shape of the graph is similar to that of woollen cloth: a gentle increase until the middle of the sixteenth century, 1556 the peak year, and then stabilising at about the same level as in the 1500s. From the 1520s, the export of hides from Edinburgh shot up whilst those from other burghs contracted. In the 1460s, Edinburgh's share was 28 per cent of the total; by the 1590s it was 83 per cent. A large number of burghs was involved in the trade, but only on a tiny scale.

The skins of dead sheep, or in many cases, lambs, form all four main groups of skins as well as some minor ones, categorised according to when or how they died.

Of the four main groups — lambskins, schorlings, futefells and scaldings — lambskins not only were the strongest numerically (Fig. 7) but also generated the most revenue. This was so even though the rate per long hundred, 1s 8d, was a quarter of that for schorlings, the next largest group. Many of the more unusual skins passed through Edinburgh, and the greatest variety appeared in the last decade. Edinburgh was the top exporting burgh with 46 per cent of the trade over the period, Aberdeen 14 per cent, and Dundee almost 12 per cent, although from the 1570s shipments of lambskins from Dundee declined even though they were rapidly increasing from everywhere else.

Close study of the figures indicates that the level of exports of skins (Fig. 8) was flexible in the short term. Sharply increased quantities could be made available at short notice, but a sudden rise could not be sustained beyond one or possibly two years. There is some evidence to suggest that in times of high grain imports there were increasing exports of fells, hides, and particularly skins.[5] Hides and fells were less responsive and to some extent moved independently, producing very different-looking graphs. Yet on occasions they show close conformity with the movements of some of the groups of skins. It is not unreasonable to suppose that in time of dearth more animals would be slaughtered for domestic consumption anyway. The trade in hides and skins, less so with fells, was no more than a make-weight, important as a supplement but hardly capable of producing many cargoes on its own. It lacked long-term elasticity, because animal skins were really a by-product and so their production was limited.

Fishing in Scotland operated on a number of levels, subsistence, inshore, seasonal and commercially orientated. The fish were categorised into three groups: salmon, herring, which includes codling, as they were reckoned by the same method and frequently packed in the same barrels; and cod, which for these figures includes all the other types of fish mentioned occasionally in the accounts, such as ling or saithe.

The three groups of fisheries had different export patterns. For salmon (Fig. 9) the greatest volume went out in the middle decades; for cod (Fig. 10) in the period from the mid-1550s to the 1580s; for herring (Fig. 11) the greatest sustained success was from 1550 to the end of the century.

Most profitable to the crown was the salmon trade. There was a closed season for salmon fishing, from 15 August (the Feast of the Assumption) until 30 November (the Feast of St Andrew), and punishments for killing salmon at the forbidden time were severe. In 1400 it was a £5 fine for a first offence but capital punishment on a third conviction. All the fisheries were subject to detailed regulations concerning barrel sizes, quality control, market hours, type of salt to be used, and so on. In 1481 the duty on salmon was raised from 3s to 4s per barrel, that is £2 8s per last, an increase of almost 1000 per cent.[6]

Aberdeen was the top exporting burgh, with 42 per cent of the salmon trade over the period. Dundee had 13 per cent and Edinburgh 8 per cent. The other burghs which made significant contributions were principally Perth and Montrose, then Moray, Banff and Inverness.

Salted herring were exported in barrels, perhaps 1200–1300 fish per barrel, twelve of which made a last. In 1482 the rate of duty increased from 6d to 1s per barrel. Over the period the level of Scottish herring exported divided into two phases: until 1535, rarely over 200 lasts per year, then a marked increase to consistently over 800 lasts in the closing part of the century. Only herring out of the three groups of fish maintained growth through to the end.

Cod fishing was important, although in Scotland, as elsewhere, it came second to herring. The technique universally applied for catching cod was simply to hand a long line with individually baited hooks. This required minimal capital outlay, making cod fishing accessible to almost anyone living by the coast who wished to do it.[7] For customs purposes the cod were reckoned singly although packed in barrels for export. Unlike salmon and herring, cod were only lightly salted and then wind-dried. The Pittenweem group of burghs (which also included Anstruther, St Monance and Crail), although ranked first for cod, came into prominence only relatively late on: from nothing in the 1460s to over 50 per cent by the 1530s and over 90 per cent in the 70s. Edinburgh ranked second, and third was Montrose.

Both coal and salt were produced around the coasts, and had existed on a small scale long before their expansion at the end of the sixteenth century, at which point they made an increasing contribution towards Scotland's balance of payments, coal more so than salt.[8] The export trends for each of them over the whole period are not identical, but from 1574 onwards both coal (Fig. 12) and salt (Fig. 13) experienced unprecedented expansion, due partly to a degree of integration between them, as at Culross, but also to changes within the structure of the whole export trade. This was despite a series of prohibitions on coal leaving the country.

It has been calculated that more coal was consumed around the Forth in producing salt than was itself exported. Some coal-producing areas, such as Dysart, appear to have used their coal predominantly for salt production. More importantly, the burgh of Culross was producing enough coal by the 1580s to rank it first and second in salt and coal exports over the period, even though it first rendered an account only in 1580. Sir George Bruce's famous colliery there was technologically advanced, and was described in 1618 as 'this unfellowed and unmatchable work'.[9]

Coal exports generated almost £6000 revenue over the period. The rate was usually, but not always, 1s 4d per chalder until the 1570s, when the Exchequer Rolls began to distinguish different types of coal, and the rates went up. There were sixteen bolls to the chalder, which weighed approximately two tons, although standardisation of the measure for coal was as difficult as for any other commodity.

The major European salt-producing region was around the shores of the Bay of Biscay, where the method used was solar evaporation. Throughout the period Scotland produced salt for home consumption and a surplus for export, but the specialised demands of the fisheries for salt-on-salt could not be met in Scotland, and quantities of refined salt were imported. In compiling the figures great care was taken to ensure that the salt included in these figures was Scotland's own salt, and not re-exported salt from elsewhere. I received much help from Dr Chris

Whatley of Dundee University in distinguishing the different types of salt, but in some instances it was impossible to be certain.

The salt was normally reckoned at sixteen bolls to the chalder, paying 1s per chalder until doubled, in 1484, and it remained at 2s until the 1560s when the rates went up unevenly. Unlike coal, salt was not a part of the period of growth that for a number of commodities began around 1550. At that point salt exports had already been through two 'mini-booms', and were to remain depressed until 1574. The eight years 1574–1582 were outstanding, coinciding with political troubles in Europe and a rise in Bay of Biscay salt prices. This ability of the Scots to move quickly into the market as suppliers of salt when other suppliers failed had already been demonstrated in 1485 when Bay salt had gone up to forty merks a last (Scottish salt, twenty-two merks).[10]

It can be said that coal and salt made a useful, if not large, addition to the Scottish export package, especially in the last quarter of the century when the need to find replacement for raw wool was at its most acute. The late sixteenth-century integrated coal and salt works, that of Culross particularly, represent new departures in industry history.

3. Conclusions

It is often regarded as a sign of strength in the English economy that its merchants and seamen — especially those of London — were able to respond positively to the difficulties confronting them over the mid-century economic crisis by diversifying into new markets and new products, emerging stronger and more broadly based than before.[11] Within the same European market, although at a less advanced level, Scotland was faced with similar challenges, with a decline in its wool trade and a slump in cloth exports. The Scots appear to have grasped the problem in two stages: in mid-century efforts were made to compensate for the fall in wool and woollen cloth sales by exporting larger quantities of some other traditional items, and then in the 1570s this policy was renewed, together with diversification into new markets with goods that were not previously a part of Scotland's export package, except perhaps on a very small scale.

The general picture of Scottish trade which emerges from a detailed breakdown of the composition of the export package is one of much greater change than would be apparent from studying simply the totals of customs duties paid. It was not so much a policy as a complex *ad hoc* response by producers and traders to a changing market situation, in which the spur must be a continued, and perhaps increasing, demand for imports. As long as lords wanted wine and town inhabitants foreign consumer goods, means would be sought to pay for them; and when towns began to grow, as they did strongly in the century after 1550, they would need more consumer goods and, on occasion, emergency supplies of corn. These were the pressures to which merchants responded.

Scotland's industrial base was more backward than England's, and in particular it was weaker through lack of a really important and well-established cloth trade.

Scotland's military might was much less, and the possibility of a non-European trade therefore hardly arose. But within these constraints, and on a smaller stage, the merchants of Edinburgh and other east-coast burghs had already begun to do well even before the opening of the seventeenth century.

NOTES

1. S. G. E. Lythe, 'Scottish Trade with the Baltic 1550–1650', in J. K. Eastham (ed.), *Economic Essays in Commemoration of the Dundee School of Economics 1931–1955* (Dundee, 1955), 63–84; S. G. E. Lythe, *The Economy of Scotland in its European setting 1550–1625* (Edinburgh and London, 1960); J. Dow, 'Scottish Trade with Sweden 1512–1580', *Scottish Historical Review*, vol. xlviii (1969), 64–79; J. Dow, 'Scottish Trade with Sweden 1580–1622', *Scottish Historical Review*, vol. xlviii (1969), 124–150; J. Dow, 'A comparative note on the Sound Toll Registers, Stockholm Customs Accounts, and Dundee shipping list, 1589, 1613–1622', *Scandinavian Economic History Review*, vol. xii (1964), 79–85; A. L. Murray, 'Customs accounts of Kirkcudbright, Wigtown and Dumfries, 1434–1560', *Dumfriesshire and Galloway Natural History and Antiquarian Society*, 3rd series, vol. xl (1963), 136–162; A. L. Murray, 'Foreign Trade and Scottish Ports 1471 and 1542', in Peter McNeill and Ranald Nicholson (eds.), *An Historical Atlas of Scotland c.400–c.1600* (St Andrews, 1975), 48–49.

2. A. L. Murray, 'The Customs Accounts of Kirkcudbright . . . ', 154.

3. Many thanks for expert help to Angela Lamb, computer technician, Department of Psychology, and Iain Begg, Advisor, Computing Laboratory, University of St Andrews.

4. English figures from E. M. Carus-Wilson and O. Coleman, *England's Export Trade 1275–1547* (Oxford, 1963).

5. Lythe, *Economy of Scotland*, 14, 21.

6. *The Exchequer Rolls of Scotland*, vi–xxiv (Edinburgh, 1875–1908), vii, 430; viii, 317; ix, 146, 150; xxiii, 244.

7. A. R. Michell, 'The European Fisheries in Early Modern History', in *The Cambridge Economic History of Europe*, v (Cambridge, 1977).

8. S. G. E. Lythe, 'The Economy of Scotland under James VI and I', in Alan G. R. Smith (ed.), *The Reign of James VI and I* (London, reprinted 1981), 65; J. U. Nef, *The rise of the British Coal Industry*, 2 volumes (London, 1932), i, 45.

9. Lythe, *Economy of Scotland*, 47–49; Nef, *British Coal Industry*, i, 43; A. I. Bowman, 'Culross Colliery, a Sixteenth-Century Mine', *Industrial Archaeology*, Vol. viii (1970), 355.

10. S. G. E. Lythe, 'Economic Life', in J. M. Brown (ed.), *Scottish Society in the fifteenth century* (London, 1977), 78.

11. E.g. D. C. Coleman, *The Economy of England, 1450–1750* (Oxford, 1977), 61–65.

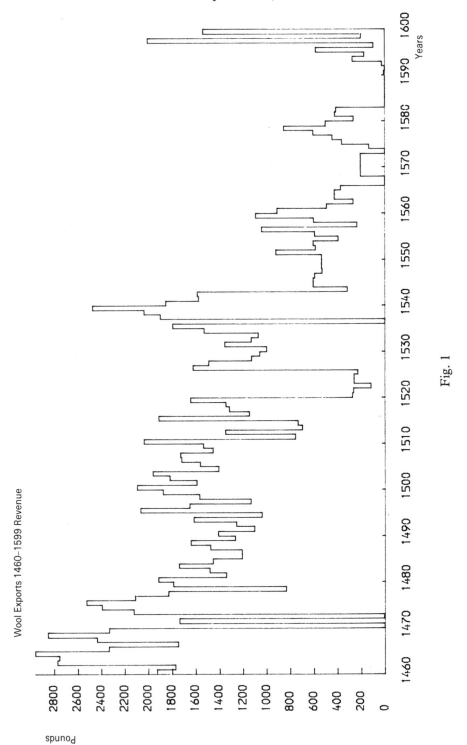

Fig. 1

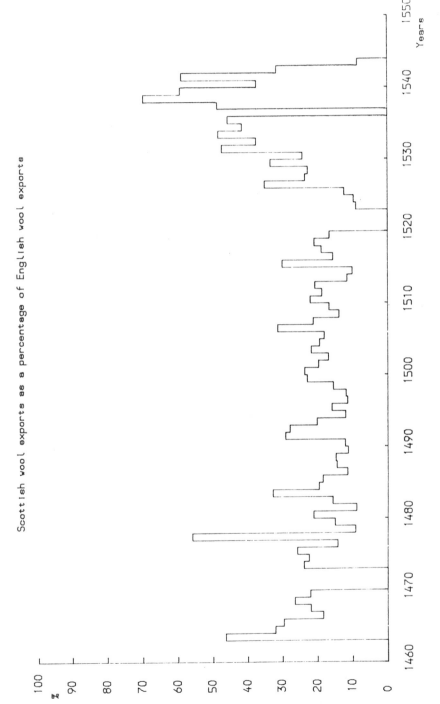

Fig. 2

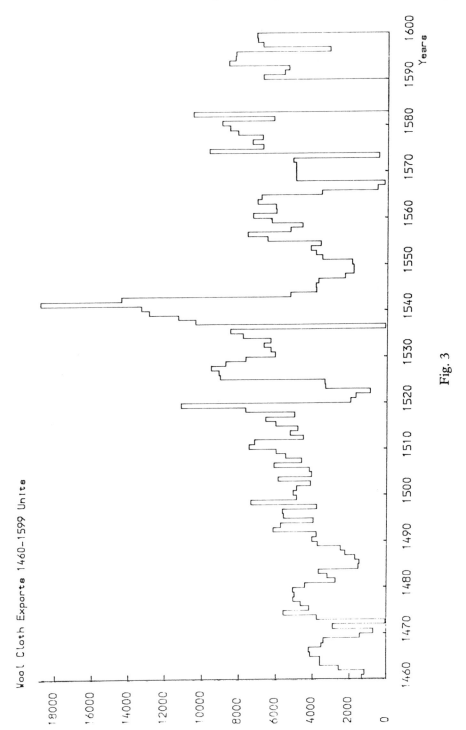

Fig. 3

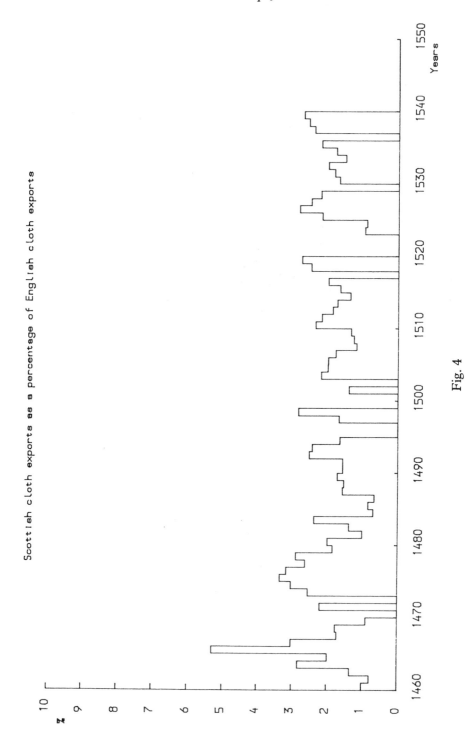

Scottish cloth exports as a percentage of English cloth exports

Fig. 4

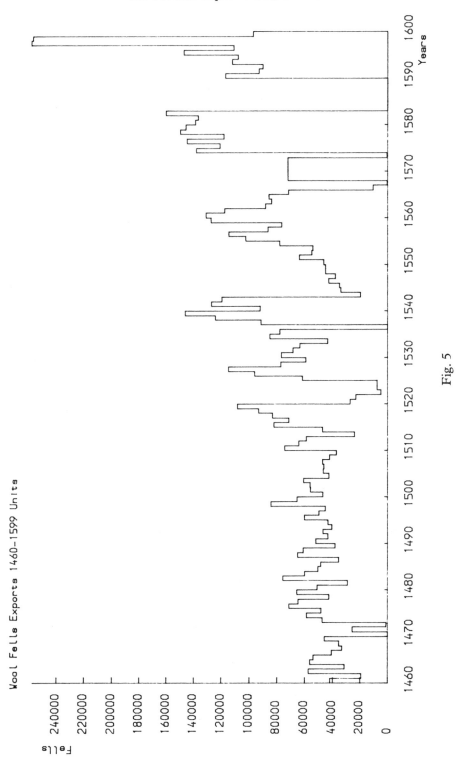

Fig. 5

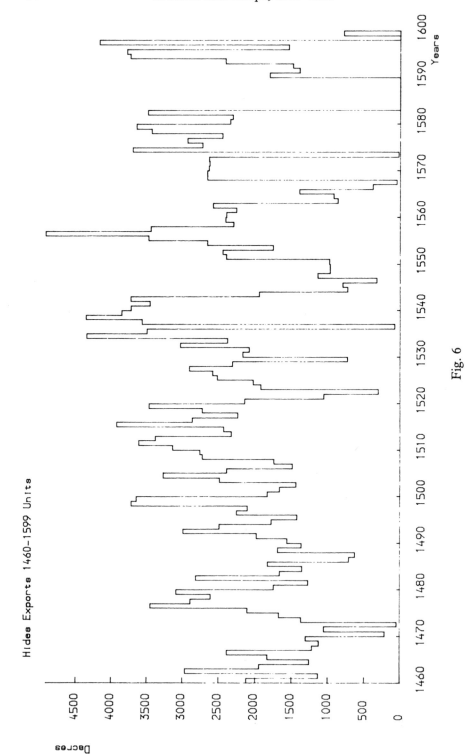

Fig. 6

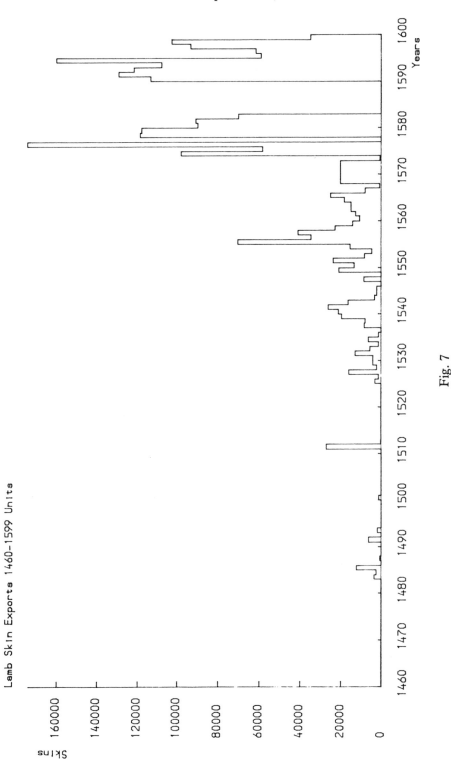

Fig. 7

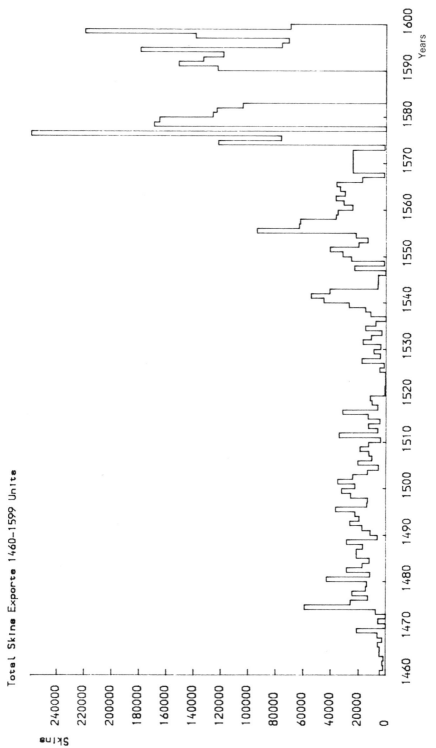

Fig. 8

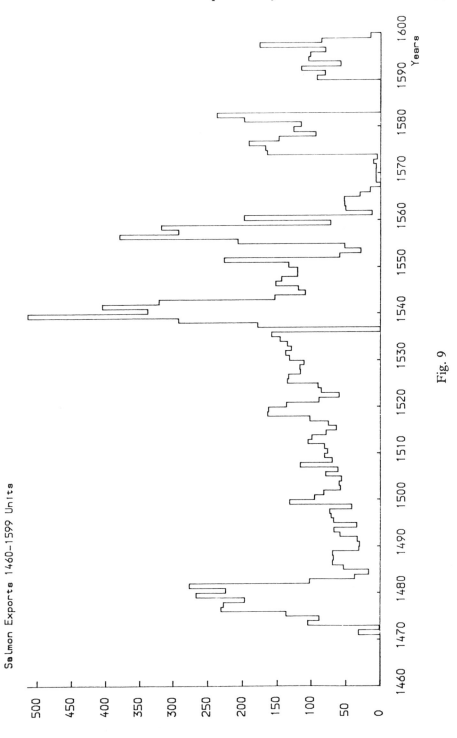

Fig. 9

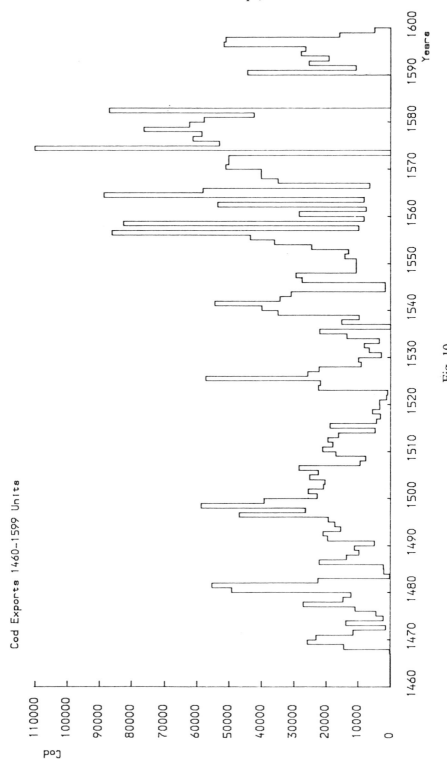

Fig. 10

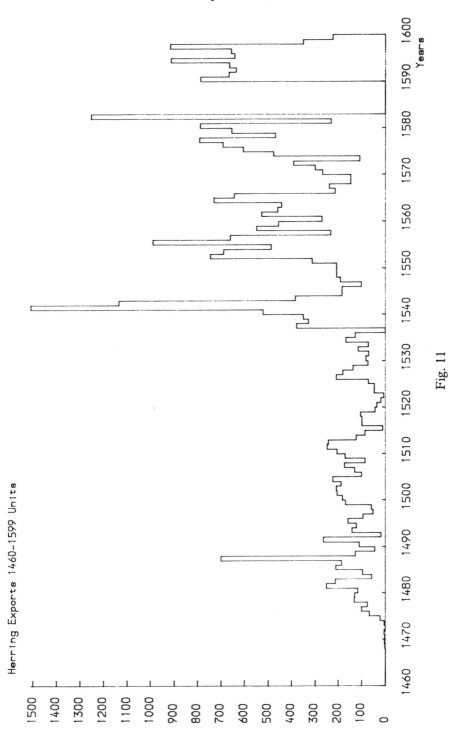

Fig. 11

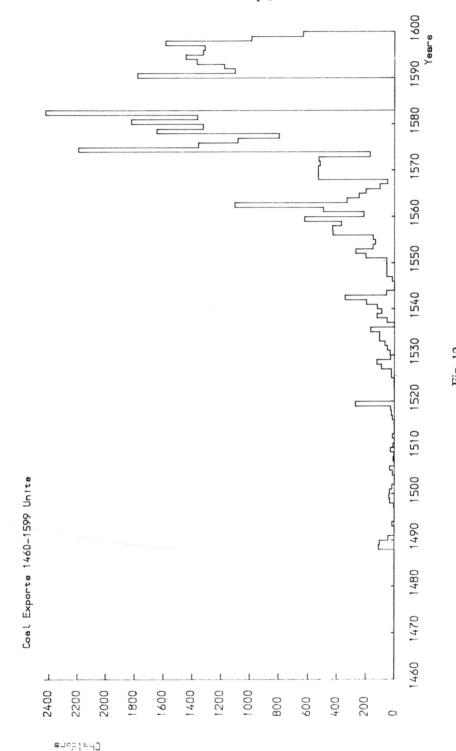

Fig. 12

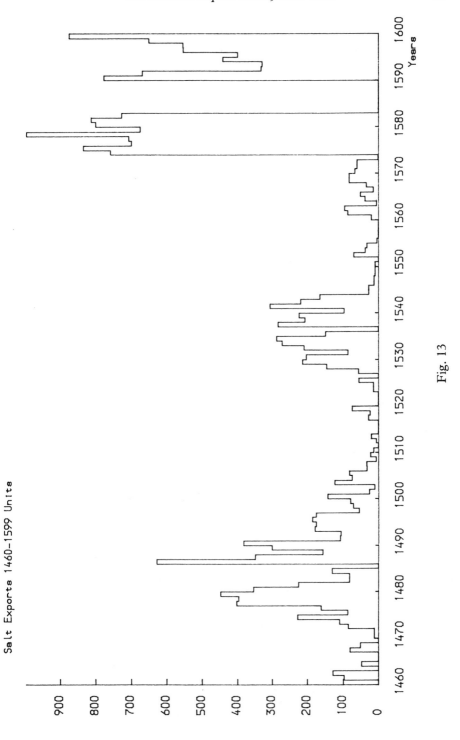

Fig. 13

5

SCOTTISH-DANISH RELATIONS IN THE SIXTEENTH CENTURY*

Thomas Riis

Among the countries comprising modern Scandinavia, only Norway appears to have had relatively frequent contacts with Scotland before the fifteenth century. The Hebrides were Norwegian until 1266; Orkney and Shetland remained so for two centuries longer. Norway's relations with England were also close from the late twelfth century. As early as the thirteenth century Norwegian timber and fish were exchanged for English grain.[1] By the end of the fourteenth century Norway, Sweden and Denmark had united under one sovereign; Sweden broke away from the union as early as the mid-fifteenth century whereas Norway remained with Denmark until 1814. It must accordingly be stressed that after 1380 the King of Denmark was also King of Norway and that Norwegian concerns may have influenced Danish foreign policy. Thus the renewal in 1426 of the treaties of Perth and of Inverness by James I and Erik of Pomerania showed the latter at work as King of Norway, taking care of Norwegian interests.

The marriage in 1468 between James III and Margaret, daughter of Christiern I, was intended to settle the differences between the governments: Christiern as King of Norway remitted all payments for the Western Isles since 1426 and promised to endow his daughter with 60,000 Rhenish florins. To cover this sum Orkney and later Shetland were pawned, leaving only 2,000 florins to be paid in cash. As her dower the Scots assigned to Margaret the palace of Linlithgow, the castle of Doune, and one third of the revenues of Scotland. We notice with interest that the parties to the treaty — which also contained a military alliance — were Scotland and Norway.[2]

The Scots had obtained much, but had of course had to make concessions compared with their claims set forth at Bourges in 1460; in particular, they had to accept a dowry much less than the 100,000 écus proposed in 1460.[3] Furthermore, the military alliance could not be invoked against countries which before the conclusion of the treaty were already allies of either party; thus the Scots could not hope for help against England, because the treaty of 1465 had established peace between Edward IV and Christiern I.[4] But, apart from this, what if anything did Christiern gain by the treaty? According to Dr Barbara Crawford, the Scots had to

*This preliminary paper presents briefly some of the results that will be contained in my forthcoming book *Should Auld Acquaintance be forgot ... Scottish-Danish relations c.1450–1707*, Odense University Press 1986.

content themselves with a good deal less than they had demanded in 1460, and for Dr Hørby the main advantage for Christiern was the fact that his diplomatic isolation was broken.[5] It should not be overlooked that the treaty might bind Scotland quite closely to Christiern's foreign policy as King of Norway, for example in moves against Sweden.

Several years elapsed after the deaths of Christiern I (1481) and James III (1488) before the treaty was confirmed. A Scottish embassy was sent to Denmark in 1491,[6] and on May 5th, 1494 the Scottish council and James IV ratified the new agreement. It confirmed the treaties concluded between James III and Christiern I and it enlarged the alliance to comprise the kings James IV and John, their realms and subjects. The alliance was to be valid in peace and war, the parties were bound to assist each other in any just war, but consultations were to be held before war was declared.[7] As to trade, the subjects of either king were allowed to trade freely in each other's dominions on condition that the customary duties were paid.[8] In this way Denmark was opened up to Scottish commercial enterprise, a fact which should be compared with the commercial treaty of 1490 with England that tried to limit English trade to a certain number of localities.[9] A few years later permission was given for two years to the subjects of King John and of his brother Frederik, Duke of Schleswig and Holstein, not only to trade throughout Scotland, but also to sell prizes taken by privateering.[10]

Under the renewed alliance Scots came to Denmark in growing numbers, settling down mainly along the principal route into the Baltic — the Sound — and from there moving to towns further away. On the whole, the years between the ratification of the treaties and the death of the two kings in 1513 represent a culmination in Scotland's relations with Denmark, while the Norwegian aspect becomes less evident. James IV tried to mediate in the conflict which set John against Lübeck and Sweden, and the Scottish alliance with Denmark was completed with treaties between Scotland and France (1491-2) and between France and Denmark (1499).

Christiern II's marriage with a Hapsburg princess meant that Denmark drifted away from the Triple Alliance, relations with Scotland remaining good, but not as close as in the days of James IV and John. Both the Scottish regency and Christiern needed military support desperately, the Danes against the Swedes, the Scots against the English. However, only Christiern received help, apparently without giving any.

When Christiern left Denmark in the spring of 1523, the Scottish government offered him asylum in Scotland,[11] but he preferred to settle in the Low Countries. Charles V owed him money for the queen's dowry and German mercenaries could be recruited more easily there. But which government should Scotland recognise? Attempts to persuade the Scottish government to recognise Frederik I were skilfully counteracted by Christiern II's Scottish-born physician Dr Alexander Kinghorn who until his death, presumably in 1529, acted as his ambassador in Scotland. It was to Christiern's great advantage that Kinghorn appears to have been related to the Chancellor, Archbishop James Beaton[12] and that an influential member of the Scottish political and naval establishment like Robert Barton supported the exiled king. Actually the Scots used the official royal titles in their letters to both kings, but allowed individuals to support Christiern II.

Thus Scotland managed to avoid committing herself before the end of the Danish civil war in 1536. Relations were then resumed, but did not regain the fervour of the previous generation. At first sight, one obvious explanation for this might be religious questions, since Denmark broke away from the Catholic faith twenty-five years earlier than Scotland, but relations did not in fact become closer after 1560, except that the Scottish government allowed the Danes to levy troops in Scotland for use in the Seven Years' War (1563-70). More important were the two countries' different positions in international relations: Scotland remained faithful to the French connection, whereas in 1544 Denmark settled her differences with Charles V who thus recognised Christian III. The Scots and the Danes no longer needed each other.

It was not till the 1580s that the two countries took a new interest in each other. The reason was that James VI, twenty years old in 1586, needed a wife. Choice Protestant princesses of some standing were rare, and among those available a Dane may have been the most suitable, as such a match might have political advantages as well. The supply of Norwegian timber was perhaps even more important now than in the Middle Ages — because of urban growth in Scotland — and Scottish trade was expanding into the Baltic. Good relations with its doorman would thus be an advantage. That trade was of capital importance for Scotland is seen from the Scots' initial claims, among which were the reciprocity of treatment for Scots and Danes in the other country and the Scots' exemption from the 1% *ad valorem* duty collected at Elsinore. The Danes avoided committing themselves at these points, stating that the Regency Council was unable to take decisions of that kind, a legally correct answer as both customs and — formally — privileges belonged to the prerogatives of kingship. The question of the Northern Isles (which the government in Copenhagen wanted to redeem) was likewise delayed until the coming of age of Christian IV.[13]

The treaty was concluded, and we know how James VI decided to sail to Norway where princess Anne had been detained by bad weather; the couple were married in Oslo and travelled later to Denmark, where they spent the winter. The most important effect of James's stay was his personal acquaintance with Danish political leaders and intellectuals, which appears to have strengthened contacts between the Scottish and Danish branches of the Republic of Letters.

Queen Anne has had an ambivalent reputation; her beauty and friendliness were recognised, but she was said to be a frivolous spendthrift.[14] The latter is by no means justified in respect of her sojourn in Scotland. It is true that, for example, for the year 1601-2 she was given the round sum of £12,000 for clothes, but during the same period her consort's clothes allowance was £10,000 — the difference is not huge and corresponds to those known for Margaret and James III in 1473-4, or for Margaret and James IV in 1507-8.[15] Much money was spent on jewels for the queen, but very often they were presents from her consort. In the cultural field her interest in theatre is well known; less familiar, perhaps, is the fact that her court appears to have been a centre for intellectual contacts between Scotland and Denmark (see Section V below).

II

Let us now turn to economic contacts, where the Baltic trade formed an important focus for Scottish-Danish relations. As Professor Lythe pointed out, the sixteenth-century Scottish merchant would be prepared to trade everywhere where ships of his town could go, and we may include those of the next town as well.[16] Perth merchants almost invariably used Dundee as their port; Dundonians might use Leith. Part-ownership of ships was the rule and caused numerous lawsuits concerning the division of loss and profit: people were in a hurry to obtain their returns in order to reinvest them, especially if a new voyage could be made before the end of the sailing season. Skipper and owner were often different persons, at least in overseas trade. A ship from Dundee might be the property of a group of part-owners obliged to furnish proportional shares of the cargo, and the skipper a professional mariner from Dundee or from some port in the East Neuk of Fife.

In the fifteenth century the sailing season had been defined as the period between Candlemas and Michaelmas (February 2nd to September 29th)[17], but in the sixteenth century it would generally begin in March or in early April and end in November. Where the skipper was a specialist in a certain type of voyage, for example to the Baltic or to Bordeaux, the ships might change skipper more than once during the sailing season, as was the case in 1615 with the *Providence* of Kirkcaldy. On September 22nd her masters paid their contributions to the Mariners' Box: James Law paid for a voyage with coal to Bordeaux as well as for two Bordeaux voyages to England, whereas William Tennant paid for a voyage from Danzig to Leith and appears also to have made one to Bristol and London.[18] The two Bordeaux voyages to England reveal that to a certain extent the Scots had become carriers for other nations. That this was not recent is seen from another Kirkcaldy case. In February 1583 the *Fortune* of Kirkcaldy, laden with herring, sailed from Scotland to London, and from there to King's Lynn to fetch grain for Bruges.[19] Even in the cases where the skipper and master (if they were not identical) may have had specific instructions, ample space was left for improvisation. This was of course more evident when skipper, master and owner were identical, which would be characteristic of the smaller enterprise. Merchants of higher rank may have had a ship and a skipper employed exclusively by them like William Kinloch of Dundee round about 1550. His ship's papers were not satisfactory to a Danish man-of-war which stopped her and consequently laid her under arrest. William Kinloch addressed himself to Christian III with a heartbreaking tale of damage suffered because of the burning of Dundee by the English, of his grief caused by his wife's death, and of his utter poverty with eleven children — and obtained in the end the release of the ship.[20] He was one of Dundee's leading merchants.

If, as Professor Lythe stated, the Scots seldom made more than one Baltic voyage a year, that was not due to incapability. As can be seen from the original manuscript Sound Toll Registers (but not from the published edition) from the first half of the sixteenth century, most ships did indeed make one voyage a year, but in 1542 John Fotheringham of Dundee and James Barker of Leith both made two, and William Home and William Richardson of Leith made three each.

Where in Denmark did Scottish ships call? The early Sound Toll Registers tell only that they passed Elsinore, but from 1557 both their cargoes and their port of departure are entered. Cases in which a Danish port was given as port of departure on a west-bound voyage are very rare, but this did not mean that they did not occasionally complete their cargoes somewhere in Denmark on their way back from Danzig to Scotland.

One town, Aalborg, attracted numerous foreigners; among the non-Scandinavians, Dutchmen and Germans were well represented, and in certain years a number of Scots. Unfortunately, the Aalborg chamberlain's accounts survive mainly for years from which few similar sources are known other than the Sound Toll Registers. We learn, however, that a cargo might be completed at Aalborg, both on the way out and on the return voyage. Thus, Constantine Arents of Montrose, perhaps a Dutchman by birth, called at Aalborg in 1594 on his way to or from Nylödöse;[21] in 1595 he bought two lasts of barley and ten lasts of herring at Aalborg, where he paid the toll that he should otherwise have paid at Elsinore. He was bound for Danzig where he presumably sold the herring, and where he purchased typical Baltic goods like tar, as well as flour: on his way back to Scotland he appears to have bought further grain in Aalborg.[22] That in years of scarcity Scottish ships made up their return cargoes with grain is quite natural, but that they might sometimes have acted as carriers for others is perhaps less well known.

Scots calling at Aalborg (individual calls)

1583	1[a]	1599	2
1586	2	1600	7
1587	6	1601	3
1588	2[b]	1602	1
1589	3[c]	1603	1
1590	2	1604	2
1592	2	1606	1
1594	3[d]	1633/4	1
1595	8[e]	1637/8	7
1596	16[f]	1643/4	3[j]
1597	6[g]	1663/4	1
1598	2[h]	1664/5	1

Source: Landsarkivet for Nørrejylland: Aalborg kæmnerregnskaber. a) Of Montrose b) One of Edinburgh/Leith c) Two paid for a stall at the Whitsun Fair d) Two of Montrose, one of St Andrews e) Three of Dundee, three of Montrose, one of St Andrews f) Three of Aberdeen, five of Dundee, five of Edinburgh/Leith; one (no home port specified) paid for a stall at the Whitsun Fair g) One of Aberdeen h) One of Aberdeen, one of Dundee i) One of Dundee j) Three of Dundee.

There must have been more like Constantine Arents, but the sources do not allow us to identify them.[23]

III

Scottish historians often state that the Scots operating within Denmark were mainly pedlars, but let us look a little more closely at the evidence. In 1496 King John prohibited Scottish, German and Danish merchants from dispatching their servants to trade in the countryside surrounding Køge (twenty-five miles south of Copenhagen, on the Sound) to the prejudice of the town's burgesses.[24] Six years later Hans Skotte, burgess of Nykøbing in the island of Falster, asked for a testimonial from Toreby parish (in Lolland separated from Nykøbing by a narrow sound). It certified that he had never been a pedlar nor a merchant in the countryside in the parish, nor had traded as far west as Maribo or elsewhere; however, the parish representatives did not pronounce on the question whether or not he had traded with the servants of Anders Tidemand, commander of the castle of Aalholm in South-east Lolland.[25] A case from Scania tells of a certain Willom Staal (probably a Scot or an Englishman called William Steel) who traded in the countryside, visiting the fairs on behalf of distinguished burgesses like the mayors Jørgen Kock of Malmø and Ambrosius Bogbinder of Copenhagen, who had furnished him with working capital to buy goods.[26]

The claim that the Scots were pedlars is therefore justified, at least for the late fifteenth and early sixteenth centuries, but so were both Danes and Germans, especially in Scania, the interior of which had not been opened up by the construction of good roads and the foundation of a town, so that itinerant tradesmen still had an important role to play.

If we consider the Scottish emigrants from Aberdeen mentioned in the testimonials published by Louise B. Taylor for the years 1589–1603,[27] we learn that in Poland the proportion of travelling Scots was larger than that of Scottish residents; in Prussia and Denmark the residents were far more numerous than the travellers; in Brandenburg and the remaining parts of Germany the shares were almost equal. Prussia was, as is well known, economically more developed than the other parts of Poland, especially the country's eastern regions. Whereas the major phase of urbanisation had been the twelfth to the fourteenth centuries in Eastern Germany and in Denmark, it was only in the sixteenth to seventeenth centuries that it took place in the peripheral regions of Europe like Norway, Sweden and Eastern Poland.[28] Thus the pedlar system appears as a characteristic of a less developed economy and as no peculiarity of the Scots.

The sources tell us about a number of important Scottish merchants established in Denmark and trading with foreign countries, sometimes with their own ships; on occasion they would become mayors or members of council. Best known among them is Alexander Lyall who had, by 1536, become mayor of Elsinore, to which charge he joined, in 1548, that of customs officer of the Sound Toll. His widespread commercial activities placed him among the few really important

Danish merchants who used bills of exchange regularly. Less spectacular, but also important, was Alexander Winton or Wenton of Malmø. In 1520 he was one of the four Danish delegates to the negotiations with Stockholm; the result was the establishment of a trading company intended to have four factories — in Copenhagen, Stockholm, somewhere near the Finno-Russian border and in the West, presumably in the Low Countries.[29] A few years later Christiern II was overthrown and nothing came of this ambitious plan.

These leading merchants belonged, however, to an élite; we know little about the other Scottish members of Danish urban society. Judging from the accounts of fees paid by new burgesses of Malmø, the cloth trades and crafts (merchant, tailor, weaver) played a considerable role for the Scots, and both in Elsinore and Copenhagen many Scots appear to have been weavers.[30] There may also have been some Scots leather workers. We should not, however, expect these categories to be exclusive. David Paterson was admitted burgess of Malmø in 1572 as a cloth dealer, but he did not disdain to export grain or malt, despite his declared profession.

IV

Let us now examine in detail the Scots in a given Danish community as a case study. Malmø in Scania is a suitable town whose burgh archives are the richest of pre-1658 Denmark: around 1500 the town was almost as important as Copenhagen and it was still one of the major Danish towns a century later. It appears to have declined in the seventeenth century, perhaps because of Copenhagen's extremely rapid growth.

Kaemner (Chamberlain) Lyder van Freden's accounts have survived for the years 1517-9, but because of arrears and other problems 1518 has been selected as perhaps the most reliable year. The municipal taxes were apparently paid by those owning houses in the town, but officials — including the mayors and councillors — were exempted.[31] With these obvious reservations we get the following figures:

1518	*Taxpayers*	*Total tax*	*Average tax/person*
1st quarter	154	2,154½	14.0
2nd quarter	114	2,152⅔	18.9
3rd quarter	143	1,519	10.9
4th quarter	201	3,056½	15.2
Malmø, total	612	8,882⅔	14.5

Taxation amounts in Danish *skilling.*Source: *Lyder van Fredens kämnärsräkenskaper för Malmö*, ed. Ljungberg.

We thus learn that the first and the fourth quarters were of average wealth, whereas the second and third quarters were its rich and poor parts respectively.

If we consider only the taxpayers of Scottish origin, we arrive at the following figures (taxation amounts in Danish *skilling*):

1518	*Scots*	*Total tax*	*Average tax/person*
1st quarter	5	134	26.8
2nd quarter	3	136	45.3
3rd quarter	4	50	12.5
4th quarter	4	17	4.3
Malmø, Scots	16	337	21.1

Source: *Lyder van Fredens kämnärsräkenskaper för Malmö*, ed. Ljungberg.

The Scots made up 2.6% of Malmø's taxpayers, but from them a larger share (3.8%) of the sum was collected. Although in the first and third quarters some Scots paid less than the average, most paid more; every Scot was above the average in the second quarter and below it in the fourth quarter. Among those whose profession we can ascertain were two merchants (the Wintons in the second quarter), one baker (David Baker) in the first quarter; in the third quarter there lived a tailor, Thomas Skotte, who in 1524 was alderman of the tailors' guild, and in the fourth quarter two craftsmen, Jørgen Skotte and James Pennor, leather workers, and a man employed as a bricklayer's assistant in September 1519.

On May 27th, 1555 the militia of Malmø was mustered; the surviving muster roll gives us the names of 679 men, presumably exclusively houseowners. Among those listed were twenty Scots. Three were armed with guns, nine with halberds, and eight with lances; in all, eleven had armour. Compared with the militia's total we arrive at the following result:

1555	*Scottish militiamen*	*Militia total*
Guns	3	115
Halberds	9	259
Lances	8	286
Spears	–	11
Armour	11	140
Other equipment	–	6

Source: RA. Da. Kanc. B 43 a: Mønstringsruller og rostjenestetaksationer 1535–55.
Note: As some of the militiamen were equipped with, e.g., both armour and a weapon, the totals of the categories exceed the number of Scots (20) and of militiamen (679) respectively.

We notice that the Scottish element in Malmø was 3.0% of the total population, virtually unchanged since 1518. In 1555 the Scots again appear to have been more prosperous than the average inhabitant, as their greater use of armour reveals.

During the second half of the sixteenth century, however, the Scottish element declined, both in numbers and, generally, in wealth, as is evident from the coronation tax list of 1596:

1596	*Taxpayers*	*Total tax*	*Average tax*
Total	930	91,630	98.5
Scots	9	682	75.8

Source: Malmö Stadsarkiv: Stadens enskilda räkenskaper A I a:7 (Kämnärsräkenskap 1596), fol. 24v.–43r. *Notes*: Tax is calculated from the assessment figures multiplied by 22 in order to give the amounts to be collected. The Scottish figures exclude, however, one very rich individual David Paterson who paid 1,232 *skilling*; were he included, the Scots' contribution would be 1,914 *skilling* or an average of 191.4 *skilling*.

The number of Scots in Malmø decreased during the second half of the sixteenth century until in 1596 they made up little more than 1% of the town's taxpayers, and their economic force had diminished as well. Only two of the ten were above the town's average, although one must admit that David Paterson's contribution of 1,232 *skilling* is rather impressive. No wonder that this merchant, who was admitted as a burgess in 1572,[32] was elected councillor and later mayor of Malmø, as well as alderman of St Canute's guild. In 1617 he had a memorial made for St Peter's Church to commemorate his parents; he is represented there as a well-dressed elderly gentleman.

The history of the Scottish colony of Elsinore has also been studied for the second half of the sixteenth century and shows a trend that is not unlike that at Malmø, although the point of departure was different. In Elsinore the majority of Scots were of modest condition (weavers, grocers, hatters, skinners, butchers, porters), whereas a small number had done extremely well — leading merchants serving on the town council and marrying into each other's families. By the end of the century these differences within the Scottish community had been accentuated. The colony was now larger, but a larger part of it was now of modest condition compared with the situation forty years earlier; there were still some leading merchants among the Scots. The tax lists allow us to trace this social development within the Scottish colony; from 1556 to 1577 the Scottish inhabitants were richer than average, although to a diminishing extent from the mid-1560s. In 1578, the Scots first became poorer than average, a phenomenon which occurred again frequently from 1583 to the end of the century.

One might explain these facts by harder conditions for foreigners in late sixteenth-century Denmark, but we should not overlook the fact that the Dutch began to settle in larger numbers during the second half of the sixteenth century and that, at least at Elsinore, they did well. Every year from 1556 to 1599, their taxation share exceeded their share of the population, although the distance between the two narrowed for the very last years of the century.[33]

Probably several factors were at play in the decline of the Scottish communities during the sixteenth century. One of the reasons may have been the competition from the Dutch, to whom the Baltic trade was the 'mother trade', whereas for Scots it was only one among three or four important trades; furthermore, the Low Countries were, in the second half of the sixteenth century, the major trading nation of Northern Europe in almost every respect. Another reason is perhaps a change in the social structure of the group of Scottish immigrants to Denmark; for

Danzig it has been established that merchants were numerous in the early phase of Scottish immigration, whereas in the later phase craftsmen and workers were more abundant.[34] If immigration to Denmark followed the same pattern it could explain the decline in average wealth of the Scottish community during the second half of the sixteenth century.

V

Lastly, let us glance at the intellectual relations between the two countries. A few Scots found employment in the University of Copenhagen from its foundation in 1479. One of its first teachers was Peter Davidson of Aberdeen, who was probably recruited at Cologne like other Copenhagen teachers of the first generation. He worked in Copenhagen for about forty years till his death in 1520; respected, always content with his modest revenues because he had always been poor, unswerving in his loyalty towards Catholicism, Aristotle and the Schoolmen, and for the latter reason slightly outdated as a university teacher.[35]

Whereas Peter Davidson's employment arose from his association with Cologne, close Scottish-Danish relations around 1500 may have led Denmark to look for other teachers in Scotland itself. Thus Thomas Allen taught in Copenhagen's faculty of arts and Dr Alexander Kinghorn in that of medicine.

A few Scots took the road to Denmark for religious reasons: Alesius fled from Scotland in the early 1530s and stayed for some time at Malmø before leaving for Germany, whereas John Gaw settled in the Scanian town and published *The Richt Vay to the Kingdom of Heuine* (1533), a translation into Scots of Christiern Pedersen's *Den rette Vej til Himmeriges Rige* (first published in Danish in Antwerp in 1531).[36]

Best known among the exiled Scottish divines is John MacAlpine who was prior of the Blackfriars of Perth from 1530–4. He fled to England in 1534 where he lived for some years as canon of Salisbury; he married, thus becoming the brother-in-law of Myles Coverdale. In 1539, for security reasons, he resigned and left with his wife for Germany. He spent some time studying at Cologne, until he matriculated in Wittenberg in November 1540. He appears to have worked mainly with Melanchthon who gave him, perhaps as a pun on his Scottish name, that of Machabeus by which he became known in his later years. It was possibly in 1541 that Christian III asked Bugenhagen (who had helped to organise the Lutheran Church in Denmark) for a qualified person for a chair of Divinity in the University of Copenhagen. The king's attention was drawn to MacAlpine, who had already been offered a post in Strasbourg (and refused it); in the end he accepted Copenhagen. One of the reasons was the problem of language: MacAlpine felt that his German was not sufficient for the German town of Strasbourg, but that it might do in Denmark! The former Blackfriar took up his new work in 1542, continuing till his death in 1557. The major part of his production has been lost, but his most important activity must be considered his work with the Lutheran bishop of Zealand, Peder Palladius, as dogmatic councillors to the Danish government.[37]

Towards the end of the sixteenth century closer contacts between Scotland and Denmark meant new friendships between Scottish and Danish men of learning who happened sometimes to have important charges in politics or administration. The best example is James VI's former preceptor Peter Young who undertook more than one diplomatic mission to Denmark in the years about 1590. From the Danish side Nicolaus Theophilus and Niels Krag, professors of law and Greek respectively, were sent on missions to Scotland. We might perhaps consider these three persons as the main bearers in the 1590s of the relations between Scottish and Danish intellectuals. Among the latter must be mentioned the astronomer Tycho Brahe and the governor of the Duchies, Heinrich Rantzau. On the Scottish side the physician and mathematician John Craig corresponded regularly with Brahe until he happened to offend him; more enigmatic are Brahe's relations with George Buchanan, to whom he sent his publication on a new star. Several letters appear to have been lost, but from the surviving sources we learn that Tycho Brahe admired Buchanan. In 1590 he reminded Peter Young of his promise to send him his biography of the late scholar; he had already received from Young a portrait of Buchanan, a likeness which James VI recognised when he visited Uraniborg.[38]

King James had himself met some of the learned Danes, among them the famous divine and former professor, Niels Hemmingsen, but the royal acquaintance proved more fruitful for Tycho Brahe. Well briefed by Peter Young, the King of Scots granted to Brahe the copyright in Scotland of his works and even wrote him two poems as preface to his *Astronomiae Instauratae Progymnasmata*.[39] Niels Krag also received the sign of royal favour, being admitted, in 1593, to the Scottish nobility.[40]

One of the major reasons for the close intellectual contacts between learned men from either country must have been their personal acquaintance due to the frequent embassies and to King James's sojourn in Norway and Denmark for about six months. At least two of the Scottish friends to whom Krag would send his regards had accompanied the king in 1589–90; but as we saw in the case of Tycho Brahe and Buchanan, there were other ways of establishing relations. The great majority of these intellectuals were *dilettanti*, often gentlemen of independent means with a wide range of interests; it could be seen as a sign of modernism that theological matters seldom appear in the letters. This explains why the famous professor Andrew Melville did not belong to the circle: he was too much of a professional to match the Scottish-Danish gentlemen.

Scottish education had, however, a great influence on certain Danes sent abroad to study. As in other fields, two periods were of special interest: the beginning and end of the sixteenth century. Two young Danes were educated at the court of James IV towards the end of his reign; one was the nephew of King John, the other the nephew of the Danish chancellor. Both took Scottish wives, but the prince,[41] after being made Baron of Brechin, met an untimely death: the chancellor's nephew, Mogens Løvenbalk, did not have the brilliant career that one might have expected.[42]

The main period during which Danes went to Scotland for education was, roughly, from 1590 to 1615. Most studied at St Andrews, although two went to Marischal College in Aberdeen. In the cases where we know the students' social background we find that administration and clergy were almost equally prominent, leaving the nobility and the bourgeoisie far behind. Of the twelve Danes in St Andrews, one became a Master of Divinity, six obtained their Bachelorship and two continued to the Mastership of Arts. The great majority were subsequently employed in the Church or in secondary education, but only one in higher education and one in public administration. The noblemen's stay in Scotland must have been only part of their grand tour.[43] The number of Danes in St Andrews has been attributed to the reputation of Andrew Melville,[44] which is unlikely as most Danish students studied after 1606. Melville was however *praeses* of the Mastership of Divinity thesis presented in 1595 by Christopher Dalby.[45] In this case Melville's renown must have attracted Dalby and his travelling companion Andreas Schwendi. Among the other Danes, however, only one definitely met Melville, and one more may have done so.

VI

Looking back at Scottish-Danish connections in the sixteenth century, we realise that both the last twenty years of James IV's reign and the 1590s were periods of especially close relations between the two countries. In the former case the treaties of the 1490s paved the way for many kinds of cooperation. In the latter case this was to a great extent due to the royal marriage. If we ask about the balance of giving and taking, we find that in the economic sphere Denmark offered possibilities that would have been limited in Scotland and Denmark received a number of immigrants who sometimes introduced new techniques, as in shipbuilding. Christian IV had in his service two shipbuilders of Scottish orgin: David Balfour and Daniel Sinclair. Each Scot was expected to teach his craft to twelve apprentices for four years. At the end of this period they would be ships' carpenters, and the brightest among them would have been taught the elements of geometry as well. When David Balfour's son Henry wanted to enter his father's trade and to that purpose intended to study in Great Britain, Christian IV wrote him an introduction to the Great Admiral of Great Britain.[46]

In the political-military field Scotland was the giver; Denmark kept out of the numerous Scottish-English conflicts, and Scotland generally did so in the conflicts in which Denmark was involved. Scotland did, however, send mercenaries and other kinds of support that could be given without engaging the government (a topic too large to be dealt with in this brief paper). Further, Scotland gave Denmark some university teachers and education to a number of adolescents, which was a one-way movement. Only where the late sixteenth-century *dilettanti* were concerned were the two countries equals.

It is clear that the Scottish demographic surplus made her a potential source of manpower, especially of mercenaries, but we should not expect other types of immigration to have involved very large numbers; moreover, as between 1483 and about 1660 access to land was generally prohibited to the bourgeoisie, the towns would have had to absorb the immigrants.

In higher education (as well as in shipbuilding) Scotland appears to have been the more advanced of the two countries. Since the mid-thirteenth century Denmark's cultural horizon had gradually narrowed, almost integrating her into North German civilisation, as manifested especially in the art of the later fifteenth century. We may view the introduction of the Reformation in its Lutheran, not its Calvinist form, as the culmination of this trend.

Scotland, on the other hand, had old and well-established relations with the Low Countries and especially with France. She was thus able to offer to Denmark something different from the civilisation of Northern Germany. Conditions were favourable about 1500; in James IV Scotland had a king of international outlook, and Denmark was simultaneously trying to liberate herself from Hanseatic domination. The Danish civil war of 1534–6 brought a definite solution: the Hansa's influence was curbed, although cultural dependence upon Northern Germany continued for at least another generation through the influence of the Reformation. Towards the end of the sixteenth century the new group of *dilettanti* intellectuals was formed, in Denmark and Scotland as elsewhere; despite personal piety they were mainly secular in their intellectual concerns, internationally minded and at home everywhere with their equals. Europe about 1600 was regaining her lost cultural unity of the Middle Ages, but on a secular basis; it was thus no totally blind fate that made Johan Rhode, a merchant's son of Copenhagen, study at St Andrews and end his days as physician and researcher in Padua.[47]

NOTES

1. Knut Helle, 'Anglo-Norwegian Relations in the Reign of Håkon Håkonsson (1217–63)', *Mediaeval Scandinavia*, Vol. I (1968) 102–6, 114.

2. *Diplomatarium Christierni Primi* (ed. C. F. Wegener, Copenhagen 1856), 201–7. Despite the words of the treaty, it is stated by both Reidar Marmøy (*Vårt Folks Historie* IV (Oslo, 1963), 104) and Ole J. Benedictow (*Norges Historie* V (Oslo, Cappelen, 1977), 183) that the pawning of Orkney and Shetland was undertaken without the consent of the Norwegian authorities.

3. 100,000 *écus* would correspond to 453 kgs fine gold, while 60,000 Rhenish florins would give only 166.2 kgs, cf. Friedrich Frhr. v. Schrötter (ed.), *Wörterbuch der Münzkunde* (Berlin-Leipzig 1930), 170, 229, 371.

4. *Dipl. Christierni Primi*, 163–9 (1465 3/10).

5. Barbara E. Crawford, 'The pawning of Orkney and Shetland. A reconsideration of the events of 1460–9', *Scottish Historical Review*, Vol. XLVIII (1969), 50–2; Kai Hørby, 'Christian I and the pawning of Orkney. Some reflections on Scandinavian foreign policy 1460–8', *Scottish Historical Review*, Vol. XLVIII (1969), 62.

6. *Acts of the Parliaments of Scotland* (*APS*) II, 224 c. 4 (ambassadors nominated 1491 18/5); the aim was 'the renouacioun of the confederacioun maid of before for the gude of merchandiss'; see also James IV to King John 1491 24/5, *Missiver fra Kongerne Christiern I's og Hans' Tid*, ed. W. Christensen, Vol. II (Copenhagen, 1914), no. 94.

7. *Repertorium Diplomaticum Regni Danici Mediaevalis*, II Række, ed. W. Christensen (quoted as *Rep. II*), no. 7650 (after the original Scottish ratification in Rigsarkivet, Copenhagen): ' . . . ita tamen quod unus nostrum bella non attemptet sine alterius consilio et assensu . . . '

8. *Ibid*: ' . . . Item quod regnorum nostrorum homines possint predicta regna nostra secure mutuo uisitare necnon mercari aliasque negociari iuxta consuetas consuetudines regionum. saluis de iure et de more soluendis . . . '

9. Rymer: *Foedera*, ed. Holmes V, part IV, 6–8 (1490 20/1, cf. for emendations of text *Rep. II*, no. 6667).

10. *Rep. II*, no. 8116 (after the original in Rigsarkivet, Copenhagen) dated March 8th 'anno regni nostri 9' which in *Rep.* is rendered as 1496 8/3 instead of the correct 1496–7 8/3 (Scottish) or 1497 8/3 (Danish).

11. Rigsarkivet, Copenhagen (hereafter RA), Münchenersamlingen C pk. 17 læg 9 no. 457/291 = *Letters of James V*, ed. Hay, 92 (1523 20/4); RA. Münchenersamlingen C pk. 8 læg 11 no. 4054/684.

12. *Letters of James V*, ed. Hay, 127–8.

13. *Danmark-Norges Traktater*, III, ed. L. Laursen (Copenhagen, 1916), 10–11 and 21–4.

14. *D.N.B.* I, (London, 1885), 431–41 (A. W. Ward).

15. S.R.O. E 21/76 fol. 178 v., cf. *T.A.* I, 1–75 and IV, 26 and 32.

16. S. G. E. Lythe, *The Economy of Scotland in its European Setting, 1550–1625*, (Edinburgh-London, 1960), 125.

17. *Ibid.*,134.

18. Kirkcaldy Burgh Archives 1/9/4: Minute Book 1612–74, 1615 22/9.

19. Kirkcaldy Burgh Archives 1/1/1: Council Records 1582–5, fol. 90v.

20. RA. TKUA Skotland A II 3, two undated letters (*c.* 1549–51).

21. Landsarkivet for Nørrejylland (hereafter NLA.): Aalborg kæmnerregnskab 1594; James Dow's papers (Dept. Scottish History, University of Edinburgh).

22. NLA. Aalborg kæmnerregnskab 1595; RA. Øresundstoldregnskab 1595, 459 and 483.

23. Also in Scottish trade with Sweden the movements may have been more complex than revealed by the surviving customs accounts; cf. James Dow, 'Scottish Trade with Sweden, 1512–80', *Scottish Historical Review*, Vol. XLVIII (1969), 74–5.

24. *Danmarks gamle Købstadlovgivning*, ed. Erik Kroman, III (Copenhagen, 1955), 211 (Køge no. 19).

25. *Rep. II*, no. 9618 (1502 29/5).

26. *Malmø Stadsbok 1549–1559*, ed. Einar Bager (Copenhagen, 1972), 66–7; cf. *Kjøbenhavns Diplomatarium*, ed. O. Nielsen, I (Copenhagen 1872), 275.

27. Louise B. Taylor, ed. 'Testimonial Book of Aberdeen: "Testimonialis Grantit be ye Bailies sen ye last day of Merche 1589" ', *Miscellany of the Third Spalding Club*, II (Aberdeen, 1940), 1–86.

28. Maria Bogucka, 'Les villes et le pouvoir central en Pologne aux XVe–XVIIe siècles. La place de Gdańsk dans la république nobiliaire', in Thomas Riis & Poul Strømstad, eds., *Le pouvoir central et les villes en Europe du XVe siècle aux débuts de la révolution industrielle. Actes du colloque de la commission internationale pour l'histoire des villes au Danemark*, 1976 (Byhistoriske Skrifter I, Copenhagen, 1978), 14–18; Thomas Riis, 'Conclusions', in *Ibid.*, 103–4.

29. N. J. Ekdahl, ed., *Bihang till Christiern IIs Arkiv . . .* IV (Stockholm, 1842), 1329–33.

30. Allan Tønnesen, *Helsingørs udenlandske borgere og indbyggere ca. 1550—1600* (Ringe, 1985), 23.

31. Leif Ljungberg, ed., *Lyder van Fredens Kämnärsräkenskaper för Malmö 1517–1520* (Malmö, 1960), 10–11. Ljungberg gives the number of taxpayers for 1518 as 586, but if arrears are added, one arrives at 612. About the same time Copenhagen had 811.

32. Malmö Stadsarkiv. Magistratens arkiv H I a:1: Räkenskaper: Borgmästare och råds 'rettighed' 1563–76, 139.

33. Tønnesen, *op.cit.*, 73–80.

34. Hedwig Penners-Ellwart, *Die Danziger Bürgerschaft nach Herkunft und Beruf, 1536–1709, Wissenschaftliche Beiträge zur Geschichte und Landeskunde Ost-Mitteleuropas*, 13 (Marburg/Lahn, 1954), 157.

35. 'Chronicon Skibyense', in Marius Kritensen & Hans Ræder (eds.), *Skrifter af Paulus Helie VI* (Copenhagen, 1937), 81–2; cf. *Dansk Biografisk Leksikon*[3] XI (Copenhagen, 1982), 337–8 (Bjørn Kornerup). Despite his modest condition he left to his sister 522 marks Danish and 102 *ounce wt* of silver (Aberdeen City Archives: Town Council Register XI, 338, 386, 418–9, 422, 616).

36. Lauritz Nielsen, *Dansk Bibliografi 1482–1550 med særligt Hensyn til dansk Bogtrykkerkunsts Historie* (Copenhagen-Kristiania, 1919), 102.

37. Fuller documentation in Riis, *Should Auld Acquaintance be Forgot . . .* , Chapter 4. MacAlpine's refusal of Strasbourg, see *Aarsberetninger fra det kongelige Geheimearchiv*, ed. C. F. Wegener, I (Copenhagen 1852–5), 221–2 (1542 6/1, Christian III to Bugenhagen).

38. I. L. E. Dreyer *et al* (eds.), *Tychonis Brahe Dani Opera Omnia*, VI, 255 and 269; VII, 282–3 (1590 27/10, Brahe to Peter Young).

39. *Ibid.*, II, 11–12.

40. Bodleian Library, Ms. Smith 77, 429–32. I gratefully acknowledge my debt to Professor James K. Cameron, St Andrews, who drew my attention to this manuscript.

41. Christopher in Scottish and Christiern in Danish sources; for fuller documentation see Riis, *Should Auld Acquaintance be Forgot . . .* , Chapter 10.

42. In Scottish sources often mentioned as Mawnis (Beild, Lawrence), cf. William Christensen, Mogens Bille — Mogens Lauridsen Løvenbalk, *Personalhistorisk Tidsskrift* 5 Rk., Vol. III (1906), 272–81.

43. Fuller documentation in Riis, *Should Auld Acquaintance be Forgot . . .* , Chapter 12.

44. Harald Ilsøe, 'Danske Studerende ved St. Andrews i Skotland 1595–1610, med et tillæg om de studerende i Oxford 1603–22', *Personalhistorisk Tidsskrift*, Vol. LXXXII (1962), 24, referring to R. Pitcairn (ed.), *The Autobiography and Diary of Mr James Melvill . . .* (Edinburgh, Wodrow Society, 1842), 418.

45. Christoph. Iohannides Dalby, *De Prædestinatione. Sive De Causis Salutis et damnationis aeternae disputatio . . .* , Edinburgh (Robert Waldegrave), 1595; cf. Ronald Gordon Cant, *The St Andrews University Theses 1579–1747. A Bibliographical Introduction* (Edinburgh Bibliographical Society, *Transactions*, II 2 (1941=1942)), no. 42.

46. Kanc. Brevbøger 1625 6/5; RA. TKUA Alm. del 1 no. 10: Latina 1616–31, fol. 15v.–16r. (1616 25/11, Christian IV's introduction for Henry Balfour).

47. Egill Snorrason, *Danskeren Johan Rhode i det 17' århundredes Padua*, (Copenhagen, n.d. (*c.* 1964–5), 14–20.

6

THE SCOTTISH-NORWEGIAN TIMBER TRADE IN THE STAVANGER AREA IN THE SIXTEENTH AND THE SEVENTEENTH CENTURIES

Arnvid Lillehammer

The subject of this chapter is the timber trade from the district of Ryfylke in Norway, from the middle of the sixteenth to the beginning of the eighteenth century, which brought Swedish, Danish, German, Frisian, Dutch, French, Spanish, Irish and English in addition to Norwegian and Scottish vessels to the fjords north and north-east of Stavanger. In spite of the variety of nations taking part, this trade is still traditionally called 'The Scottish Trade', and the sixteenth and seventeenth centuries are still called 'The Scottish Period'. 'The Scottish Trade' is an unambiguous concept that has lived on in oral tradition for 150 years after the trade ended, underlining how close the connection must have been between the east coast of Scotland and south-west Norway.

A traditional story from the farm of Ropeid, some 60 kms NNE of Stavanger, illustrates how one family got to know the trading foreigners so well when they arrived in their vessels during the summer that they looked upon them almost as relatives. A particular Scotsman came to this farm almost every year with his wife. One year the Scot came alone and was in a hurry because he had left his wife at home expecting a baby. When the farmer's wife heard this, she made the best kind of 'barselgraut', porridge traditionally brought to a woman after childbirth, which she put in a covered wooden pot and wrapped in an eiderdown coverlet before the ship left. The Scot thanked her, put the pot in his cabin with extra cloth around it, and left the fjord: he was lucky, got a favourable easterly wind and after a few days was back in Scotland. As soon as possible he took the wooden pot home and found his wife in bed, with a three-day-old boy in the cradle. 'Look,' he said, 'I have brought you some childbed porridge from Norway; the nice Ropeid woman made it and asked me to bring her best regards.' 'Oh, bless you, and bless the Ropeid woman,' she answered, 'bring it to me so I can taste it.' And when he unwrapped it and removed the cover, it was still piping hot. It would be wrong to use such a tradition uncritically, but it undoubtedly reflects the fact that the timber trade in the sixteenth and the seventeenth centuries tied the two areas on each side of the North Sea closer together than perhaps ever since.

Ryfylke was, of course, not the only part of Norway where the timber trade played a significant role in the economy of the time. The neighbouring districts Agder and Sunnhordland were also involved as well as Telemark in eastern Norway and the area around Oslofjord — and later the Møre-Trøndelag districts further north.

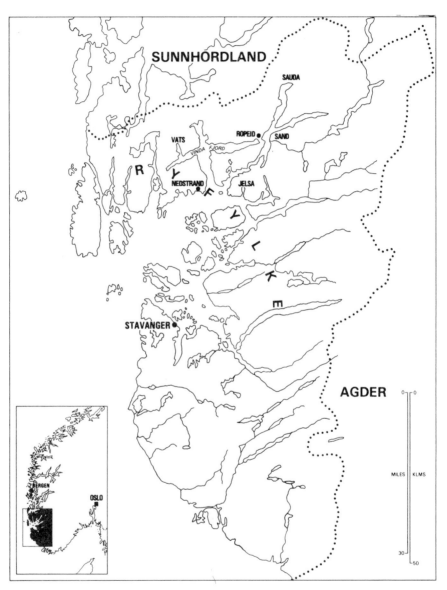

The Stavanger Area

In the sixteenth century, Norwegian farmers administered most of the forests themselves. At first, despite some small-scale timber trade to small towns and to districts poor in wood, forestry was first and foremost run for the subsistence needs of the farmer. The degree of exploitation was low, and the profit from sales modest. By 1600, however, forestry had become, as it has remained, one of the principal industries of Norway. The explanation for this is to be found in the increasing need for imported wood from Western Europe as the centre of European trade moved from the Mediterranean to the North Sea, to the benefit of mercantile communities in the Low Countries and Britain.

The consumption of wood in western Europe increased rapidly as Dutch and English towns grew and came to need great quantities of beams for the frames of houses and commercial buildings. Housebuilding also required an increasing number of boards, or 'deals' as they are called in the customs books. The shipbuilding industry needed deals, beams, planks, masts, tar and pitch; the fisheries needed barrel staves and barrel hoops, and the mining industry needed timber to shore up galleries. Firewood was also needed for heating dwelling houses, and wood was used in most of the tools of the time. The great consumption of wood led to shortages in the neighbourhood of big towns, and timber had to be brought from a distance by ship, which partly explains why Ryfylke, with its easily accessible forests, came to play a prominent part in this trade.

Early in the sixteenth century, the district reached the bottom of the crisis which Norwegian historians refer to as 'the depression of the Late Middle Ages'. After a vigorous expansion of farming up to about 1300, the Black Death and other plagues of the fourteenth and early fifteenth centuries led to a marked decrease in population, followed by the desertion of a great many farms. This process of desertion was especially severe in the parishes furthest from the coast. Research has shown that in some parishes in Ryfylke more than 70 per cent of farms were 'deserted' (that is completely depopulated) in the opening years of the sixteenth century. While this crisis may have led to a change of farming system that placed more emphasis on animal husbandry, in the vast areas emptied by plague, rough grazing, meadows and fields became after a few generations overgrown with a dense wood which, according to early seventeenth-century testimony, had to be cleared again before deserted farms could be brought once more into cultivation.

In addition to this, Ryfylke has heavy rainfall. In Sauda, in the north-eastern corner of the district between high mountains at the head of a fjord, the average rainfall is more than 2000mm a year. Moreover, the topography is characterised by steep hillsides, so that the rain falling in the mountains has only a short way to travel down to the sea. Throughout the fjords rivers and burns abound, many of them suitable sites for a sawmill.

In the Middle Ages the finishing of a log was very demanding. Using an axe, the log would be cut into two thick boards, which took time and wasted raw material. The advent of sawmilling was therefore an important technological advance for Norway. The technique may have been introduced to Sweden as early as the 1460s, probably from Germany. In Norway we have the first information about sawmills from 1503, and from the 1530s onwards we may assume that they were known and used over most of southern Norway.

The sawmills of the sixteenth and seventeenth centuries were constructed on very simple principles. A long saw blade of iron, set in a wooden frame, was moved vertically by a water wheel. This made it possible to produce boards much faster than by hand, and allowed a log to be cut into five, six, seven or even eight boards, instead of just two. Thanks to this new method of production, Norway (and Ryfylke with it) came to play a large part in the wood processing of Northern Europe. These boards, or 'deals' as they were also called, were the most important end-product of sawmilling, but not the only one, as we shall see later.

The evidence for sawmills in the Ryfylke area is rather scanty in the sixteenth century. In an account book for the Cathedral in Stavanger we find that the Bishop received boards from Vats, Jelsa and Sand in 1554. Those boards must have been fabricated on sawmills because the same book names a Martin 'sagmester', i.e. sawmiller. A Tax Book from 1563 mentions, somewhat unexpectedly, only one sawmill in the whole of Ryfylke, while we find nine in the neighbouring district of Sunnhordland. In 1567 we find a Hallvard sawmiller as a citizen in Stavanger. Occasional sawmills are mentioned both in the 1580s and in the 1590s, but it is not until after the turn of the century that the evidence makes it possible to follow the development in sawmilling activity in detail. Then suddenly, we can imagine the creaking and squeaking of saw blades in all the fjords in Ryfylke. A river did not need to be particularly large to have a sawmill on it. For a farmer who owned his own land, the only tool he had to buy was the saw blade, which was easily paid for when a few dozen timber logs had been sawn and sold as boards.

Most of Ryfylke's precipitation falls as rain in autumn and as rain or snow in winter. Consequently the sawing was done by flood water during autumn and during the melting season in spring. This made the sawing easy to combine with other farm work.

A systematic search through all available evidence that might provide information on sawmills in the district of Ryfylke for the two centuries under study reveals about 135 sawmills operating for shorter or longer periods between 1550 and 1700. Some were only in use for a year or two, others have run continuously from the 1560s to our own century. Most were concentrated in the Vindafjord and in the Jelsa-Sand-Sauda fjord systems. The majority were situated close to the sea, but in the most active period some sawmills were built up to 25 kms from the mouth of rivers. The profit must have compensated even these sawmills for the extra transport costs over land to the fjords.

In 1606 there were 64 sawmills in use in Ryfylke, a remarkable increase from the single one mentioned in 1563. Even if there were a few more unrecorded sawmills in 1563, this seems to demonstrate that the last decades of the sixteenth century were a lively period of establishment and expansion in sawmilling activity. Unfortunately lack of evidence prevents us from following this development in detail. Only after 1600 is it possible to quantify the sawmills in operation on an annual basis. From 64 in 1606 we can follow an increase to a peak of 83 in 1621. From the end of the 1620s, on the other hand, sawmilling seems to have faced a crisis: only 41 sawmills are mentioned as taxable in 1628, while 21 are referred to as deserted. Later there was again a small increase, and between 1631 and 1644 between 50 and 60 sawmills were working yearly. The falling trend resumed, however, towards the end of the century: in the 1660s and the 1670s between 30 and 40 sawmills were recorded in use each year, and after 1684 only between 15 and 20. One explanation for this may be marked deforestation.

Several factors, therefore, played an important part in explaining why Ryfylke for 150 years had a major role in the Norwegian timber trade. The district had forests, sawmills to exploit them and easy access to the commodity. Timber was a bulk cargo, low in price compared to weight and volume, and transportation costs (especially overland) would thus strongly influence the market price. In Ryfylke the forests were located close to suitable harbours mostly free from ice except in midwinter, and the distance to the market was short. With a favourable wind a ship would not take more than a few days to cross the North Sea, either to Germany, to the Low Countries or to Britain.

Another important factor was political. The timber trade was exempted from government attempts to strengthen the position of the towns by conducting commerce solely through citizens and burghers. In Stavanger's grant of privilege of 1579 the Danish-Norwegian King Frederik II placed the town, with its burghers, inhabitants and goods under his protection, enjoining that no merchant, farmer or farmer's servant be allowed to trade outside its bounds. For various reasons, however, it was impossible for the authorities to direct the timber trade through the towns. The producer was allowed to sell wood directly to whoever he or she might wish. This explains why German, Dutch and Scottish ships in most cases sailed past the small town of Stavanger and directly into the fjords, at least in the sixteenth and the seventeenth centuries.

Buyer and seller thus made direct contact without intermediaries. Most of the sellers and producers were farmers. Ryfylke was a district characterised by a high percentage of farmers who owned their own land: in some parishes, around 1660, farmers might be the owners of more than 60 per cent of the land. But even if the farmers lived as tenants, it was still possible for them to exploit the forests. Other landowners were the King, monasteries (before the Reformation) and churches: on their land the burghers of Stavanger often put up sawmills. All the same, the best localities for sawmills were mostly to be found on farmer's land. In the timber trade, therefore, there was often a conflict between the rural and the urban population.

So, in the sixteenth and the seventeenth centuries, foreign ships sailed directly to the fjords of Ryfylke to trade in timber with the producers, mostly the farmers. The oldest source to quantify this navigation is a list from 1567. In that year 38 vessels visited Ryfylke; 1 Frisian, 4 German and 4 Dutch: but no fewer than 28 were Scottish. Not until after the turn of the century, however, are there Customs Books that provide fuller details of this trade over a longer span of time. Apart from an incomplete book from 1601, the current Norwegian Customs Books start in 1602 and exist for most of the century. Their content changes in the middle of the century, but between 1602 and 1646 very detailed information is given about the ships: the tonnage, their arrival and departure dates, the names of skippers and their origin, and the volume of the commodity; before 1624, the names of the sellers, and after 1630, the names of the vessels are also given.

A good deal of work has been done on analysing this very rewarding material from different angles. Though not yet complete, some of the preliminary results can be presented here.

First of all, if the 1567 list is representative of its time, it is clear that the number of vessels calling shows a considerable increase over the last decades of the sixteenth century, which fits in well with the trend we have seen in sawmilling. From 38 vessels in 1567 the calls almost triple to 104 vessels in 1602–3 (the tax year ran from 1 May to 30 April). In no single year before 1646–47 did the calls drop to the level of 1567. In 17 out of the 34 years in this period which it is possible to examine in detail there were more than 100 calls of ships, and only for 3 years did the total fall below 70. The top years were 1610–11 and 1619–20 with 158 and 183 ships respectively. On average the fjords of Ryfylke saw 95 vessels each year in the first half of the seventeenth century. The graph of calls shows, not unexpectedly, strong fluctuations, but the trend appears to be as follows: the number of vessels after increasing from the middle of the sixteenth century, reaches a high point between 1610 and 1630, and then shows a slight decrease in the 1630s and 1640s. This again mirrors the sawmill statistics.

The vessels were of different origins. Now and then we find a Spanish ship, one or two French and some English in addition to rather more Scandinavian. Generally, however, the most important were the German, the Frisian, the Dutch and the Scottish. Of these, without doubt, the dominating ones were the Frisian and Dutch, which are best regarded as one group, and the Scottish. Each of the 34 years between 1602 and 1646 which is possible to quantify saw 29 or more Scottish vessels in the fjords. In the tax-year 1619–20 alone as many as 115 Scottish voyages were coming to buy timber from this small part of the long Norwegian coast. The number of Scottish calls follows the same trend as the total number of calls; that is an increase up to about 1620 and perhaps a slight decrease in the 1630s.

There is a further interesting feature. If we compare the number of Scottish calls with the rest, and particularly with the Frisian/Dutch, we find that Scottish calls constituted an increasing share of the total during the first four decades of the century. While they often constituted less than 50 per cent in the first decade, after 1610 they constitute more than half of the total calls each year, with an increasing trend. The Frisian/Dutch on the other hand show an opposite development, and almost disappear after 1635.

Nevertheless, even though Scottish vessels made more than half the calls, they did not necessarily carry more than half the tonnage. In some years they did, as between 1612 and 1621 and after 1633, but otherwise they carried less than their numbers would lead one to expect. The structure of the Scottish fleet in Ryfylke differed from both the Frisian/Dutch and the German fleets. The Scots came in great numbers but in small vessels. The others came in fewer but larger vessels. Before 1639 we do not find any year that shows an average tonnage for the Scottish vessels higher than 20 lasts — that is, about 40 tons. In most years before 1639 the average tonnage lies between 10 and 14 lasts (20 and 28 tons). Now and then in summer we find small fishing boats down to 6, 5 or even 4 lasts (8 tons) making the journey across the North Sea. The Frisian and the Dutch vessels seldom drop below an average of 20 lasts (40 tons). The trend of increasing average tonnage for the Scottish vessels from about 1640 could be explained by better registration of the tonnage, but it could also be explained by a change in the Scots form of trade involving large ships, a point we will return to later.

At first sight it may appear strange to find evidence of strong trade connections between the east coast of Scotland and south-west Norway. Both were areas of similar natural endowment and based their economy mainly on grain-growing, animal husbandry and fishing. All the same we do find differences that make trade seem natural. In Scotland there was a great need for easily accessible timber, while Ryfylke was a district deficient in grain. Even if all farmers in Ryfylke sowed grain in their fields each spring, this did not guarantee that there would be enough cereals for their own use during winter as well as seed corn for the following year. Cereals were exactly what the Scots could offer. While information about the import of grain to Ryfylke is not as comprehensive as information about the export of timber, it is rich enough to present a clear picture of imports as a whole and of the difference between the Scots and other importers.

Information on imported goods is given in the Customs Books between 1601 and 1605, in 1611 and 1612 and then again from 1643 to 1646. The evidence for the first period, while giving no quantities, is unambiguous that the Dutch, Frisians and Germans mainly traded timber for currency, but the Scots instead brought goods, particularly cereals or cereal products, mostly grain, flour, malt and bread. Later on, in 1611–12 and 1612–13, and in 1643–44, 1644–45 and 1646–47 the different goods were quantified. The Dutch, Frisians, Germans and others still paid for timber mainly in money, and occasionally in small quantities of goods, such as a little liquor, half a pound of hops, some linen cloth, or, as in 1644–45, two barrels of walnuts. A coin hoard found in 1961 at the farm of Haavik in Skjold parish gives the same impression: it contained 120 coins, two Norwegian, one Danish, one Polish, 47 German or Austrian and 69 Dutch. The earliest coin was from 1585, the latest from 1666. Even though currency at that time was not restricted by national borders, and Dutch and German coins passed in Britain too, it is striking that no English or Scottish coin was found in this hoard.

The Scottish skippers could of course also settle a deal in hard cash, but their most important medium of exchange was cereal products, of which malt seems to have been the most significant. In 1646–47, for instance, the Scots imported at least 317 barrels of malt into Ryfylke, as well as at least 594 barrels of grain, 24½ barrels and 20 sacks of flour and 59 barrels of bread. In all, at least 994½ barrels and 20 sacks of cereal products were shipped to the fjords of Ryfylke in this particular year. The grain alone — 594 barrels or 87,000 litres — was equivalent to the total amount of seed corn on all the 130 farms in Sauda and Suldal parishes.

More than 90 per cent of the grain cultivated in Ryfylke at that time was oats. The imported grain, when accurately specified, not surprisingly often included barley, wheat and rye. Thus in 1644–45 one finds specified 161 barrels of barley,

121 barrels of rye and one barrel of wheat. The small quantities of wheat were supplemented by another commodity, wheat rusk and wheat bread, or as it was also called, Scottish bread. Wheat bread or Scottish bread is found in the Customs Books in each of the years with quantified information; in 1644–45 the import of wheat bread was 74 barrels. The rye, however, can hardly have originated in Scotland, and must have been a Baltic re-export.

Besides the cereals, textiles played some part in the import, particularly linen cloth, of which 1020 ells occurred in 1646–47. In the first decades of the seventeenth century one also finds 'Scottish shoes', and by the middle of the century the trend is clearly towards a multiplication of goods. In addition to the cereals and the linen, it is more common to find liquor, bar iron, iron pans, knives, peas, beans, soft soap etc. In the second half of the century this trend became even stronger.

Let us now turn to the export trade. From 1602, oak was forbidden to be shipped from Norway, as the use of oak was vital to the Danish-Norwegian royal fleet. This valuable wood was therefore of little significance to the Scottish trade in the seventeenth century, although one must of course allow for some smuggling to have taken place on a scale impossible to quantify. The types of wood which were mainly of interest, therefore, were hazel, birch and pine. Whole trees, or logs, were seldom in the lists: the wood was normally processed before export, and four types of goods dominate the Scottish trade — boards or deals, beams or baulks, barrel hoops and firewood.

The most valuable of these were the boards, prepared at the sawmills in the spring or in the autumn, but beams of different sizes, from 6 to 12 ells long, made up a great deal of the volume. The boards and the beams were pinewood. The hoops on the other hand were the most numerous items, although they only accounted for a small part of the value of the exports. They were hazel, and were used in the production of barrels and other wooden vessels. The firewood was birch, and did not play any significant role either compared to boards and beams.

A detailed study of five years picked at random serves to illustrate the trend of trade in these commodities. To start with the firewood, it was evidently not of the same importance to the Scots as to the Germans or the Dutch, but was used rather to fill up space in the Scottish ships after other commodities had been loaded. In 1631–32 the Scots in 53 vessels exported 188 cords of firewood. Thirty-nine of these vessels — almost three-quarters — took away only three cords of firewood or less, while only one carried more than 10 cords, in this case 24. On the other hand, of 37 Dutch, Frisian and German ships, only three took out three cords or less. Twenty-nine of the continental vessels took out more than 10 cords — one of these as many as 70 cords. The Scots simply do not seem to have had much interest in birch firewood from Ryfylke, perhaps because of their abundant supply of coal at home.

We find the Scots more strongly represented in barrel hoops. In all five of the years examined they handled more than 50 per cent of the total export — in 1631–32 nearly 84 per cent — while in 1620–21, 420,000 out of 680,000 were sent on Scottish vessels.

However, the most important kind of timber in terms of volume for the Scots trading in Ryfylke was the beams. Until around 1630 beams 9 and 12 ells long dominated the trade. The longest, though, were comparatively few in number; one year most of them went to Scotland, another year to some other country. Beams of 9 ells length were on the other hand a typical Scottish commodity. In 1641–42, a year with an export of about 28,000 beams, almost 91 per cent left Ryfylke in Scottish vessels. In the early 1630s the length changed, and from then onwards most were of 6 or 8 ells. At the same time contemporary sources call the beams 'skottebjelker', Scottish beams, showing where their primary association lay.

For the boards, nine years were selected for examination. In none of these did the Scots take even half the export. The highest percentage was reached in 1635–36 and again in 1641–42, both with about 43 per cent. It was the Dutch, the Frisian and the German vessels that left the fjords with most of the sawn boards. Even though the Dutch and the Frisians almost disappeared after 1635, the Germans, the English and the Danes or Norwegians, thanks to their larger vessels of 40, 50, 60 and even more lasts, managed to capture most of the production. Perhaps the most interesting of the nine years was 1641–42, when out of a total of about 170,000 boards shipped from Ryfylke, 74,000 went on Scottish vessels.

From the beginning of the 1630s the figures also seem to indicate a proportionate increase in the export of boards and beams, at a time when the Dutch and the Frisians stopped trading with Ryfylke. This may, paradoxically, be connected with deforestation in the district, which meant that the products had to be made smaller, of 6–8 not 9–12 ells in length. The larger trees must have been cut down first in the vast exploitation of the first decades of the century. The Dutch and the Frisians may have been interested mainly in the larger sizes, and therefore turned to trade elsewhere along the Norwegian coast, while the Scots still found it worthwhile and profitable to obtain timber from Ryfylke.

Thus in the first half of the seventeenth century between 50 and 100 Scottish vessels crossed the North Sea yearly to exchange cereal products and linen cloth for timber, mainly boards, beams, hoops and firewood. Naturally one wants to know whence in Scotland these vessels came. Fortunately the Norwegian Customs Books also give detailed information on this: occasionally, a vessel is said to be only of Scottish origin, but in most cases the records name the actual place of origin. Even though the records show that most of the vessels came from the central part of Scotland's east coast, some also came from a wider area between the Northern Isles and the English border.

As early as 1567 the pattern was apparent. The 28 vessels of that year came from seven different localities: Orkney, Montrose, Dundee, St. Andrews, St. Monans, Kirkcaldy and Leith. As many as 11 of them came from Dundee, without doubt the most important town in this early phase of the timber trade. Between 1601 and 1647, the evidence fortunately makes it possible to follow the skippers' journeys on an annual basis. From this period we know of between 35 and 40 different towns or harbours in Scotland with connections with Ryfylke. Even Glasgow is mentioned, but only twice, once in 1633–34 and once in 1646–47. Not unexpectedly the other towns or harbours are all on the east coast, from Kirkwall in the north to Dunbar in

H

the south, but the distribution is uneven. While vessels from both Shetland and Orkney were common in Bergen and Sunnhordland (the district north of Ryfylke), one does not know of any ships from Shetland and only a few from Orkney in Ryfylke itself. The north-east does not figure much either, even though in the first decades of the century Fraserburgh and Aberdeen had repeated contact with the area. On the southern shores of the Forth the leading town was, not unexpectedly, Leith, the harbour of Edinburgh. Nevertheless, the centre of distribution was to be found along the coasts of Tayside and Fife. The Customs Books give information on 16 burghs here: Montrose, Arbroath, Dundee, St. Andrews, Crail, Anstruther, Pittenweem, St. Monans, Elie, Largo, Leven, Wemyss, Dysart, Kirkcaldy, Burntisland and Culross. The distribution is most dense between Dundee and Elie, with, as I have mentioned already, Dundee as the main port. Until the 1620s it was not unusual to find that one out of four Scottish vessels trading timber in Ryfylke came from Dundee. After 1630 a shift took place southwards towards the coast of Fife. In only one year before 1624, the 13 known burghs in Fife had more than 50 per cent of the Scottish trading vessels. Between 1630 and 1646 these ports were responsible for less than 50 per cent of the vessels in only 3 of the 17 years. In 1632–33 as many as 77 per cent of the Scottish vessels in Ryfylke appear to originate in the burghs of St. Andrews, Crail, Anstruther, Pittenweem, St. Monans, Elie, Largo and Leven alone. The importance of Crail, Anstruther and Pittenweem in particular grew after 1630.

The first Scottish vessels used to appear in the fjords of Ryfylke in March or April, and the last used to leave in September. The ships first passed the Customs House at Nedstrand, sailed from there into the fjord of destination, lay at anchor for a week or two, then returned to the Customs House at Nedstrand before sailing for Scotland. It is also possible to follow the individual skippers on their journeys; two skippers from St Andrews may serve as examples.

The annual number of visits from St Andrews varied from one vessel in 1632 to 10 in 1619. In the years studied in detail, there is information on about 180 voyages, involving between 70 and 75 skippers from this town between 1602 and 1646. Many of the vessels crossed the North Sea to Ryfylke more than once. Between two-thirds and three-quarters of the skippers from St Andrews are mentioned only once, the rest making two or more journeys. These included such men as Stephen Arnot, Henry Deirs, James Furrat, Andrew Masterton, James Morton, Andrew Steenson, David Walker and James Watt. Let us dwell upon David Walker and Henry Deirs.

David Walker was first mentioned in connection with a long stay in Norway between 4 August 1635 and 13 June 1636. He had arrived at Drarvik in Hylsfjord in 'an old decayed vessel which he had bought in Stavanger and which he got the authorities permission to improve with pinewood, and which he had done'. In spring the following year he was back at Drarvik on 8 April, stayed there for 18 days loading timber, was away again for six weeks, but returned on 5 June, this time at Eide in Sandsfjord and stayed there for 14 days till 19 June, then left once more — this time for nine weeks, but returned for the third time on 22 August at Drarvik and loaded timber for the last time that year. He finally left Norway that year on 6 September. Thus the records tell us that David Walker managed three trips to Ryfylke in one year, ventures which to him were clearly not an isolated commercial enterprise. In 1643 he again made three calls to Ryfylke, but in general he seemed to have made one or two journeys a year. In 1642 he again stayed longer. That year he arrived on 16 April and did not leave until 8 August — almost four months later. The reason this time was 'his old rotten and depraved vessel which he was to improve and repair'. Ironically the name of his vessel was *The Gift of God.*

It is evident that frequent calls and long stays such as those of David Walker must have resulted in close connections between seller and buyer, between the east and the west side of the North Sea, just as the oral tradition reveals. Indications of a strong connection are clearly seen when looking at the distribution of the ports where David Walker loaded his timber. Between 1635 and 1646, 12 out of his 16 voyages were to Drarvik (three times), to Eide (six times), to Tengesdal (once), to Sand (once) and to Vandvik (once), which meant that all twelve calls were made to the same parish. The other four calls were made to Kvaløy, situated in another fjord, but only 11 kms from the ports of Sand and Eide. Another interesting observation concerning David Walker, which lacks a satisfactory explanation, is the markedly longer duration of his stays in the 1640s compared to the 1630s, from an average of 15 days before 1641 to an average of 28 days after 1641.

These observations are further supported by the trade routes of another skipper from St Andrews, Henry Deirs. Between 1616 and 1624 he is recorded in the Customs Books eleven times. Except for his first visit, which was to Jelsa, all his trading was done in Sauda parish. During these years the Customs Books also mention the names of the sellers of timber. The same farmers are recorded year after year selling to Henry Deirs, notably Torger Hovland, Orm Søndenå, Anders Søndena, Saebjørn Abø, Ola Birkeland and Hermann Amdal. This indicates that contact between buyer and seller could not have been based on mere chance: the Scottish skippers must have known where to go beforehand. Contacts must have been established deliberately and after some plan, and arrangements made from one year to the other. When Henry Deirs left Sauda on 29 April 1623, Torger Hovland and Hermann Amdal must have known of his plans to return and made arrangements for the delivery of timber in time for his next arrival, for they were both among the sellers when Henry arrived next on 2 June. It is also interesting to note that out of 163 ventures involving St Andrews where we have enough information, only 16 were to anywhere outside the Jelsa-Sand-Sauda fjord system.

There is no space here to touch upon another interesting aspect of the Scottish-Norwegian connections, the immigration in this period from Scotland to the Stavanger area, but such immigration did take place, both to the town of Stavanger and to the rural district of Ryfylke.

Let us next turn briefly to the period after the 1640s. Unfortunately after 1646 the information in the records at hand is less detailed, and there are also gaps in the material. No Customs Books spanning the years between 1646-47 and 1665 have yet come to light, and from 1665 to the mid-1680s the Customs Books do not contain detailed information, providing only the export totals for each commodity in a way that makes it impossible to quantify the share of different countries in the trade. There is no reason to believe that the Scots lost their dominance. What instead seems to have happened was further deforestation in the easily accessible woods in Ryfylke. Take for instance the export of boards and beams. In the first years of the seventeenth century the total number of exported boards was between 33,000 and 43,000 each year. During the 1630s the export volume was rising, reaching a peak of between 90,000 and 160,000 boards each year between 1635 and 1645. In the second half of the century, on the other hand, the number of sawmills decreased, as we have already seen, as did the export of boards. The volume fell from between 48,000 and 66,000 at the end of the 1660s, to between 20,000 and 36,000 each year at the end of the 1670s. By the middle of the 1680s the volume was down to betwen 8,000 and 12,000 yearly. With beams, the same drastic fall was not apparent, but the trend was the same and export was falling during the last half of the century. Thus the timber taken out of forests of Ryfylke did not amount to the same volume at the end of the century as in the beginning, and foreign traders had to turn to other districts in Norway for their timber.

The later Customs Books seem to indicate other changes in the Scottish timber trade. First of all the exported timber gradually became more manifold in type. More important is the fact that the variety of imported goods increased at the same time. The trade was no longer so distinctly dominated by cereals or cereal products. Among other things there was also trading now in hemp and tobacco, tobacco pipes, red wine and liquor, earthenware, onions and carrots, sugar, rice, prunes, figs and raisins. Many of these goods came to Ryfylke from Holland on Scottish vessels, which suggests that the Scottish trade changed from a predominantly two-way trade into one with more of a triangular element involving the east coast of Scotland, the Low Countries and south-west Norway. This can be directly deduced from the Customs Books, for instance in 1668 when some of the imported goods are said to be 'Scottish goods and from Holland, which later are exported to Scotland', which means that the Scottish vessels sailed from the burghs along the shores of the Forth and Tay, to Holland, traded there, and on their way back sailed to Ryfylke in order to change some Dutch goods with Norwegian timber before returning home to Scotland. Possibly this triangular trade started after the Dutch and Frisians left the fjords of Ryfylke in the mid-1630s, but more research into this particular aspect is needed.

Finally, we should touch upon the last important factor governing the trade conditions of the time, namely the relationship between the town of Stavanger and the district of Ryfylke. We mentioned earlier that, except for the timber trade, all trade in the region was legally the privilege of the burghers of Stavanger, or of Stavanger together with Bergen. Even though the timber trade was so exempted, this did not prevent the inhabitants of Stavanger from taking part. Burghers erected sawmills on land owned by the king or by the churches and monasteries. Logs were bought from farmers to saw into boards which later were sold to foreigners. At the end of the sixteenth century and during the first decades of the seventeenth century Stavanger expanded from a small stagnant harbour into a thriving trading centre. After 1620, more and more timber was recorded being brought through Stavanger on its way out to the European market, even though the volume from Stavanger never, at this period, equalled the amount exported from the fjords of Ryfylke itself.

By the middle of the century, Stavanger's aspiration to control the timber trade as a whole became more and more evident. In 1662, the town was given a monopoly of the timber trade, but with one important exception: the small loading ports inside the fjords were still allowed to continue as exporting harbours as before, with the reservation that the citizens of Stavanger sent trading agents to them to control the trade. During the period of the 1660s to the 1680s the struggle between the merchants of Stavanger and the farmers of Ryfylke, who were thus deprived of their rights to trade directly with the foreigners, continued. The trade, however, was difficult, not to say impossible, to control, and it is reasonable to think that the farmers continued to sell timber directly to the incoming vessels. By 1686 the situation had not improved, and the Customs House at Nedstrand was closed. Thereafter vessels had to sail to Stavanger to clear inwards and outwards. To cut a long story short, in 1717 a royal resolution was passed which ensured the privileges of Stavanger and forbade the Scots to trade in the fjords. From then on all timber in the region had to be transported to Stavanger before being shipped abroad, and the number of Scottish vessels in the whole of Rogaland dropped remarkably. Already as early as 1733, only twenty-six years later, the County Court Judge called the period before 1717 'The Scottish Period', indicating that the times of the distinctive Scottish trade connections of the sixteenth and the seventeenth centuries were already being looked upon as bygone days.

This chapter is intended as no more than a preliminary report on the timber trade between Norway and Scotland, and a more extended publication is planned in the near future. At least, however, it will serve to give an indication of the character and importance of this branch of commerce over the North Sea.

SCOTTISH BOATS IN RYFYLKE, 1601–1647

Year	Total	% of all ships	Lasts	% of all lastage	Average lasts
1601	5	71.4	89	66.9	17.8
1602–03	46	44.2	792	35.0	17.2
1603–04	42	56.0	649	31.7	15.5
1604–05	38	50.0	638	39.9	16.8
1605–06	29	43.5	459	29.7	15.8
1610–11	74	47.5	1054	31.6	14.2
1611–12	61	59.2	849	43.8	13.9
1612–13	70	72.2	1041	58.4	14.9
1613–14	5		80		16.0
1614–15	74	70.5	1050	58.1	14.2
1615–16	62	55.9	777	39.6	12.5
1616–17	52	65.0	674	50.3	13.0
1617–18	54	60.4	590	45.3	10.9
1618–19	76	70.4	1021	56.3	13.4
1619–20	115	68.8	1557	45.6	13.5
1620–21	69	64.9	939	51.1	13.6
1621–22	88	75.2	1061	58.0	12.1
1622–23	54	60.7	627	32.0	11.6
1623	74	74.7	890	52.0	12.0
1623–24	78	71.6	1059	46.9	13.6
1630–31	72	56.7	955	32.6	13.3
1631–32	52	68.4	453	42.9	8.7
1632–33	55	65.4	614	43.1	11.2
1633–34	85	81.7	1014	57.5	11.9
1634–35	85	85.0	1087	66.6	12.8
1635–36	93	80.9	1559	59.5	16.8
1636–37	79	69.3	1302	51.4	16.5
1637–38	88	82.2	1622	69.9	18.4
1639–40	53	67.1	1053	40.1	19.9
1640–41	38	59.4	772	35.0	20.3
1641–42	72	75.0	1884	57.7	26.2
1642–43	76	69.1	2106	51.6	27.7
1643–44	53	73.6	1481	61.7	27.9
1644–45	41	71.9	1082	54.4	26.4
1646–47	55	77.5	1410	55.7	25.6

PORTS OF ORIGIN OF SCOTTISH SHIPS IN RYFYLKE

Port	1567	1602-03	1603-04	1604-05	1605-06	1610-11	1611-12	1612-13	1613-14	1614-15	1615-16	1616-17	1617-18	1618-19	1619-20	1620-21	1621-22	1622-23	1623-24	1630-31	1632-33	1633-34	1634-35	1635-36	1636-37	1637-38	1639-40	1640-41	1641-42	1642-43	1643-44	1644-45	1646-47
Glasgow																																	1
Orkney	2																											1						
Caithness				1			1																	3			1		1				2
Elgin												1			1													1	2				
Banff			1		1	3			3			1	1	6	10	9	5	4	5	3	5	5	9	4	8	7	3	9	4	7	3	5	
Fraserburgh							2	1	1	1			1	1		1	2	3	1	7	16	5	11	9	7	10	4	9	6	3	9	7	5
Peterhead				1		1		2								1	2	1	1	6	12	15	11	15	10	20	7	10	9	9	1	7	5
Newburgh														1						5	4	8	14	8	8	3	1	4	3	1		6	2
Aberdeen	1		1	1	2	2	1	1	1	2	4	2	2	6	6	5	1	1	1	3	2	1	5	3	1	1	1	3	7	3	2	3	
Stonehaven															1	2		2	2	2		1					1					1	
Montrose	2	4	5	8		6	7	8		14	9	10	4	4	7	4	11	2	6	2		6	4	7	5	10	4	8	2	7	7	2	3
Arbroath		2	2	2		2	1	1	2	2	1		1					1		1	1	2	2	3	1	1	1	1	2	2	7	2	3
Dundee	11	12	12	4	7	7	11	17		17	15	12	16	23	27	18	26	11	18	13	6	16	15	11	15	20	5		9	6	9	9	16
Tayport	5	5	1			11		5	5	9	5	9	5	6	10	9	1	5	8	7	1	3	5	4	4	8	1	6	4	7	3	4	5
St Andrews		7	2	5	2	2					2	2	5	1	4	1	7	5	7	3	5	5	9	9	11	7	3	9	6	3	3	5	
Crail		1					2	2	6	4	4	3	5	4	3	1	5	5	6	7	16	15	11	15	11	10	4	3	10	9	9	7	5
Anstruther	3	1	3	2	1	2	2	2	6		1	1	3	5	5	1	5	2	5	6	12	11	11	8	12	8	7	9	9	3	9	7	5
Pittenweem	3	3	2	5		7	3	3		6	2		6	6	9	4	2	4	4	5	3	2	14	9	10	3	6	2	3	3	3	6	2
St Monans	3	1	1	1		2	1	3		2	4	2	5	5	7	7	4	1	10	3	6	3	5	3	3	5	2	4	4	1	1	2	2
Elie			1	2		2	4	1	2	2	2		2	4	5	4	2	3	3	3	6	6	10	4	6	5	3	2	4			
Largo		1		1		1	4	3	2	2		1		5	10	4	4	1	3	5	2	2	4	3	3	1	3	3	5			
Leven		2		2		4	3						1	1	1	2	3		2	3	6	6	3	2	6	1						
Wemyss	2	1	1			1			1	1					2	2		1	2		2	2	1	3	2	1	1	1	2	2		2	
Dysart	2	2	1	9		5	5	1	3	3	2				2	2	2		1		4	4	1	1	3	2	1		2	1	2	4	
Kirkcaldy	3	5	2	2		2	2	4	2	1	1		2	2	2		2	2	1		2		1	3	1	2		1		1	1	2	2
Burntisland		1					1	1					2	2		2	2		1	1				1					2		1		
Culross			1					1	1	1	1																1				1		1
Kincardine									2											1													
Bo'ness		2	1	1										1		1	1		1							1	2	2	1		5	4	5
Queensferry		1	2			1										2												2	2				
Cramond				1	1	1																											
Edinburgh			1																														
Leith	2	2	2	2		2	5	6		1	2		1	2	6	2	1		2	1	1	1	1	1	5	2	1	6	6	5	2		2
Fisherraw														1		2	1	1	1			1	1	5	1	1		1	2				
Mussellburgh		1					1			2			1	1								1											
Prestonpans						1										2												1		2			
Berwick						2	2	1		2	5	1	2								2	2	1		2								
Dunbar																																	
Unknown	2	1				3	3	2		2	1	1	1	2	5	9	2	3	6	6	2	2	4	2			3			1	1		

7

SCOTTISH MERCHANTS IN GOTHENBURG, 1621-1850

Elsa-Britta Grage

1. The Seventeenth Century

Scots have played an important role in the commercial life of Gothenburg right from its foundation in 1621 and, even before then, in the trade of Gothenburg's predecessors, the towns of Lödöse and Nya Lödöse, as has been amply demonstrated through the research carried out by our late colleague, James Dow.[1]

Gothenburg in its early years is first and foremost known as a town built on a Dutch model for Dutch merchants, all in accordance with the intentions of the founder, King Gustav Adolf. What is less often recalled is the part played by the Scots in the early development of the city. Two out of twelve seats in the Town Council in 1624 were reserved for Scots. The first two to hold these were Thomas Stewart (formerly a councillor of Nya Lödöse) and Hans Jung (Young), later succeeded by Hans Macklier (in 1633) and Hans Spalding (in 1636).

Several Scottish merchants who had been residents in Nya Lödöse such as Hans Carnegie and Jakob Merser, besides Thomas Stewart, came over to the new town. Among the first burghers were also George Ogilvie (Jöran Ugleby), Hans Feiff, Anthonius Kennedy, Jakob and Hans Lindsay and Alexander Murray.[2] In a somewhat antagonistic position to the merchants we find the litigious customs inspector, Henrik Sinclair,[3] and in the 1630s also Jakob Kinnaird, a master mariner, who had arrived from Denmark with his wife, Elisabeth Wedderburne.

The sudden great influx of Scottish merchants to Gothenburg in the 1620s was certainly due to the fifteen years of tax freedom granted to the burghers of the newly founded town. At the end of this period of privilege in 1636 some of them left, not having fulfilled their obligation to build a house in the city. Jakob Lindsay, for example, went to nearby Marstrand but returned later.

It has been suggested to me that some of the early Scottish settlers in Gothenburg came from Baltic ports, and this seems plausible enough since many of their family names also appear in Danzig and other Baltic towns, but I have not been able to find any proof of such a connection in particular cases. The town records of Gothenburg are very faulty for these early years, and we do not have those wonderful series of birth-briefs that are to be found in Polish towns. The situation with regard to sources is somewhat better when an immigrant Scot happened to be ennobled, as not a few of them were. This was the case with Hans Macklier, ancestor of the agricultural reformer, Rutger Maclean of Svaneholm, and with the children of Macklier's colleague in the Town Council, Hans Spalding.

The German-speaking Hans Macklier (died in Gothenburg 1666) had an uncle, who was a merchant in Stockholm with good connections among Scottish commercial circles in Poland.[4] Besides supplying arms to King Charles II and helping with the equipment of Montrose's expedition from Gothenburg in 1649–50 (for which he was favoured with the title of baronet, with the designation 'of Dowart') Hans Macklier made himself very useful to Queen Christina through large provisions — on credit — to the fleet and army during Sweden's war with Denmark. For these faithful services he was ennobled in 1649 and favoured with endowments. Early in his career he had large sums of money at his disposal which, at that stage, he seems unlikely to have derived from his export-import business in Gothenburg, although he later showed himself to be a tough dealer with monopolistic inclinations.[5] He also had dealings with the extremely wealthy and powerful Louis de Geer. He ended as the owner of several estates in the country, chiefly in the province of Halland, just conquered from the Danes. None of his many children continued his commercial activities, but a son Johan (1639–1696) was elected President of the Town Council.

As to Hans Spalding (died in Gothenburg 1667), he was born in Scotland, the son of George Spalding and Helena Ogilvie, and had a brother, Andrew, who was a merchant and councillor in Plaue, Mecklenburg. His son Gabriel (1659–1698), also a merchant in Gothenburg and President of the Town Council, was ennobled in Sweden but does not seem to have had any economic success. A nephew of Hans, Jakob Spalding (1625–1676), was called to Gothenburg by his uncle but later settled in the town of Norrköping.

The commercial activities of this first generation of Scots in Gothenburg followed — as far as they are known — the familiar pattern from Nya Lödöse: exports of wooden products and iron (although bar iron, not osmund iron, was now the most important article) and imports mainly of cloth, salt, herring, corn and wine. Unfortunately, the customs books for Gothenburg are almost entirely missing for the whole period of enquiry.[6] There is, however, an excellent substitute for these in *Göteborgs tolagsräkenskaper*, accounts of town dues for every item exported or imported (with certain exceptions), giving name and date for every ship entering or leaving, tonnage (in lasts), name and home port of skipper, last port of call and/or destination, merchant's name, nature, quantity and official customs value of article imported or exported. An almost continuous series of accounts exists from 1649 to 1696 and again from 1719 to 1856. There are also accounts of exported goods for 1638, 1641, 1645 and 1646 (the last rather damaged).

Judging from sparse material, Hans Macklier was in those years by far the most important of the merchants of Scottish extraction, handling 20–30 per cent of Gothenburg's exports of iron and very large amounts of deals, barrel staves, tar, pitch and butter. In 1645 a large part of his iron — 130 tons — and wood was sent to Scotland, but otherwise Amsterdam was the most important market. He was also engaged in extensive entrepôt trade in articles like wine, salt and coal. He seems to have been one of the largest ship owners in Gothenburg and was also a partner of the first ropery and sail cloth factory in the town. At this time the export business was clearly concentrated into a few hands, not leaving much room for smaller dealers.

So far I have dwelt mainly on Scottish merchants who became burghers in Gothenburg. Foreign traders who did not want to settle in Swedish cities were, according to the *Handelsordinantia* of 1617, not allowed to stay for more than eight weeks yearly and had to deal only in wholesale trade and exclusively with the burghers of the 'ports of staple'. The enforcement of these regulations was rather lax in Gothenburg during the first fifteen years. In 1636 there were complaints that 'a multitude of young foreign merchants [*köpmandrängar*] had settled all the year round under pretext of recovering debts following unlawful trading', and in 1638 it was discovered that more than seventy persons had been engaged in trade for up to twelve years without becoming burghers. The trade of the foreign factors was to be a recurring cause of complaint from the Gothenburg burghers for another 175 years.

At the heart of the matter lay the scarcity of Swedish capital both for trade and for working iron and timber. This made the government wary of enforcing the law too strictly, since the attraction of foreign capital to Sweden was one of the main objects of the foundation of Gothenburg. In pursuit of this the Swedish government made special efforts to encourage the trade of the English in Gothenburg, starting in 1635, when a charter was given to an English trading company. The company was an immediate failure, but the high-flying hopes of making Gothenburg a staple for English goods were revived in 1643 and again in 1652, although they were only first realised for a brief period during the Napoleonic wars.

The legal basis for an expansion of Anglo-Swedish trade was created through commercial treaties in 1654 and 1665. Of special importance to Gothenburg was the agreement on mutual freedom of storage for entrepôt goods, in force until 1681. At the same time the export of timber from Gothenburg was furthered by London demand for timber after the Great Fire.

The favouring of the English at the expense of other nations, especially the Dutch, may possibly also have had an adverse effect on Scottish immigration to Gothenburg, since I have not found any trace of Scottish merchants settling there from the late 1630s until 1670, although Scots established themselves as important merchants in Stockholm during the same period.

In the 1670s English factors played a very dominant role in the exportation of Swedish iron and wooden products, and in 1675 there were English factories both in Stockholm and in Gothenburg.[7] The years 1675–79, when Sweden was at war with the Netherlands, Denmark and Brandenburg, were the heyday of the English carrying trade. Those years were also very favourable to the Scots. The number of ships arriving from Scotland to Gothenburg jumped from 13 in 1670–74 to 76 in 1675–79, and those departing for Scotland rose from 17 to 99 in the same years

(Table 1). In the 1670s there were again Scottish merchants applying for citizenship in Gothenburg, and in 1689 the largest iron exporter was a Scottish factor, James Craig.

During the last decades of the century the struggle between the burghers and the foreign factors was intensified. In 1661 an association of indigenous merchants had been formed in Gothenburg in order to promote the trading interests of the burghers. On the other side we soon find the British merchants organised in the British Factory. Regrettably the records of the British Factory (which are now kept at Landsarkivet in Gothenburg) do not go back further than 1699, so we are at a loss concerning its earliest members.

In 1694 the government issued further restrictions regarding the foreign factors, but after Dutch and British diplomatic representations it was induced to prolong their stay to a period of four months which was then rigorously enforced (4 Dec. 1795). Prosecution now followed against those overstaying the stipulated period. In Stockholm this made several Scots apply for citizenship, while others sought refuge in Elsinore for the winter months.[8] In the burgher list of Gothenburg I have not found any Scottish names for the whole period 1682–1720 except David Kinnaird, who was a grandson of Jakob Kinnaird, one of the early settlers. There is no trace of the factor Robert Heriot, mentioned by Professor Smout,[9] which may of course be due to faulty registration of the new burghers.

The seventeenth century thus ends with a question mark as to how many Scottish merchants were really residents and how many were just visiting the town for shorter periods.

2. The Eighteenth Century

The new century started with the abolition of all restrictions on foreign factors immediately after the outbreak of the Great Northern War when Sweden again had to rely heavily on British shipping. Although British ships were withdrawn from Sweden during the wars against France and Spain, British trade flourished thereafter, and Gothenburg's export of iron and deals culminated in 1713 with 1,615 tons of iron and 23,000 dozens of deals.[10] The export trade now seems to have been heavily concentrated into the hands of a few British merchants, first and foremost Henry Maister, representative of the large merchant house of Maisters in Hull, and also by John Chambers and his partner, William Pierson. John Chambers, who settled for good in Gothenburg, was the father of Sir William Chambers who — as the achitect of Kew Gardens — clearly drew inspiration from his earlier travels to China as a supercargo in the Swedish East India Company.

During the years 1715–1717 Sweden's commercial exchange with Britain was complicated by Charles XII's political links with the Jacobites. In 1716 a ship arrived from Scotland full of Scottish officers seeking a haven in Gothenburg, but none of these seems to have settled in the town.[11] Early in 1717 King George issued a proclamation prohibiting all trade with Sweden. In that year and the next Swedish exports for Great Britain were to a large extent transferred to Holland.[12]

It is most regrettable that the Tolag accounts are missing for the whole period 1697-1718, so that we cannot study the effect either of those exceptionally good or exceptionally bad years on Scottish shipping and trade with Gothenburg.

Immediately after the war, the complaints of the Gothenburg merchants against foreigners were renewed and the question was raised in the Diet both in 1719 and 1726. A special cause for alarm was the establishment by the English of 'contoirs' in Gothenburg in spite of the fact that they themselves did not settle there or use the returns of their trade to benefit the city. No fewer than thirteen to fifteen foreigners were said to dwell there at the same time. The most important of these was still Henry Maister of Maister, Henworth & Co., who beside their business in Gothenburg had two warehouses in Stockholm and one in Fredrikshald in Norway. After them was mentioned the firm of Maule, Montgomerie & Fenwick,[13] though it is not clear whether this firm actually had its seat in Gothenburg. At any rate the three Scots do not appear in the records of the British Factory in Gothenburg, which seems to have been made up chiefly of Englishmen until 1729 when Hugh Ross became a member.[14] That year can be said to mark the beginning of a new era of much closer ties between Scotland and Gothenburg.

Gothenburg's commercial expansion in the eighteenth century was very closely related to the demand for iron and deals in Great Britain. For obvious geographical reasons the British market played a much more dominant role in the foreign trade of Gothenburg than it ever did in that of Stockholm. From 1720 onwards, 75-90 per cent of Gothenburg's iron and from 1745 as much of its deals were sold to Great Britain. While the British market was certainly very important to Stockholm too, it did not usually take more than slightly over half of the iron exported from there[15] (Table 2).

After 1750 Stockholm's trade with Scotland began to dwindle. This shift coincided with a change in the organisation of foreign trade in Stockholm, where British merchants were steadily being squeezed out of the export business.[16] There was still room for them in Gothenburg. There they were helpful in establishing the necessary contacts with the expanding British market and provided much needed capital for growth in trade and production (Table 3).

The goods in the traffic between Gothenburg and Great Britain were to an overwhelming degree carried in British ships — as had also been the case in the previous century. This was certainly true with regard to both England and Scotland. In the years 1745, 1755 and 1775 virtually none other than Scottish ships were used between Gothenburg and Scotland, although in 1771, seventeen Swedish ships left for Scottish ports.[17] The ships were rather small, mostly around 30 lasts, although there were some larger ones in the 1770s, mainly from the Glasgow area. These were involved in a triangular trade, Scotland-Gothenburg-Ireland, carrying tobacco to Gothenburg, Swedish herring to Ireland (chiefly for negro slaves in the West Indies), and iron and deals to the west coast of Scotland.

In Gothenburg — as was also the case in Stockholm — the export business was concentrated in the hands of a limited number of larger merchants (often of foreign extraction), while the import business was taken over by a great number of lesser merchants, mostly of Swedish origin. This was not the case, however, in Scottish-Swedish trade, where the shipowner or owners were anxious to secure an out-freight as well as the usual home-freight of iron and deals and maybe some East India commodities. The Gothenburg correspondent of the Scottish importer was thus more or less pressed to import such commodities as malt, barley, butter, wine and lead in the first half of the century and lead, coal and tobacco in the second half. The Scottish merchants in Gothenburg in this way helped to widen the market for Scottish commercial goods to some small extent.

In the late 1720s and 1730s we find a new generation of Scots in Gothenburg who were to play a leading role in the commercial development of the city. Among the first to arrive was Hugh Ross, soon followed by George Ross, Thomas Anderson who was said to be a Scot of noble birth, William Chalmers senior and James Tailyour. Thomas Anderson soon took a partner, Benjamin Hall, whose origin is unknown. In the late 1740s a nephew of Benjamin's, John Hall senior, also appears in Gothenburg, and soon yet another member of the Hall family, Robert Hall, arrived, possibly from Hull. They were all great exporters of iron and deals. The son of Benjamin, John Hall junior, became the founder of the most important merchant house in Gothenburg of the century, with widespread ramifications into iron-working, saw-milling and herring-curing. The trade with Scotland and the close relations of the Scottish merchants in Gothenburg with the Scottish market are shown in Table 5.

Another, perhaps more glamorous, side of Gothenburg's commercial expansion was the China trade of the Swedish East India Company, which attracted a large number of Scots. This company was founded in 1731 by the Stockholm merchant, Henrik König, Niklas Sahlgren, merchant of Gothenburg, and Colin Campbell who, after having been involved in the South Sea Bubble, had left London and worked as a supercargo for the Austrian Ostend Company (suspended in 1727). Colin Campbell became one of the three original directors of the Swedish East India Co. and was appointed *Ministre Plenipotentiare* to the Emperor of China, Great Mogul and other Asian Princes in 1731. He was soon joined in the company direction by his brother Hugh and by a Scottish friend, Charles Pike. Among other Scots serving in the East India Co. as supercargoes or officers were, in 1740, Charles Irvine, James Maule, James Moir, John Pike and, as surgeon, George Bellenden, all of whom later settled as merchants in Gothenburg.[18] The company's most successful periods of charter were the first, 1731–1745, and the second, 1746–1765. In the second period, however, the Swedes dominated the company.

If the Swedish East India Company, after 1745, functioned no longer in the same way as an outlet for enterprising young Scots, there were other reasons to make them come to Gothenburg in search of a new life.[19] After Culloden a new wave of Scots arrived. Among them were James Carnegy, Laird of Balnamoon, and his younger relative, George Carnegie of Montrose. The latter settled as a merchant in Gothenburg. Employed in his 'contoir' we find in the 1760s Thomas Erskine (the later Lord Kellie), John Hall junior and James Carnegy Arbuthnot, son of the above-mentioned James Carnegy. In 1769 George Carnegie returned to Scotland and bought back the family estates, Pittarow and Charleston. He married Susan Scott, and in 1786 they sent their son David to learn the trade in the merchant house of John Hall junior where David Carnegie stayed until 1806, eventually building up an export firm of his own, David Carnegie and Co.

James Carnegy Arbuthnot in 1771 took over the business of an Englishman, William Williamson, who returned home to Hull with a large fortune. Until 1779 James Carnegy carried on an extensive export trade to the English and Scottish markets. He then returned to Balnamoon, Brechin, where the correspondence and other papers from his Gothenburg business were preserved (they are now in Aberdeen University Library).

In fact, many Scots went back to Scotland after a decade or two in Gothenburg. Most of these merchants had not been burghers there. Their stay in Sweden was eased by new regulations in 1741 to the effect that foreign merchants were permitted to stay if they brought in ready money to buy and to ship metals and other Swedish products.

Among those who left Gothenburg were several who had been in the service of the East India Co., such as Hugh Campbell, Charles Irvine, James Moir (of Stoneywood) and Charles and John Pike, although they had all been naturalised as Swedes before entering the Company. Others left after having been engaged in foreign trade as 'handelsexpediter' (they were no longer called factors). Among these were James Cleghorn, William Douglas, Robert Innes, Thomas Irvine, David Johnston, John Sibbald and James Tailyour. Others again had been burghers like George Carnegie, James Carnegy, Thomas Erskine, John Hall senior, Robert MacFarland and John Scott senior. In the last case they had to leave a part of their fortune to the town authorities before their departure.[20]

While Swedish legislation with regard to the British merchants became more lenient, the character of the British Factory in Gothenburg also slowly changed. From the 1730s Britons who had become burghers were nevertheless admitted as members of the Factory, although they were excluded from the administration of the British Poor Box. In 1794 the Factory was at a loss to find a British-born treasurer for the Poor Box and had to make an exception to its rules with regard to Laurence Tarras, the Swedish-born son of John Tarras senior.[21] By then it seems to have been customary to become a burgher before being admitted as a member of the Factory.

In 1769, Thomas Erskine had taken the initiative in forming the Bachelors' Club in Gothenburg, together with eleven other bachelors of British descent. Their names illustrate the great number of young Scottish merchants living in Gothenburg at that time. They were William Chalmers junior, George Fletcher, John Fraser, Henry Greig, Robert Innes, David Low, David Lyall, John Scott junior, William Shepherd (an Englishman), John Sibbald and John Smith.[22] The members of the Bachelors' Club were or became members of the British Factory.

At the end of the century times were bad for trade. English demand for Swedish iron almost disappeared overnight. The number of Factory members was at an ebb: George Fletcher had died already in 1775, Henry Greig went bankrupt in

1794 and died a few years later, Robert Innes settled in Newcastle in 1795, Thomas Erskine left Gothenburg in 1799 in order to take over Cambo House between St Andrews and Crail, from where he kept in close touch with his old friends.[23] The business in Gothenburg was carried on by his partner, David Mitchell from Montrose, who died in 1803. That was the firm that David Carnegie took over and made into one of the largest merchant houses of nineteenth-century Gothenburg. Erskine was succeeded as British Consul by John Smith of the important firm of Low and Smith who stayed on in Gothenburg. Another Scottish merchant active for a few years in the 1790s was James Christie, son of John Christie of Arbroath, but he died in 1806.

There was thus a very marked reduction among the Scottish merchants in Gothenburg around the turn of the century, and many of the well-known names disappeared altogether.

3. The Nineteenth Century

In the early years of the nineteenth century Gothenburg was hit by a series of misfortunes. A large part of the town was destroyed in two great fires in 1802 and 1804, and large sums of capital were consequently tied up in its rebuilding. The herring fisheries, which had directly or indirectly been a very important source of income to the inhabitants of Gothenburg since the late 1760s, came to a sudden end involving at the same time the herring export and the salt-carrying trade. Finally, the East India Co. after its fourth period of charter ended in miserable failure, which was a severe blow to — among others — its most energetic director, William Chalmers Jr., who followed the company into bankruptcy. Before his death in 1811 he was nevertheless in a position to make large donations to the Sahlgren Hospital, still the largest hospital in Gothenburg, and to the Chalmers industrial school, later to become the Chalmers Institute of Technology.

For those engaged in foreign trade, however, happy times were again just around the corner. After the Peace of Tilsit in 1807 the old dream of Gothenburg as the staple for British trade with the Continent became true for a few incredibly hectic years. In 1810 Sweden had to conform to Napoleon's Continental Blockade, but the British fleet occupied the islands of Fotö and Vargö off Gothenburg, and on these small islands an enormous exchange of goods took place. At times 400 to 500 ships anchored at Vinga. In 1808 the total number of ships leaving Gothenburg had been 431: in 1810 it was 1,231. In those years the Scots in Gothenburg did very well indeed. Among the 35 merchants or firms paying the highest municipal taxes ('*sammanskottsmedel*') were, in order of amount paid, David Carnegie and Co., Alexander Barclay (who had been obliged to leave Hamburg when Napoleon took the town), Laurence Tarras, Low and Smith, Robert Dickson, Thomas Kennedy (of Kennedy and Åberg), and Scott and Gordon.[24] This was of course a new period of great influx of British merchants into Gothenburg, but most of them left little trace in the town, and after 1814 they soon disappeared again.

The trade depression that followed was severe, and it hit both well consolidated merchant houses like Low and Smith and more recently established merchants such as Robert Dickson, James Gavin, William Gibson, William Gordon and David Scott. Laurence Tarras had died in 1814 and was thus spared the collapse which befell his partner, Charles Blaurock.

The post-war commercial depression acted as something of a watershed in the economic life of Gothenburg. With commercial profits dwindling, enterprising spirits turned towards industry. The activities of William Gibson are a good example of this. Born in Arbroath, he got his first commercial training with James Keiller, merchant in Dundee. At the age of 14 he was sent to James Christie in Gothenburg. After Christie's death in 1806 he did some trading on a commission basis and also tried his hand at various industrial enterprises. During Napoleon's continental blockade he went into shipping, which was to remain one of his main interests. The other was to be the production of sailcloth (and other textiles), which he started in 1826. With the help of Alexander Keiller (son of the above-mentioned James Keiller of Dundee) as managing engineer and partner, Gibson also established a mechanical spinning-mill. The production was transferred to Jonsered outside Gothenburg in 1835, and this was the beginning of the Jonsered Factories which were to play a leading role in the industrialisation of the Gothenburg area. Modern machinery for the workshops there were designed and built by Keiller or smuggled out of Britain. To the textile factory was added a foundry for the manufacture of machinery and tools. The wood-processing machines of William Gibson and Sons became world-renowned and got the highest award at the London Exhibition of 1862.[25]

In 1839 Alexander Keiller left the company and founded the first engineering works in Gothenburg, later to develop into its largest shipbuilding yard, the Götaverken. From 1842 Alexander Keiller was also engaged in foreign trade. We thus find that both William Gibson and Alexander Keiller had one foot in the traditional activities of the Scots in Gothenburg, shipping and commerce, and one foot in industrial development. The same is true of other very remarkable figures in the economic life of Gothenburg in the nineteenth century, such as the Dickson brothers and David Carnegie Jr.

A merchant by the name of Richard Dickson had been a member of the British Factory in the 1770s and 1780s, but it is unclear whether he was a relative of Robert Dickson of Montrose who arrived in Gothenburg in 1802 and his younger brother James who soon followed. The two brothers each started separate export and import businesses in the traditional way. Iron and deals were the chief exports; the imports consisted mainly of colonial wares. In 1816 the firm of J. Dickson and Co. was established by the two brothers and expanded swiftly. Shipping was soon added to the commercial activity of the firm, and its fleet of sailing ships became at one time the largest in Sweden. Ironworks and sawmills were integrated into the business. James's son, also called James, was appointed leader of a London branch, Dickson Brothers, in the 1830s, until he too became a partner of the Gothenburg firm in 1840. Another son of James, Oscar, was put in charge of vast areas of forests and numerous sawmills in the north of Sweden. The tough and energetic son of Robert Dickson, James Robertson Dickson, also joined J. Dickson and Co. Their vast and differentiated enterprise was at its height just before and during the Crimean War. The Dickson name is connected with large donations to cultural and social institutions in Gothenburg, and Oscar Dickson, who was a great patron of the natural sciences and supported several Arctic expeditions, gave his name to Dickson Bay at Spitzbergen and to Dickson Island at the mouth of the river Yenisei.

Equally remarkable is the story of David Carnegie junior who came over from Scotland at the age of 17 to work with his uncle, David Carnegie senior. Six years later, in 1836, he became a partner of D. Carnegie and Co., and in the same year he bought a sugar refinery and a porter brewery at a bankruptcy auction and started a business of his own in partnership with a cousin, William Robertson, in Scotland. In 1841 the two Carnegie firms merged. The export of iron and wooden products along traditional lines was carried on until 1845. Thereafter the activity of D. Carnegie and Co. was concentrated on shipping and the production of sugar and porter. In 1838 David Carnegie junior had introduced the method of vacuum-boiling into Sweden, which permitted the use of cheaper qualities of Brazilian and Cuban raw sugar, and was thereafter through price-cutting able to capture a large part of the Swedish sugar market. The porter brewery was the only one in Sweden and thus provided for the whole country. Bottle glass was imported from Leith. In 1841 David Carnegie moved back to Scotland where he bought several estates. From Stronvar he continued to direct the import of raw sugar and the shipping business while the sugar production in Gothenburg was taken care of by Swedish managers.[26] After his return David Carnegie kept in close contact with his friends in Gothenburg, where he is remembered by his generous gifts making possible the foundation of Göteborgs Högskola, later the University of Gothenburg.

There were many other prominent Scots in nineteenth-century Gothenburg, the Sinclairs and the Seatons for instance, but it would take too long to go into their different stories. I have chosen only a few examples to illustrate the change from commercial to industrial activity which took place among immigrant Scots of this period. Keeping close relations with Britain — as they had always done — they were able to play an important part as disseminators of new techniques in the industrial field, just as they had done earlier in international trade.

The Scots in Gothenburg thus became in the nineteenth century integrated into the economic and social life of the town to a higher degree than before. As early as 1825 the British Factory in Gothenburg replied to an investigation by the British Minister at Stockholm that it would not be to their advantage to be granted the privileges of British-born subjects.[27] The original purpose of the British Factory, to protect its members against Swedish authorities and interest groups, was no longer valid: the Scots had become Swedish themselves.

NOTES

1. J. Dow, 'Scottish Trade with Sweden 1512-1622', *Scottish Historical Review*, Vol. XLVIII, 1969.

2. E. Långström, *Göteborgs stads borgarelängd 1621–1864* (Gothenburg, 1926).

3. The name of Sinclair is known from the fourteenth century in nearby Marstrand, then a Norwegian trading centre.

4. B. Hildebrand, 'Bidrag till släkten Makeléer (Macklier) — Macleans historia', *Personhistorisk tidskrift*, Vol. 60 (1962): J. N. M. Maclean, *The Macleans of Sweden* (Edinburgh, 1971); E. Spens, 'Maclean alias Macklier', *Västsvensk genealogi och personhistoria* (Gbg, 1972).

5. H. Almquist, *Göteborgs historia. Grundläggningen och de fösta hundra åren*, I, 1619–80, 597 (Gbg, 1929).

6. Extracts from the customs ledgers were compiled before their destruction and published by J. Bergwall, *Historisk underrättelse om Göteborgs betydligaste varuutskeppningar* (Gbg, 1821).

7. S. E. Åström, *From Cloth to Iron. The Anglo-Baltic Trade in the late 17th century* (Helsingfors, 1963) Vol. I, 135, 140.

8. *Ibid.*, 148.

9. T. C. Smout, 'Commercial Factors in the Baltic at the end of the 17th century', *SHR*, Vol. 39 (1960).

10. Almquist, *op.cit.*, II, 324.

11. Th. A. Fischer, *The Scots in Sweden* (Edinburgh, 1907), 150.

12. E. Ekegård, *Studier i svensk handelspolitik under den tidigare frihetstiden* (Uppsala, 1924) 177.

13. Memorial till K. Kommerskollegium ang. Göteborgs handels närvarande tillstånd. Acta vid Riksdagen 1726. I. Göteborgs stads arkiv. Landsarkivet. Göteborg.

14. Until 1728 the Poor Box, administered by the Factory in aid of poor British sailors, was called 'The English Poor Box'. This was later substituted by 'The British Poor Box': S. Townsend and H. J. Adams, *History of the English Congregation and its Association with the British Factory, Gothenburg* (Gbg, 1946), 26–7.

15. Occasionally as in 1756/60, 58% and 1761/65, 57%: S. Högberg, *Utrikeshandel och sjöfart på 1700talet. Stapelvaror i svensk export och import 1738–1808* (Lund, 1969), 63, 73.

16. Åström, *op.cit*, 140; K. Samuelson, *De stora köpmanshusen i Stockholm 1730–1815* (Stockholm, 1951), 43.

17. A special study of the Tolag accounts of Gothenburg for the years 1745, 1755, 1771, 1775 and 1780 was made possible for me by a grant from Statens Samhällsvetenskapliga Forskningsråd. See table 4.

18. A. A. Cormack, 'Scots in the Swedish East India Company', *Aberdeen University Review*, Vol. XLII:I (1967). C. Koninckx, *The First and Second Charters of the Swedish East India Company 1731–1766* (Bruges, 1980).

19. See further G. Behre, *Göteborg-Skottland och Vackre Prinsen. Göteborg förr och nu. 16* (Gbg, 1982).

20. H. Fröding, *Göteborgs Köp- och Handelsgille: Handelssocietet: Handelsförening: Handelskammare, 1661–1911*, (Gbg, 1911), 88–9. James Carnegy and Thomas Irvine were among the merchants most highly taxed with respect to their trade, only surpassed by three great Swedish merchant houses and by John Hall and Co.

21. Townshend, *op.cit.*, 31 and 72.

22. L. H. Ulvenstam, *The Royal Bachelors' Club 1769–1944, Minnesskrift* (Gbg, 1947).

23. A film copy of the letters is kept at Nordiska Museet, Stockholm. Some of the letters are printed in B. Stjernsvärd, 'Lord Kellies arkiv på Cambo House i Skottland', *Personhistorisk tidskrift* (1957), 122–145.

24. C. A. Tiselius, *Göteborg under kontinentaltiden Perioden 1808–1810* (Gbg, 1935).

25. The Gibson family papers, also including some papers concerning Alexander Keiller and John Barclay, are kept at Landsarkivet, Göteborg. Their story has been told by John Gibson, *William Gibson 1783–1857, och hans barn* (Offset-print, 1962).

26. A. Attman, *D. Carnegie and Co., En hundrafemtiårig merkantil och industriell verksamhet 1803–1953* (Gbg, 1953).

27. Townshend, *op.cit..*, 78.

Table 1. Ships departing from Gothenburg to England and Scotland, 1649–1703
Source: J. Lind, *Göteborgs handel och sjöfart 1637–1920* (Gbg, 1923), Tables 69–70.

Year	To Scotland				To England				All ships	
	Number	Lasts	% of total	Av. size lasts	Number	Lasts	% of total	Av. size lasts	Number	Lasts
1649	7	221	4.4	32	5	238	4.7	47	94	5,011
1650/54	31	867	3.4	28	52	3,572	14.1	69	490	25,251
1655/59	24	441	2.2	18	87	4,191	21.4	48	378	19,557
1660/64	14	252	1.1	18	112	5,507	24.4	49	384	22,526
1665/69	12	356	1.3	30	174	10,818	39.5	62	564	27,368
1670/74	17	377	1.5	22	171	10,984	43.7	64	570	25,089
1675/79	99	2,645	11.4	27	272	12,085	52.3	44	550	23,096
1680	8	200	3.6	25	41	1,401	25.2	34	150	5,547
1684	8	218	4.7	27	37	1,888	41.1	51	109	4,583
1685/89	27	621	2.8	23	156	7,728	35.5	50	610	21,714
1690/94	15	424	1.3	28	202	11,324	34.5	56	776	32,823
1695/99	20	688	1.9	34	225	14,336	39.7	64	727	36,032
1700/03	18	361	1.3	20	259	14,569	54.1	56	600	26,909

Table 2. Exports of iron to Scotland and England from Stockholm and Gothenburg, 1720–1737 (Eng. ton)
Source: Kommissionen ang. järnhandelns upphjälpande 1743. 'Bergsbruk': Riksarkivet, Stockholm.

Year	To Scotland from			To England from			All iron from	
	Sthlm	Gbg	Total	Sthlm	Gbg	Total	Sthlm	Gbg
1720	1,048	367	1,415	10,850	3,835	14,685	20,510	5,185
1721	1,756	419	2,175	7,860	4,695	12,555	20,095	7,740
1722	580	610	1,190	9,540	7,585	17,125	17,980	9,785
1723	385	333	718	9,465	8,320	17,785	18,375	9,765
1724	732	339	1,071	9,330	4,645	13,975	16,590	6,080
1725	738	393	1,131	7,455	6,755	14,210	19,505	9,380
1726	925	441	1,366	10,965	6,490	17,455	21,360	7,710
1727	661	570	1,231	8,610	5,460	14,070	19,520	7,120
1728	693	429	1,122	8,195	7,130	15,325	20,425	8,930
1729	835	1,022	1,857	8,680	7,450	16,130	21,595	9,905
1730	240	940	1,180	9,890	7,620	17,510	23,100	9,645
1731	1,160	455	1,615	9,520	8,640	18,160	21,895	10,170
1732	925	687	1,612	8,400	7,970	16,370	21,170	9,940
1733	928	745	1,673	9,925	8,765	18,690	24,195	11,500
1734	678	628	1,306	10,645	7,185	17,830	23,215	9,070
1735	975	451	1,426	11,420	7,260	18,680	27,010	10,515
1736	1,274	918	2,192	10,030	9,380	19,410	24,135	12,215
1737	1,060	563	1,623	12,425	9,070	21,495	24,990	11,185

Table 3. Gothenburg's exports to Scotland, 1771–1800
Source: Exportlistor i Göteborgs stads arkiv: Landsarkivet, Gothenburg.

Year	Bar iron Eng. tons	Forged iron Eng. tons	Colonial wares Riksdaler	Deals Dozens
1771	2,200			10,559
1772	1,930		2,935	8,500
1773	2,135		3,852	9,246
1774	1,910		4,825	5,616
1775	2,280	45	12,069	7,362
1776	2,350		8,039	9,161
1777	2,060		3,594	12,224
1778	1,575		1,272	13,285
1779	1,850		519	11,424
1780	2,035	40	–	13,595
1781	1,980	30	5,209	11,548
1782	2,010	55	1,445	10,336
1783	1,440	50	1,485	9,409
1784	2,065	75	4,186	13,236
1785	2,275	65	6,121	14,512
1786	2,360	40	1,414	11,827
1787	3,435	70	1,113	13,922
1788	2,780	40	2,160	9,193
1789	3,160	20	3,888	9,375
1790	4,335	60	351	10,428
1791	3,245	95	162	11,564
1792	3,950	110	132	13,196
1793	2,345	20	65	6,975
1794	3,710	35	115	9,711
1795	3,720	20	33	9,675
1796	3,150	30	101	7,445
1797	2,730	8		5,801
1798	3,160	20		9,491
1799	3,015	25	125	6,203
1800	2,920	30		8,224

Table 4. Scottish ships leaving Gothenburg arranged according to home port of skipper
Source: Göteborgs stads tolagaräkenskaper: Landsarkivet, Gothenburg.

	1745	1755	1771	1775
Aberdeen	1	2	3 + 1	5 + 3
Airth		3	1	4 + 2
Alloa		2 + 1	3 + 1	2 + 1
Anstruther	3 + 1		1	
Arbroath			1	
Ayr		1	1	2
Banff		2		
Bo'ness	1	1 + 1	2 + 1	
Burntisland	1		1	

(*cont. overleaf*)

Table 4 *continued*

	1745	1755	1771	1775
Carronwater		1 + 2	5 + 1	
Clackmannan		1 + 2		
Cockenzie		1 + 2		
Crail			1 + 1	1
Dumfries	1	3		2 + 1
Dunbar	1	1		
Dundee	2	9 + 2	7 + 5	4 + 3
Dysart	1		1 + 1	1
Elphinstone		1		
Eyemouth		3	1	
Findhorn			1	1
Fraserburgh		2		
Gardenstown		1	1	
Garmouth				1
Glasgow		2 + 1	5	2
Greenock	1		1	6
Hamilton		1		
Inverkeithing	1	2 + 5		
Inverness		2		
Irvine	2 + 1	1	1	1
Johnstone		1		
Kinghorn		2	1	1
Kincardine			2	2
Kirkcudbright		2		
Kirkwall		2		1
Leith	1	12 + 2	13 + 4	10 + 4
Leven	2	1	3	1
Limekilns		2 + 1		
Loch Broom			1	
Montrose	2	3 + 5		1
North Berwick		2 + 3		
Perth		1 + 1	1 + 1	5 + 6
Peterhead		3	1	4 + 1
Pittenweem	2 + 2			
Portsoy		2 + 1	1	2
Prestonpans	1			
Queensferry				3
Saltcoats			1	1
St. Andrews		1	1	
Shetland	3			
Stirling			2	
Stonehaven		1		
Torryburn	1 + 2	1 + 1		
Wigtown				1
In all (number of voyages)	33	104	77	92
Average size in lasts	30	28	33	28

N.B. The first figure is the number of separate ships from each Scottish port, the second figure gives additional journeys. Thus in 1755 there were two boats from Alloa, one of which appeared once, one appeared twice.

Table 5. Exporters of bar iron and deals (all kinds) to Scotland
Source: Göteborgs stads tolagsräkenskaper: Landsarkivet, Gothenburg

	1745		1755			1771		1775		1780
	Iron Ton	Deals Dozens	Iron Ton	Deals Dozens		Iron Ton	Deals Dozens	Iron Ton	Deals Dozens	Iron Ton
Anderson & Hall	600	1,853			Chr. Arfvidsson	602	3,240	364	2,100	340
Chr. Arfvidsson	6	57	295	1,602	Beckman, Beyer & Co.		105	5		335
Bagge, Wilson & Hall			413	3,670	Geo. Bellenden		118			50
Geo. Bellenden			240	3,445	James Carnegy	39		60	225	
Geo. Carnegie			158	1,042	Geo. Fletcher			397	1,155	
Wm. Chalmers Sr.	24	87	445	1,935	Henry Greig			10	285	
Robert & John Hall			50	17	John Hall & Co.	886	3,598	1,030	2,965	1,260
John Jarratt			317	80	Thomas Irvine	44	115			
James Moir			225	1,791	D. Johnston & Co.	118	626	40	180	
Bob. Parkinson	24				David Lyall	30	150	84		
Hugh & Geo. Ross		97			Scott & Fraser	223	1,012	160	245	
John Scott Sr.			186	1,286	John Sibbald	234	1,646			
James Tailyour	206	2,240			John Tarras	24	170	130	280	
Others		88	41	182	Others					50
	860	4,422	2,370	15,050		2,200	10,780	2,280	7,435	2,035

8

SCOTTISH-DUTCH LEGAL RELATIONS IN THE SEVENTEENTH AND EIGHTEENTH CENTURIES

Robert Feenstra

This is certainly not the first time that the subject of Scottish-Dutch Legal Relations in the seventeenth and eighteenth centuries has been dealt with: there was, in particular, an important article by Sir Thomas Smith, 'Scots Law and Roman-Dutch Law, A Shared Tradition', published in 1959,[1] and another by Professor Peter Stein, 'The Influence of Roman Law on the Law of Scotland' (1963),[2] which gives special attention to the influence of some Dutch writers — mainly Johannes Voet — on the judgments of the Scottish courts. Most of the earlier contributions have been written by Scotsmen. It would seem difficult and dangerous for a Dutchman, unfamiliar with Scots law and Scottish legal history, to pretend to give much more information on the Scottish side. I will, therefore, try to add material from Dutch sources and limit myself to aspects with which I feel more or less familiar.

Before entering on the developments in the seventeenth and eighteenth centuries, it is worth considering the earlier history of the 'shared tradition' of Scots and Dutch Law. In both countries there had been considerable influence from Roman law from the end of the Middle Ages. The seventeenth-century English civilian, Arthur Duck, says in the chapter on Scotland in his treatise on the 'Use and Authority of the Civil Law of the Romans in the dominion of Christian Princes'[3] that it is generally recognised abroad that 'whereas the English decide their disputes according to their own municipal law alone, the Scots, like the other nations of Europe, use the civil law'.[4] As Professor Stein states, the extensive adoption of Roman ideas over the whole field of Scots law did not begin until the second half of the fifteenth century. At that time 'the need for more trained lawyers, both as judges and advocates, became acute'.[5] With the re-establishment of the Court of Session in 1532 this need was further increased.

A similar development is to be seen in the Netherlands, especially in the province of Holland. It should be recalled that the term 'Nederlanden' or 'Pays Bas' (which means literally 'Low Countries') has been used since the fifteenth century. In the middle of the sixteenth century it included nearly all the principalities in what is now the territory of the kingdoms of the Netherlands and of Belgium. As a result of the Revolt of the Northern Provinces the Republic of the United Provinces was established between 1579 and 1588. This Republic — just like its successor, the actual Kingdom of the Netherlands — is often called Holland. This is due to the outstanding importance of the province of Holland in the seventeenth and eighteenth centuries. It is clear, however, that this terminology should not be used in historical discussions, where a distinction should always be made between Holland and the United Provinces. In Holland, then, a Provincial Court was first established in 1428; it encouraged the use of Roman law and created a need for judges and advocates trained at the universities.

In the thirteenth and fourteenth centuries lawyers from the Netherlands, just like their Scottish colleagues, studied abroad, at first in Italy, later in France. The University of Orléans attracted most of the law students from both countries; the *natio Germanica* (to which the students from the Netherlands mainly belonged) and the *natio Scotica* played a very important part in university life at Orléans.[6] In the fifteenth century universities were founded both in Scotland and in the Netherlands, all offering teaching in canon and civil law. But while at the universities of St Andrews and Glasgow this teaching soon languished,[7] it proved a success at the University of Louvain, founded in 1425 on the model of that of Cologne. It even attracted many Scottish law students. Among the first of these was William Elphinstone, the father of the founder of the University of Aberdeen;[8] in the Library of that university there are three manuscripts with his lecture notes taken at Louvain in 1431–1433.[9] When I first came to Scotland in 1959, my attention was drawn to these manuscripts by Dr Leslie Macfarlane of the Department of History at Aberdeen; I am still under an obligation to publish a study of these documents, which not only can be considered as an illustration of the influence that Louvain University may have had on Scots Law in the fifteenth century, but which also contain a very important addition to our knowledge of the position of civil law at Louvain University itself.

In the sixteenth century many Scottish law students continued to go to France. From the 1530s they seem to have preferred the University of Bourges, the centre of Humanist Jurisprudence, where Roman Law was studied according to the *mos gallicus* (as distinct from the traditional Italian method, *mos italicus*). Bourges also attracted students from the Netherlands. In 1572 the heyday of Bourges came to an abrupt end through the flight of prominent Huguenots such as Hotman and Donellus during the Massacre of St Bartholomew. The part France and Bourges had played in the development of jurisprudence was taken over by the Republic of the United Provinces and by Leyden in particular, where a university was founded in 1575.[10] To quote a much used cliché: the torch of European jurisprudence, which had been lit in Italy, from where it had gone to France, was taken over in the seventeenth century by the Dutch Republic, which finally passed it on to Germany at the end of the following century.[11] The link is shown *inter alia* by the Leyden preference for Protestant Humanist lawyers who had taught at Bourges, which made itself felt in the invitation of Hotman to Leyden and — after Hotman's refusal — in the appointment of Hugo Donellus in 1579.

It would seem that the Scottish law students did not switch allegience as quickly as Donellus. It should be remembered, however, that Donellus, who between 1572 and 1579 had taught at Heidelberg, did not stay long at Leyden: he was discharged in 1587 because he had repeatedly voiced his opinions on topics of a religious and political nature. His enforced departure had a markedly negative effect on interest in the study of law at Leyden. His successor Everardus

Bronchorst, who had studied at Marburg, Erfurt and Wittenberg, introduced German teaching methods and was not at all in the French tradition of Humanist Jurisprudence. However, in this period none of the European universities were prospering. In Germany especially the universities declined. Leyden soon managed to overcome the crisis, whereas in Germany no revival occurred until the second half of the seventeenth century. In the first half of that century Leyden had already a well-governed university, in which the study of law was thoroughly organised. Credit for this should be given, among others, to Bronchorst, who had initiated this organisation. However this may be, Leyden did not immediately attract Scottish law students. They only arrived in larger numbers from the middle of the seventeenth century; the peak of their inscriptions at Leyden lies in the last quarter of that century and the first four decades of the eighteenth.

There is some confusion as to the number of Scottish law students at Leyden University.[12] J. C. Gardner, in the chapter on 'French and Dutch influences' in *An Introductory Survey of the Sources and Literature of Scots Law*,[13] writes that E. M. Meijers, a well-known professor of law of Leyden University, gave him the information that 'between 1600 and 1800 some sixteen hundred Scottish students studied law at Leyden University'. This must be a mistake; sixteen hundred might perhaps be right for the total number of Scottish students at Leyden in these two centuries (accounting for the fact that not all were matriculated, the number of matriculations being only about 1440), but not for the law students only. Sir Thomas Smith, in his article mentioned at the beginning of this essay, tacitly amended Gardner's statement in this way;[14] however, he does not give a number for Scottish law students. Figures were published in 1976 by N. T. Phillipson for the period 1660–1800;[15] he divided this period up into ten-year periods. I had myself made some calculations at an earlier date,[16] breaking up the period 1675–1800 into twenty-five-year periods. I preferred this periodisation because it allows a comparison with the total number of Scottish students at Leyden, as given in a table by H. T. Colenbrander.[17] The result is shown in Table 1:[18]

Table 1. Scottish law students at the University of Leyden, 1575–1800
(figures in brackets refer to the total number of Scottish students at Leyden)

1575–1600	9	(21)	1701–1725	187	(406)
1601–1625	10	(35)	1726–1750	115	(252)
1626–1650	24	(72)	1751–1775	26	(55)
1651–1675	89	(188)	1776–1800	1	(12)
1676–1700	235	(419)			

This gives a total number of 696 law students, but these figures are very rough. On the one hand it should be kept in mind that the matriculation lists are far from complete; on the other, some matriculations may have come from people who did not in fact study law for any length of time in Leyden.

Are any checks on these figures possible from other sources? At first sight one would be tempted to look at the numbers of degrees in law that were conferred on Scots in Leyden. Counting these degrees is not very easy, however. There are lists of Leyden degrees in general, but they are incomplete,[19] and the law degrees are mixed up with other degrees. On the basis of these lists, total numbers of Leyden degrees acquired by Scots have been published;[20] these numbers are very small in comparison with the matriculations. My impression is that they include practically no law degrees. Scottish law students, therefore, do not seem to have taken a degree at Leyden;[21] some may have taken it elsewhere on the continent, but many would not have troubled to take a degree of any kind.

This leads us to the only possible check that would seem more or less reliable: the number of Scottish law students at Leyden who were later admitted to the Faculty of Advocates in Edinburgh. This admission usually took place after examination on a title of the Digest by a committee of examiners appointed by the Faculty;[22] there was thus no use in getting law degrees abroad. Records of these admissions for the period 1661–1750 can be found in the *Minute Book of the Faculty of Advocates*, which has recently been published by the Stair Society.[23] It is easier, for checking the names of the lawyers who had studied at Leyden, to use the alphabetical list of members of the Faculty of Advocates that was published in 1944 by the Scottish Record Society and which covers the period 1532–1943.[24] In 1973 J. Yokoyama, a young Japanese scholar who studied for a short period at the University of Glasgow,[25] started research on this subject, but unfortunately he did not bring it to a conclusion. He made available to me a provisional list, established by identifying names of Scottish law students found in the *Album Studiosorum* of Leyden University with names of advocates shown in the publication of the Scottish Record Society. The results[26] are shown in Table 3 below, in which I have incorporated figures from other Dutch universities.

For universities other than Leyden no previous research of any importance has been done. J. C. Gardner did not give any numbers for Scottish students outside Leyden, although this might have been possible to a limited extent for the universities of Groningen and Utrecht, for which matriculation lists had been published;[27] this was not the case for the University of Franeker, whose *Album studiosorum* appeared only in 1968.[28] Phillipson adds figures of Scottish law students at Groningen and Utrecht for the period 1660–1800 to those for Leyden mentioned before.[29] He drew all these figures from lists which were prepared for him 'on the instructions of the Deans of the three Law Schools'. Unfortunately, only from Leyden did he get a list limited to Scottish students in the Law Faculty.[30] Utrecht and Groningen would seem to have provided him with lists of Scottish students in all faculties.[31] For Utrecht there was no other solution because the faculty is not mentioned in the matriculation lists.[32] The Groningen matriculation list, however, usually adds the faculty, so further specification would have been possible. The same holds true for the University of Franeker, which was not dealt with by Phillipson (wrongly, because for law students Franeker was at least as important as Groningen in the period covered by Phillipson's lists;[33] the fact that the University of Franeker did not survive after the Napoleonic wars[34] and that its matriculation list was only recently published may, however, account for this omission).

In an attempt to remedy these deficiencies, I have myself noted Scottish students[35] in the Franeker *Album studiosorum,* and used a manuscript list of English and Scottish students at Groningen which was very kindly made available to me by the Groningen University Museum.[36] I have tried to correlate the names of the Scottish students — together with those of Scottish students at Utrecht[37] — with names of members of the Faculty of Advocates at Edinburgh, in the same way as had been done for Leyden.[38] The results for all four universities in the period 1661–1750[39] are given in Tables 2 and 3.

Table 2. Scottish law students matriculated
(figures in brackets indicate the number of students later admitted to the Faculty of Advocates)

	at Leyden		at Franeker		at Groningen		at Utrecht	
1661–1670	34	(17)	2	(0)	–		–	
1671–1680	72	(25)	10	(6)	–		–	
1681–1690	94	(33)	10	(6)	–		4	(3)
1691–1700	103	(39)	5	(5)	–		13	(13)
1701–1710	63	(37)	–		5	(3)	3	(1)
1711–1720	76	(30)	2	(1)	2	(2)	3	(3)
1721–1730	90	(32)	3	(2)	12	(8)	2	(0)
1731–1740	61	(22)	–		11	(4)	1	(1)
1741–1750	11	(3)	–		2	(1)	1	(1)
	604	(238)	32	(20)	32	(18)	27	(22)

Table 3. Admitted to the Faculty of Advocates
(figures in brackets followed by a letter L indicate the number of students at Franeker, Groningen and Utrecht who were also matriculated at Leyden)

	from Leyden	from Franeker	from Groningen	from Utrecht
1661–1670	16	–	–	2
1671–1680	19	5 (4 L)	–	–
1681–1690	28	3 (2 L)	–	2
1691–1700	34	4 (3 L)	–	11 (1 L)
1701–1710	50	3 (2 L)	2 (1 L)	4
1711–1720	34	2 (1 L)	3 (2 L)	3 (1 L)
1721–1730	34	1 (1 L)	7 (6 L)	–
1731–1740	16	–	2 (1 L)	1
1741–1750	10	–	3	1
	241	18 (13 L)	17 (10 L)	24 (2 L)

The total number of Scottish law students is given as far as it could be determined: the number is more or less reliable only for Leyden; for Franeker and Groningen there may have been additional law students under those for whom no faculty is given, and for Utrecht it was not possible to give any figures except those of students who could be identified as law students by using the list of the Faculty of Advocates or, exceptionally, by other means. Some Scottish law students were matriculated in more than one university; there were several examples among the future advocates as well as among the other law students.[40] I have therefore refrained from adding a column 'total' (as Phillipson did). Of course many more law students may have visited the universities than those who matriculated.[41]

In the period 1661–1750 the total number of candidates admitted to the Faculty of Advocates was 663,[42] of whom 275 candidates, or about two-fifths, are known to have studied in the Netherlands.

What lies behind a simple entry in sources like matriculation registers and minute books can be illustrated by individual cases where material has survived in the form of letters[43] and diaries.[44]

An example from the seventeenth century is to be found in the letters of Colin Mackenzie of Coul to his uncle John Mackenzie, one of the Clerks of Session.[45] Colin first studied at the University of Utrecht;[46] in May 1692 he wrote to his uncle: 'our professour[47] has been thir two year bygone offering our countrymin for whom he pretends to have kindnes, a colledge off Feudal Law, with a strict inquirie into Craig whom he sayes he studied upon our accounts; but for me I think it not convenient to mix different studies till I come some greater lenth then the next colledge (which he designes to begin) will bring me . . .'. In 1698 he writes from Leyden:[48] 'If you pleased I should wish all ye books I have treates of ye feues were sent to me some time or the nixt spring, that (if it pleases God we live) I may hear a colledge of them then; for my professor is thought very good on that subject and pretends to correct Craig, tho he hes a vast opinion of him'.

The reference is to the *Jus Feudale* by Sir Thomas Craig of Riccarton (1538–1608), who in 1563 was admitted a member of the Faculty of Advocates and for a period of more than forty years applied himself to the study and practice of law.[49] The book was published for the first time in 1655, nearly fifty years after his death. It became well known on the Continent; in 1716 a second edition was published at Leipzig by Luther Mencken, a Leipzig professor. The Leyden professor to whom Colin Mackenzie refers may have been Johannes Voet (1647–1713), who in his *Commentary on the Pandects* — which is the result of his lectures on Roman and Roman-Dutch law — inserts a *Digressio de feudis* of more than fifty pages; we find him indeed citing 'Thomas Cragius in tractatu juris feudalis'.[50]

The courses given by the Utrecht and Leyden professors on feudal law were probably private courses; they would seem to have been general courses on feudal law, not special ones on Scots law, as has been suggested by Sir Thomas Smith.[51]

Another example from a later period might be James Boswell who studied law in Utrecht in 1763–1764.[52] On the advice of Sir David Dalrymple he had chosen Utrecht instead of Leyden: ' . . . it was hoped that he might also improve himself generally in culture and manners; and for this purpose Utrecht was thought to offer advantages over Leyden'.[53] While studying in Utrecht with Professor Trotz (a German who taught there from 1754 to 1773) he had the plan of translating into Latin the *Principles* of John Erskine.[54] The plan was never accomplished, despite the encouragement of Trotz, who was prepared to discuss the Latin text with Boswell and to write notes to Erskine's text. Boswell wrote in his diary: 'Consider:

it is a plan that may be of use to you for a whole life. It is to take a *privatissimum* on the law of your country with one of the ablest lawyers in Europe, who by comparing it with the Civil and Dutch, will give you a complete knowledge of law. It is only remaining here a month longer'.[55]

Apart from these examples taken from letters and diaries there are two cases of Scottish lawyers who spent a number of years in Holland for other purposes than studying at a university. The first is that of the great Scottish jurist James Dalrymple, Viscount of Stair. He came to Holland as a political refugee in 1682 and lived in Leyden until about 1688. At that time he already had a twenty-years' career as a judge behind him and had just published his major work, *Institutions of the Law of Scotland* (1681). He was well acquainted with Dutch legal science. Among the authorities which were being quoted to him as a judge in the period from 1660 to 1680 we repeatedly encounter Dutch authors, above all Arnold Vinnius, who was a Leyden professor from 1633 to 1657 and whose most important work was a commentary on the Institutes of Justinian.[56] In his *Institutions* Stair often quotes Hugo Grotius's *De iure belli ac pacis*, a work that was less apt to be used in the courts. At a number of places he disagrees with Grotius's view, but my impression is that at other places he is often inspired by Grotius even when he does not quote him. This impression would seem to be confirmed by what Professor Gordon has said recently;[57] he suggests that insufficient stress has been laid on the role of natural law and equity in the *Institutions*, in mediating Roman Law. I have not found any evidence that Stair also used Grotius' *Inleidinge tot de Hollandsche Rechtsgeleerdheid* directly; the fact that this book was written in Dutch might have made it less accessible to him. However, indirect influence is possible. A number of ideas and definitions of Grotius penetrated into the writings of jurists outside the Netherlands through the medium of other Dutch authors who wrote in Latin and quoted Grotius. In that way they may also have reached Stair. This would seem more probable than that he had indeed read the *Inleidinge* as was suggested by Sir Thomas Smith,[58] who had otherwise rightly drawn a parallel between the two authors:[59]

> Each — Grotius and Stair — had considerable experience of law in action: Grotius as Advocaat-Fiscaal of Holland, Stair as Lord President of the Court of Session. Both men were widely read and deeply learned — Grotius the greater scholar, Stair the more experienced Court lawyer. The great institutional works on their countries' laws which they produced were written — not in Latin — but in the everyday language of their countrymen. These works were written as creative treatises set out according to original schemes of arrangement and were not overloaded with citations after the fashion of some of their contemporaries.

Whatever the influence of Grotius and other Dutch jurists on Stair may have been, there is no evidence that later jurists in the Netherlands took notice of Stair's work. This is not surprising, as Professor Luig has recently pointed out that no copy of Stair's work is available in the old stock of any of the European libraries of the eighteenth century.[60]

This aspect may lead us to the second case of a Scottish lawyer who spent a part of his life — indeed much longer than Stair — in Holland: Alexander

Cunningham. He did not write a book on law as Stair did, but he planned to do so and his name appears not only in contemporary correspondence of Dutch legal scholars but also in the *Commentary on the Pandects* of Johannes Voet. It is apposite to quote the passage in Voet which has already been used by Sir Thomas Smith (though his interpretation may not be completely right):[61]

> This is in accord with a conjecture suggested to me quite lately in a friendly conversation by the distinguished Scot named Cunningham. He was formerly one of the most beloved attendants at my lectures, and is now keenly bent on the embellishment of our civil jurisprudence, and on cleansing the Corpus of the Roman law still more from faults.[62]

The name Cunningham without a Christian name might at first sight present problems of identification, since during the period in question at least three law students by the name of Cunningham were enrolled. None of these, however, is a likely candidate for the person meant by Voet.[63] On the other hand there is overwhelming evidence in favour of identification with a man whose name cannot be traced in the Leyden matriculation register,[64] viz. Alexander Cunningham, born between 1655 and 1660, son of the Rev. John Cunningham, minister of Cumnock in Ayrshire.[65] After having been educated probably both in Holland and at Edinburgh, he was selected by the first Duke of Queensberry to be tutor to his youngest son, Lord George Douglas. He accompanied the latter on his grand tour,[66] which started in April 1686 with a stay of nearly a year at the University of Utrecht. Most of the time was spent there on private lessons in Roman law which Lord George received from Cunningham; traces of this instruction[67] can be found in a copy of Arnoldus Vinnius' edition of Justinian's Institutes (Leyden, 1646) with numerous marginal notes in the hands of both Lord George and Cunningham, which is now among the Advocates' Manuscripts in the National Library of Scotland.[68] There is no matriculation of either of them at Utrecht.[69] In the spring of 1687 they left for the continuation of their tour around Europe,[70] from which they returned in January 1693. Lord George died soon afterwards, probably in July 1693. Cunningham was appointed by the Crown to be professor of civil law in the University of Edinburgh about 1698. I have found no trace of his teaching, and it may be questioned whether he did teach at all.[71] From correspondence between Dutch scholars it can be inferred that he travelled around Europe for several years in the first decade of the eighteenth century. He may have got the appointment as a protégé of the Duke of Queensberry; he probably lost it in 1709, when the Duke was out of favour. He then established himself at the Hague, where he lived until his death in 1730, supported by the rents of his estate and probably by an annuity from the Queensberry family. He devoted himself to chess[72] and to study of the classical authors; he would also have continued his work on an edition of the *Corpus iuris civilis*. This work had already been started at the time of his tutorship of Lord George; it is mentioned in a letter of 1689.[73] In 1705 he dealt with Amsterdam publishers; one of them asked the advice of Cornelis van Bynkershoek and of two Dutch law professors (Noodt and van Eck). This appears from a letter of Bynkershoek, dated at the Hague, 10 January 1705,[74] in which mention is also made of Cunningham's close friendship with Johannes Voet (who was not to be asked as an adviser because the publisher did not have a high opinion of his critical competence). In 1708 he was again in Holland for a few months;[75] he asked Bynkershoek for the use of his manuscript of the Digest and other materials from his library. Bynkershoek had no great confidence in the realisation of Cunningham's edition. The project is even mentioned in a letter of 1709 from Leibniz,[76] who, however, does not seem to have had a direct knowledge of Cunningham's work. The edition was never finished,[77] and no traces have been found of Cunningham's interleaved copy with all his notes.[78] In 1725 Cunningham is mentioned by Everardus Otto in the preface to the first volume of his *Thesaurus juris romani*; together with Henricus Brenkman he is thanked for his help.

Scottish-Dutch legal relations thus appear to have been of greatest importance in the last quarter of the seventeenth century and in the first quarter of the eighteenth. The influence of Roman-Dutch law on Scots law, however, continued after the period in which personal contacts were frequent. That influence has been thoroughly dealt with in the studies of Sir Thomas Smith and Professor Stein, to which the reader is referred. One legacy remaining to the present day is the great significance of Scottish libraries for studies in the history of Dutch law.[79]

NOTES

1. *Acta juridica* (Capetown, 1959), 36–46, reprinted in T. B. Smith, *Studies critical and comparative* (Edinburgh, 1962), 46–61.

2. *The Juridical Review*, N.S. Vol. 8 (1963), 205–245.

3. *De usu et authoritate juris civilis Romanorum in dominiis principum Christianorum libri duo*, II, 10 (first edition London 1653; I used the ed. Lugduni Batavorum 1654).

4. *Op. cit.*, II, 10, 15 (ed. 1654, 429); translation taken from Stein, *op. cit.*, 205.

5. *Op. cit.*, 213. On the reception of Roman Law in Scotland see also Stein, *Roman Law in Scotland* [=Ius romanum medii aevi, Pars V, 13b, Mediolani 1968], and A. Watson, *Legal Transplants* (Charlottesville, [1974]), 44ff.

6. On Scottish students in Orléans see T. B. Smith, 'The influence of the 'Auld Alliance' with France on the Law of Scotland', in his *Studies critical and comparative* (Edinburgh, 1962), 28–45 (French version, 'L'influence de la Vieille Alliance sur le droit écossais', in *Actes du congrès sur l'ancienne Université d'Orléans* [Orléans, 1962], 107–121). Smith quotes earlier studies on the subject; add C. Duveau, 'Les suites de la 'vieille alliance': Orléans et l'Ecosse', in *Bulletin de la Société archéologique et historique de l'Orléanais*, no.49, année 1978, 153–171.

7. Cf. Stein, *op. cit.* (above, n.2), 214; in Aberdeen, the third Scottish university founded in the 15th century, teaching in law did not begin until the 16th century. On the study of law at Scottish universities see also Stein, *Roman Law in Scotland, op. cit.* (above, n.5), 42ff.

8. William Elphinstone junior studied law at Orléans in 1470, cf. Duveau, *op. cit.* (above, n.6), 154, and L. Macfarlane in his forthcoming book, *William Elphinstone and the Kingdom of Scotland, 1431–1514*, Chapter I.

9. Mss. 195, 196 and 197; see L. Macfarlane, 'William Elphinstone's Library', in *Aberdeen University Review*, 37 [1, no. 118, Spring 1958], 253–271, at 264ff.

10. For the early history of the Leyden Law Faculty see R. Feenstra and C. J. D. Waal, *Seventeenth-Century Leyden Law Professors and their Influence on the Development of the Civil Law, A Study of Bronchorst, Vinnius and Voet* (= [Verhandelingen der]

Koninklijke Nederlandse Akademie van Wetenschappen, Afd. Letterkunde, Nieuwe Reeks, Deel 90) (Amsterdam and Oxford, 1975), 16ff, from which some of the following passages have been taken and where further references are given.

11. Cf. F. Wieacker, *Privatrechtsgeschichte der Neuzeit*, 2nd ed. (Göttingen, 1967), 169.

12. See Feenstra and Waal, *op. cit.* (above, n.10), 82ff. and footnote 404 at 81.

13. The Stair Society, Vol. I, Edinburgh 1936, 233–234.

14. *Op. cit.* (above, n.1), 40 [= 51]. Watson, *op. cit.* (above, n.5), 46, speaks of matriculation in the Law Faculty.

15. 'Lawyers, Landowners and the Civic Leadership of Post-Union Scotland: An Essay on the Social Role of the Faculty of Advocates 1661–1830 in 18th Century Scottish Society', in *The Juridical Review*, 1976, 97–120 (also in D. N. MacCormick (ed.), *Lawyers in Their Social Setting*, Edinburgh 1976, 171–194), at 120 (cf. 107, where, however, there is a misleading printing error: 'Between 1690 and 1730' should be read as 'Between 1660 and 1730'). On Phillipson's sources, see below, n.29.

16. Cf. Feenstra and Waal, *op. cit.* (above, n.10), 82 n.405. Use was made of a manuscript list, 'Schotse studenten in de rechten te Leiden', made by Mrs. O. C. D. Idenburg — Siegenbeek van Heukelom in the early 1950s (a copy is available in the Academisch Historisch Museum, Leyden University; another copy should be at the Signet Library in Edinburgh, but it could not be found in 1983). This list was also used by W. F. de Waal, 'Hands across the Herringpond, Scotsmen at the Dutch Law Schools', in *New Zealand Law Journal*, Vol. 30 (1954), 384–385. An earlier manuscript list of *all* Scottish students — 'Names of Scottish Students who studied at Leiden' — is to be found in Edinburgh, National Library of Scotland, Ms. Adv. 20.2.12; on the title-page are two notes: 'Deposited 17 Dec. 1908' and 'M. P. Rooseboom, 10 Buccleuch Place'. Unlike the later list — which is in chronological order — this list is in alphabetical order. Both lists are excerpted from the *Album studiosorum Academiae Lugduno Batavae 1575–1875* (Den Haag, 1875).

17. 'De herkomst der Leidsche studenten', in *Pallas Leidensis MCMXXV* (Leiden, 1925), 273–303, at 294–295; cf. Feenstra and Waal, *op. cit.* (above, n.19), 81 n.404 (where, due to a printing error, 'for 1676–1700, 419,' has been omitted. I did not check Colenbrander's figures.

18. My calculations are based on the list of Mrs. Idenburg (see above, n.16). Checking this list against a list of members of the Faculty of Advocates I found some omissions (cf. below, n.26); I also added four students matriculated in 1683 whom I believe to have been Scottish law students (Mrs. Idenburg's list gives no names for 1683 because for that year indications of town and/or country of origin are lacking). On the other hand I counted only once the students who matriculated twice. This may explain the differences between the figures given in Feenstra and Waal, *loc. cit.* (above, n.16) and those in the present table.

19. For the period 1610–1654 no list is available.

20. Colenbrander, *op. cit.* (above, n.17), 298–299: 1575–1600: 2; 1601–1625: 4; 1626–1650: 2; 1651–1675: 12; 1676–1700: 19; 1701–1725: 10; 1726–1750: 13; 1751–1775: 9; 1776–1794: 4.

21. I may mention one of the few exceptions: John Murdison, who matriculated as a law student at Leyden in 1599, became a lecturer in physics at the University in the same year and a professor of logic in 1603; in 1604 he took a law degree. I may return elsewhere to this interesting man, whose fate after 1604 is somewhat mysterious.

22. For the historical development of the admission procedure see *The Minute Book of the Faculty of Advocates*, Vol. 1, 1661–1712, ed. John Macpherson Pinkerton [=The Stair Society, 29], Edinburgh 1976, IX–X. Cf. Nan Wilson, 'The Scottish Bar: the Evolution of the Faculty of Advocates in its Historical Social Setting', in *Louisiana Law Review*, Vol. 28 (1968), 235–257, at 237, and J. W. Cairns, in his article quoted below, n.54, at 95ff. Until 1692 candidates could also be admitted simply by bill, without examination; from that year candidates wishing to be admitted by bill were to be examined by the Faculty on the municipal law. In 1750 examination in Scots law was also made obligatory for those who had taken an examination in civil law. From 1692 the Latin theses on civil law, upon which

the examination took place, had to be printed, see *Minute Book*, I, 119–121. Before 1692 these theses may have been presented only in manuscript; I found such a copy by chance in the National Library of Scotland, Ms. 1101 (John Mackenzie, admitted to the Faculty on 6 December 1681, see *Minute Book*, I, 58).

23. Cf. the preceding note; vol. II, 1713–1750, was published in 1980 (The Stair Society, Vol. 32).

24. *The Faculty of Advocates in Scotland 1532–1943, with genealogical notes*, ed. by Francis J. Grant [=Scottish Record Society, part 145] (Edinburgh, 1944). On the imperfection of this genealogical dictionary, see N. T. Phillipson, 'The Social Structure of the Faculty of Advocates in Scotland 1661–1840', in A. Harding (ed.), *Law-Making and Law-Makers in British History, Papers presented to the Edinburgh Legal History Conference, 1977* (London, 1980), 146–156, at 147.

25. He visited Leyden University in March–April 1974.

26. I checked Mr. Yokoyama's list against Mrs. Idenburg's list of Scottish law students; in this way I found some omissions in the latter. I rejected some of Mr. Yokoyama's identifications and made some corrections; I did not, however, re-check the list of the Scottish Record Society against the Leyden *Album Studiosorum* (as I did for the matriculation lists of the other Dutch Universities, see below).

27. *Album studiosorum Academiae Groninganae* (Groningen, 1915); *Album studiosorum Academiae Rheno-Traiectinae 1636–1886* (Utrecht, 1886). The Utrecht matriculation list is rather defective; one of the inconveniences is that as a rule it does not specify the faculty in which the student was enrolled. A matriculation list has also been published for the University of Harderwijk: *Album studiosorum Academiae Gelro-Zutphanicae, 1648–1848* (Den Haag, 1904); this list, however, does not seem to contain any names of Scottish law students.

28. *Album studiosorum Academiae Franekerensis (1585–1811, 1816–1844)*, I: *Naamlijst der studenten* (ed. S. J. Fockema Andreae and Th. J. Meijer, Franeker 1968). Vol. II, which is to give biographical annotations, has not yet been prepared.

29. Above, n.15.

30. Probably he received a copy of Mrs. Idenburg's list, cf. above, n.16.

31. Cf. below, nn.36 and 37.

32. Cf. above, n.27.

33. Cf. the figures, given below, n.40.

34. From 1816 to 1844 there was, however, an *Athenaeum*, where law and other disciplines could be studied but which could not confer degrees.

35. Not only those who were matriculated as law students but others also who were enrolled without indication of a faculty; the list of advocates has enabled me to identify some of the latter as law students.

36. This list may have been the basis of the list sent to Dr. Phillipson, cf. above at n.31.

37. A list of Scottish students at Utrecht seems to have been drawn in the early 1950s, at the same time as Mrs. Idenburg's list for Leyden (cf. above, n.16); no copy could be found, however, in the Utrecht University Museum. This list, which might have been sent to Dr. Phillipson (cf. above, at n.31), will only have been a list of *all* Scottish students, as the faculty is not mentioned in the matriculation register. I went through the *Album studiosorum* myself, in the same way as I did for Franeker (cf. above, n.35).

38. Above, at nn.25 and 26.

39. The main reason for limiting both tables to this period has been that before 1661 and after 1750 matriculation of Scottish law students at Dutch universities apart from Leyden as well as admission to the Faculty of Advocates of former law students in the Netherlands (Leyden included) was very occasional.

In Leyden 64 Scottish law students were matriculated before 1661, 27 after 1750. In Franeker there were no Scottish law students outside the period 1661–1750, in Groningen 1 before 1661 and 2 after 1750, in Utrecht 2 before 1661 and none after 1750.

At the Faculty of Advocates before 1661 only 4 or 5 possible former Leyden students were admitted, after 1750 only 7. From Franeker, Groningen and Utrecht there are no possible candidates at all outside the period 1661–1750.

In Table 2 I have added in brackets the numbers of students who were later admitted to the Faculty of Advocates. These numbers do not correspond with the numbers given in Table 3, because usually admission to the Faculty took place a few years later than matriculation at the Dutch universities (there are only a few exceptional cases in which Dutch universities were visited after admission).

40. I may give, with all reserve, the following figures of Scottish law students visiting more than one university (figures in brackets indicate future members of the Faculty of Advocates): Leyden and Franeker: 20 (13); Leyden, Franeker and Groningen: 2 (0); Leyden and Groningen: 14 (10); Leyden, Groningen and Utrecht: 2 (0); Leyden and Utrecht 5 (2); Franeker and Groningen: 1 (0); Groningen and Utrecht: 1 (0). All these figures concern the period 1661–1750; outside that period there are only two cases, i.e. for Leyden-Groningen: 1 before 1661, 1 after 1750.

41. Phillipson, *op. cit.* (above, n.15), 107, thinks that 'at least as many more' (as the 658 Scotsmen he supposes to have matriculated in the law schools of Utrecht, Groningen and Leiden between 1660 — not 1690, cf. above, n.15 — and 1730) 'paid private visits to those cities'. I have some doubt whether it would really have been 'as many'.

42. My calculation is based on Grant's list (cf. above, n.24).

43. Of course fictitious letters should be excluded. It is tempting, however, to quote John Buchan's novel *John Burnett of Barns* (first published 1898; I used the Edinburgh and Vancouver edition of 1978). John Burnett, who stays in Leyden for the study of law during the time of Lord Stair's exile there (between 1682 and 1688), writes in a letter, after having mentioned the presence of Stair: 'There were also not a few Scots Lords of lesser fame and lesser fortune, pensioners many of them on a foreign king, exiles from home for good and evil causes. As one went down the Breedestraat of a morning he could hear much broad Scots spoken on the causeway, and find many fellow countrymen in a state ill-befitting their rank' (94).

44. I have refrained from doing systematic research on the subject of lecture notes from Scottish law students who studied at Dutch universities. After having delivered my paper my attention was drawn to manuscripts 887 and 888 of the St. Andrews University Library, which were bought in 1949; they contain 'Notes of lectures on Books 28–39 of the Digesta [and on Book 2 of the Institutes] of Justinian, delivered by A. Rotgersh at the University of Leyden, 1716–1717, and taken down by Alexander Leslie, later 5th Earl of Leven and 4th Earl of Melville'. I hope to come back to these manuscripts on another occasion. Alexander Leslie was also owner of notes of lectures by Gerard Noodt: National Library of Scotland, Adv. Ms. 28.4.9.

45. Quoted in the Translator's Note in *The Jus Feudale by Sir Thomas Craig of Riccarton, . . . A Translation by James Avon Clyde*, I (Edinburgh and London, 1934), XVII–XVIII.

46. His name, however, does not figure in the matriculation register.

47. Two Utrecht professors could be meant here: Lucas van de Poll (1630–1713, professor at Utrecht since 1670) and Johannes van Muyden (1652–1729; professor at Utrecht since 1680). Probably the former is the more likely candidate.

48. The name Colin Mackenzie does not occur in the Leyden matriculation register but we do find there 'Catenus Mackenizie (*sic*), Scotus, juris studiosus annor. 21' (I quote from the original manuscript), who matriculated on 21 February 1698. It is not impossible that the inscription is wrong; in the so-called 'recensie-lijsten' there is a 'Cholinus', who might have been Colin Mackenzie.

49. See A. C. Black in *An Introductory Survey of the Sources and Literature of Scots Law*, by various authors [=The Stair Society, 1] (Edinburgh 1936), 61. On Craig and his *Jus Feudale* see also J. W. Cairns, in his article quoted below, n.54, at 99ff., A. Watson, *The Making of the Civil Law* (Cambridge, Mass. and London 1981), 46f. and 56ff., and J. J.

Robertson, 'The Illusory Breve Testatum', in *The Scottish Tradition, Essays in honour of Ronald Gordon Cant* [Edinburgh, 1974], 84–90.

50. See Feenstra and Waal, *op. cit.* (above, n.10), 85 n.421; on Voet's influence on judgments of the Scottish courts see P. Stein, *op. cit.* (above, n.2), 231ff.

51. Smith, *op. cit.* (above, n.1), 41 [= 53]; cf. however Stein, *op. cit.* (above, n.2), 218.

52. Cf. Smith, *op. cit.* (above, n.1), 41 [= 52–53].

53. *Boswell in Holland 1763–1764, including his correspondence with Belle de Zuylen (Zélide)*, ed. by F. A. Pottle (Melbourne–London–Toronto (Heinemann), [1952]), 3 (another edition, typographically different, was published by McGraw-Hill (New York–London–Toronto, [1952]); in that edition the quoted passage is also on p. 3, but for other references — cf. below, notes 54 and 55 — there is a difference in pagination, which is indicated by quoting in brackets the pages of the McGraw-Hill edition).

54. *Op. cit.*, 239 [= 245]; cf. also 196 [= 201] and 200 [= 205]. Boswell speaks of translating 'the *Institutes of the Law of Scotland*' without mentioning the name of Erskine; Pottle, however, rightly identifies the work to be translated as Erskine's *Principles of the Law of Scotland* (196 n.1 [= 201 n.4]). This work is elsewhere referred to as Erskine's *Institutes*, by James Boswell himself (31 [= 32]) and by his father, Alexander Boswell (63 [= 65]); Erskine's larger work, *An Institute of the Law of Scotland*, was not published till 1773, cf. Pottle, 31 n.1 [= 32 n.5]. It seems not improbable that *Institutes* was used as referring to an elementary introduction to the law, cf. J. W. Cairns, 'Institutional Writings in Scotland Reconsidered', in *The Journal of Legal History*, Vol. 4 (1983), [number 3, reprinted by A. Kiralfy and H. L. MacQueen (eds.), *New Perspectives in Scottish Legal History* (London, 1984]), 76–117, at 79.

55. *Op. cit.*, 200 [= 205].

56. Feenstra and Waal, *op. cit.*, (above, n.10), 84 and *passim*.

57. W. M. Gordon, 'Stair's Use of Roman Law', in *Law Making and Law-Makers* (above, n.24), 120–126, at 121. See also *addendum*, below, p. 142.

58. *Op. cit.* (above, n.1), 39 [= 50].

59. *Op. cit.* (above, n.1), 38 [= 49].

60. K. Luis, 'Stair from a foreign standpoint', in *Stair Tercentenary Studies*, by various scholars, ed. David M. Walker [=The Stair Society, Vol. 33] (Edinburgh, 1981), 239–250, at 239.

61. *Op. cit.* (above, n.1), 40 [=51]; cf. Feenstra and Waal, *op. cit.* (above, n.10, 86. The passage is also quoted by Cornelius van Bynkershoek in a letter of 2 June 1705, see below, n.74.

62. Johannes Voet, *Commentarius ad Pandectas*, 48, 19, 2 *in fine* (ed. Hagae Comitum, 1731), II, 1096; the passage already occurs in the first edition of 1704. Voet proposes to read in D. 48, 19, 7 '*vincula, verberatio*', instead of '*vinculorum verberatio*' and continues: 'prout conjecturam illam nuperrime mihi colloquio familiari suggessit Clarissimus Cuninghamius, Scotus, auditor olim inter primos charus, jurisprudentiae civilis ulterius exornandae Corporique juris Romani magis adhuc a mendis expurgando incumbens acerrime'. The translation has been taken — with slight improvements — from Gane, *The Selective Voet*, cf. Feenstra and Waal, *op. cit.* (above, n.10), 86.

63. Details in Feenstra and Waal, *op. cit.* (above n.10), 86 n.428. D. Irving, *Lives of Scottish Writers*, II (Edinburgh, 1851), 220 n.3, says of John Cunningham, an advocate who gave lectures on Scots Law and who had also studied at Leyden, that 'he kept up a constant correspondence with the celebrated Dutch lawyer Voet'; this might be a confusion with Alexander Cunningham.

64. Nor in that of the University of Utrecht. For Leyden see Feenstra and Waal, *op. cit.* (above, n.10), 87 n.430.

65. See *Dictionary of National Biography*, XIII (London, 1888), 306, and D. Irving, *op. cit.* (above, n.63), II, 220–233. Further references in Feenstra and Waal, *op. cit.* (above, n.10), 87 n.429.

66. This tour has been described by W. A. Kelly in his unpublished thesis, 'The Library

of Lord George Douglas (*c.* 1667/8–1693?)' (submitted to the University of Strathclyde for the Degree of Master of Arts, 1975). Mr. Kelly kindly permitted me to use his thesis, from which the details following in the text, up to the year 1693, have been taken.

67. Which may have been continued at places other than Utrecht.

68. Cf. already Feenstra and Waal, *op. cit.* (above, n.10), 88 n.431 (where, however, no mention is made of the fact that a part of the manuscript notes is not written by Cunningham).

69. Nor at Leyden, to which they may have passed; cf. a letter of Jacobus Gronovius of 9th May 1687, quoted by Irving, *op. cit.* (above, n.63), 224 n.2.

70. Among many other places they visited Florence, where Lord George 'gave a good account of himself in reading the Florentine Pandects' (Kelly); Cunningham himself may have used this visit for his own critical studies.

71. Cf. Irving, *op. cit.* (above, n.63), 221–222.

72. He should not, however, be confused with another chess-player called Alexander Cunningham (1654–1737), a historian who also resided in the Hague, see *Dictionary of National Biography*, XIII (London, 1888), 306, and H. J. R. Murray, *A History of Chess* (Oxford, 1913), 844.

73. From Robert Moray to Cornelius van Eck, dated Edinburgh 23 August 1689 (Utrecht, University Library, Ms. 1000): 'Nihil hic novi quod sciam molitur Minerva praeterquam quod de Cuningamo quodam Scoto dicitur, quem aiunt commentarium in universum jus Romanum esse editurum, in quo statuit, totam jurisprudentiam in meliorem ordinem redigere, quin etiam omnia juris aenigmata crucesque se clare et distincte explicaturum legesque contrarias explicaturum pollicetur. Quod certe si effecerit opus erit utile. Ipsum ego Cuninghamum non novi sed non mediocris esse doctrinae fertur'. This letter was kindly brought to my attention by my Utrecht colleague G. C. J. J. van den Bergh, who quotes it in his forthcoming book on Gerard Noodt which he kindly made available to me in manuscript. Cf. already B. H. Stolte Jr., *Henrik Brenkman (1681–1736), Jurist and Classicist*, thesis, Utrecht, 1981, 14 n.49, who, however, wrongly gives '31 August' instead of '23 August'.

74. From Cornelis van Bynkershoek to Cornelius van Eck (Utrecht, University Library, Ms. 1000): 'Cunninghamus ille, quem nosti, jam serio agit cum bibliopolis Amsterdammensibus de nova editione Corporis Juris; constituit primum solas Pandectas edere cum notis criticis, duobus voluminibus in 8°, deinde universum Corpus, tribus aut quatuor tomis in folio cum observationibus quibuscumque. Bibliopolus Amsterdammensis de eo opere explorare jussit judicium tuum, Noodtii meumque. Voetium adiri noluit, utpote cui in re critica nihil tribuit, quamvis eius quondam praeceptor et etiamnum amicus sit. Laudavit quoque Voetius, Tom. II ad ff., Cunninghami conjecturam quandam criticam ad l. 7 ff. de poenis'. This letter is also quoted by G. C. J. J. van den Bergh (cf. above, n.73).

75. See a letter of Bynkershoek to van Eck, dated the Hague, 6 September 1708 (Utrecht, University Library, Ms. 1000): 'Novarum rerum hic nihil est nisi scire attinet, huc iterum appulisse illum Coningham, Scotum, de quo nos nuper adhuc sermonem habuisse recordor. Per quinquennium abfuit in Italia, Hispania, Gallia, nunc aliquot menses hic morabitur et pollicetur, se diu cogitatum opus de nova editione Corporis Juris porro esse absoluturum eoque fini usum manuscripti Pandectarum et alia bibliothecae meae instrumenta expetiit. Est tamen, cur credam id opus numquam ad umbilicum deductum iri'. For knowledge of this letter also I am indebted to my colleague van den Bergh (cf. above, n.73); cf. as well Bynkershoek to van Eck, the Hague 21 February 1709 (*ibid*): 'Alexander Cunningham, quem novisti, promittit se brevi edicturum specimen criticae suae'.

76. G. W. Leibniz to Gisbert Cuper, dated Hannover 26 October 1709, in a P.S. (The Hague, Royal Library, Ms. 72 H 17, fol. 151 v°–152 v°). Having mentioned J. Gothofredus' statement that a true palingenesy of the Digest is still wanted, Leibniz writes: 'Id quod Gothofredus desiderat, a me factum esse, opera aliorum non indiligenti adhibita, tibi rem (opinor) non ingratam nuntio, ut aliquem vicem reddam pro laetis literariae rei

novis quae significasti. Nempe cuique autoris libro sua reddita sunt verba in Pandectas Justiniani relata. Tantum jam reliquum est ut edantur haec Redigesta, sed non sine aliquo cultu, itaque optandum foret emendationes ex Pandectis Florentinis accedere, quarum specimen dedit doctissimus Gronovius Junior. Et cum intellexerim D. Cunninghamum Scotum doctrina et ingenio valentem multum in constituendo textu laborasse, non video ubi melius uterque emendationes vel collationes suas collocare possit . . .'. The original text of the letter is mentioned by Stolte (above, n.73), 14 n.48, but he does not quote the passage concerning Cunningham. From 'Tibi rem' to 'collocare possit' the text of Leibniz' letter is quoted in a published letter of Cuper to l'Abbé Bignon, dated 12 November 1709 (G. Cuper, *Lettres* (Amsterdam, 1742), 233), of which an extract occurs in G. W. Leibniz, *Opera omnia*, V (Genevae, 1768), 571; cf. Irving, *op. cit.* (above, n.63), 229, who gives the passage on Cunningham. These editions, however, are not without errors: they read 'sed sine aliquo cultu' and omit the mention of Gronovius Junior. In his reply to Leibniz from 12 November 1709 (*ibid.*, fol. 155 v°–156 v°; see also his quoted letter to l'Abbé Bignon from the same date) Cuper mentions Henrik Brenkman's project for a palingenesy (cf. Stolte, *op. cit.*, 13 n.47) and says that he will try to contact Cunningham who is reported to be in Holland. On 27 February 1710 Leibniz writes to Cuper (*ibid.*, fol. 179 r°): 'Cuninghamum consulam per amicos Anglos'.

77. For further details on the project see Feenstra and Waal, *op. cit.* (above, n.10), 88 n.431.

78. Other pieces are now in the Advocates Library, see Irving, *op. cit.* (above, n.63), 231; cf. above, n.68, and Feenstra and Waal, *loc. cit.*

79. I am indebted to many friends for their help either before the actual delivery of this lecture or in the final preparation of text and footnotes. I cannot mention them all specifically. An exception should be made for Miss Marguerite Duynstee (Leyden), who kindly assisted me in preparing the tables, and for Professor W. M. Gordon (Glasgow), who not only provided me with valuable information but also looked closely at my English style and amended its most glaring defects.

Addendum to n.57:

On Stair's use of Grotius see now W. M. Gordon, 'Stair, Grotius and the Sources of Stair's Institutions', in *Satura Roberto Feenstra oblata* (Fribourg, 1985), 571–583.

9

PROBLEMS CONCERNING THE DEPARTURE OF SCOTTISH SOLDIERS FROM SEVENTEENTH-CENTURY MUSCOVY

Paul Dukes

Scottish soldiers entered the service of the tsars in significant numbers from the second half of the sixteenth century onwards. However, it was from the time of the War for Smolensk, 1632–4, down to the end of the seventeenth century that their contribution to the consolidation and expansion of Muscovy was most marked.[1] Near the beginning of that period of seventy years or so, one of their English comrades, Thomas Chamberlain, wrote: 'it is an ancient custome of the Russians never to lett anye strangers which serve them in theirre warrs to returne into their countreys againe'. He claimed that mercenaries never received any pay, and that they were bought and sold like horses at Smithfield in London.[2]

As the seventeenth century wore on, Chamberlain's observations were not completely borne out. Nevertheless, along with difficulties concerning their pay, problems of departure remained great and were sometimes insuperable. The central character in this paper, Patrick Gordon of Auchleuchries, made several vigorous attempts to be allowed to return to his homeland, but all of them failed. He wrote about the obstacles to leaving the service of Tsar Alexis in a passage of his diary[3] describing his entry into it in September 1661:

> I perceived strangers to be looked upon as company of hirelings, and, at the best (as they say of women) but *necessaria mala*; no honours or degrees of preferment to be expected here but military, and that with a limited comand, in the attainment whereof a good mediator or mediatrix, and a piece of money or other bribe, is more available as the merit or sufficiency of the person; a faint heart under faire plumes, and a cuckoe in gay cloths, being as ordinary here as a counterfeited or painted visage; no marrying with natives, strangers being looked upon by the best sort as scarcely Christians, and by the plebeyans as meer pagans; no indigenation without ejeration of the former religion and embraceing theirs; the people being morose, avaricious, deceitfull, false, insolent and tirranous where they have command, and being under command, submissive and even slavish, sloven and base, niggard, and yet overweening and valuing themselves above all other nations; and the worst of all, the pay small, and in a base copper coyne, which passed at foure to one of silver, so that I foresaw an impossibility of subsistance, let be of enriching my self, as I was made beleeve I should, before I came from Polland. These, and many other reasons were but too sufficient to setle myself for disengageing myself of this place. The only difficulty was, how to attaine it, which troubled me very much; every one, of whom I asked advice, alleadging it impossible.

For a short time, Gordon persisted in his efforts to depart from Muscovy, but was soon dissuaded by a sympathetic Russian official and the Colonel of the regiment to which he had been assigned, Daniel Crawford:

143

... they both tooke me aside, and among other reasons told me, that it would be my ruine to desire out of the countrey, because the Russe would presume that comeing from such a countrey, with which they were in open warr, and being a Roman Catholick, I was come to spy out their countrey only, and then returne; and that, if I mentioned any such thing, they would not only dismiss me, but send me to Sibiria or some remote place, and that they would never trust me thereafter. This, indeed, did startle me, considering the base and suspicious nature of the people; so that, with great reluctancy, I consented to accept of the orders for our comeing into the countrey.

Having arrived in Moscow in September 1661, Gordon still protested in December at the suggestion that he and his Scottish comrades should swear 'to serve his Majestie faithfully and truly all the dayes of our lyves', but he agreed with some reluctance to take an oath that he would remain in the tsar's service as long as the war with Poland continued. In his diary entry for 2 January 1662, he demonstrated that he had already learned the ways of Muscovite government by inviting the officials of the department that dealt with foreigners to a feast and presenting each of them according to their rank with a gift in sables. In this manner, 'I gained a great goodwill from them, and was ever after much esteemed by them, they being alwayes very ready to forward any business I had in the office'. Gordon also recorded the fact that he was making some progress with his social life, entertaining Colonel Crawford and his family along with other inhabitants of the German or Foreign Settlement, including Samuel Collins, the tsar's doctor: 'We sat up late and were very merry, so that one falling in fancy with a lady was not able to containe himself or conceale it'. Later in the year, in July, Gordon was involved in the suppression of the Copper Revolt, one of the periodic disturbances shaking the Russian capital and so-called because of the debasement of the coinage constituting one of its basic causes. Altogether, his life on and off duty was busy enough to keep from him much of the melancholy that had seized him at his first realisation of the difficulties of leaving Muscovy.

At the beginning of 1663, he became betrothed to a young Dutch lady, and in the summer made the close acquaintance of another Scotsman, Thomas Dalyell, who along with William Drummond had entered Muscovite service with the permission of Charles II about eight years earlier. Gordon referred to these two cavaliers, as well as to a fellow countryman of an earlier generation, in his diary entry for 11 April 1663: 'General Lesly deceasing in Smolensko, an order was sent to Lt. Genll. Dalyell in Polotsko to be Generall and to go to Smolensko to supply the deceas'ds place and another to M. Genll. Drummond to be L. Gennl'. Instead of going direct from Polotsko to Smolensk, however, General Dalyell went to Moscow, 'haveing some grievances which vexed the Boyar Elia Danielovitz not a little'. In May, according to Gordon, Dalyell had 'some high words' with the Boyar (Ilia Danilovich Miloslavsky, father-in-law to Tsar Alexis and leading member of the Muscovite government) and remained in the German Settlement 'disgusted and discontented' through into June. At the end of that month, Gordon remarked: 'I being in Mosko all this time solaced myself with good Company in a sober way, and especially with General Dalyell with whom I entred and entertained a strict friendship'. At the beginning of July, Dalyell and the Boyar were at least temporarily reconciled, and the friendship between the two Scotsmen was for the moment interrupted as Dalyell at last went off to Smolensk.

About a year later, the friendship appeared to be on the point of becoming even more remote as Gordon noted in July 1664 that one John Bruce had brought a letter from 'our king' (the recently restored Charles II) to the 'Emperour' on behalf of Dalyell and Drummond, asking for their dismissal from Muscovite service. However, on 13 January 1665, Gordon learned that an order had been sent to stop the Generals leaving because of their implication in the escape of one Colonel Kalkstein, and immediately commented: 'I verily thought it was a trick contrived by the Russes to lay such a blemish upon the Generalls to occasion their stay and that they had with Joseph caused put a cup in Benjamin's sack, for the better sort of the Russes were hugely displeased with their dismission'. Ilia Danilovich Miloslavsky was in the highest degree irritated; on the other hand, two further members of the tsar's inner entourage, Iury Alexeevich Dolgoruky and Afanasy Lavrentievich Nashchokin, were persuaded to intercede on behalf of the Scottish generals, which they did successfully.

Then, on 15 January, Gordon received a letter from Drummond describing another hitch in the proceedings. A government official in Smolensk, on orders from Moscow, had gone to Dalyell's storehouses, valued what quantity of all kinds of grain was in them, and sealed them for the tsar's use. Drummond asked Gordon to go to Nashchokin and plead with him to inform Alexis of what had transpired, and to persuade the tsar to send the government official in Smolensk his order not to molest the two Scotsmen. 'Two horses thereafter', Gordon received another letter, this time from both of them, complaining that they had been stopped and searched on account of Colonel Kalkstein and asking again for the intercession of Dolgoruky and Nashchokin. Although preoccupied by preparations for his wedding, Gordon made the representations that his fellow-countrymen had requested and duly procured an order for them to proceed without let or hindrance. However, three days after the celebration of his marriage on 26 January, Gordon received yet another letter from Dalyell and Drummond dated 25 January 'wherein they informed me that they were watched with streltsees [musketeers], their goods taken from them, their corne and provisions sealed up, that they are forced to buy maintenance for themselves, servants and horses out of the market, desiring a speedy return of the messenger though without an answer'. And so early in the morning of 30 January, Gordon went to deliver these requests to Miloslavsky, Dolgoruky and Nashchokin, of whom:

> the first seemed not well contented, the next said nothing, the last promised to do his best. Haveing solicited some days without intermission, I obtained at last that his M. Letters should be sent by Smollensko to dismiss them, but Elia Daneilowitz [Miloslavsky] being mightily incensed against them, for their petitioning out of the service, and that they had obtained their dismission by other means as his, caused another letter to be made ready, and many restrictions and troublesome inquisitions inserted therein, of which I having notice, despatched their servant in all haste with the first giving notice of the other, and advising them to make all haste possible to be gone before the other letters should come.

Just over three weeks later, Gordon learned on 25 February from an officer just arrived from Smolensk that Dalyell and Drummond had followed his advice immediately on the receipt of his letters, and had left Muscovy by way of Pskov and Riga. On their return to Scotland, of course, both of them were called upon to perform important service on behalf of Charles II.

Before taking a look at this service, let us be clear about the fact that, for all the complications surrounding it, the departure from Muscovy of Dalyell and Drummond was considered completely honourable. As proof of this, there is the patent granted to Dalyell by 'Our Czarian Majesty to the great sovereign Kings, to the Ministers of State, Dukes, Counts and to all free Gentlemen whom it may concern'. The patent, dated 16 January 1665, was loud in Dalyell's praises, indicating:

> That Thomas Dalyell Lieutenant General, formerly came over hither, in order to serve our Great Czarian Majesty, and whilst he was with us in our dominions, he did serve our great Sovereign and Czarian Majesty: He stood against our Enemies, and fought valiantly. The Military Men, that were under his Command, he regulated, disciplined, and led them to Battle himself: and he did and performed everything faithfully as becoming a noble Commander. And for these his faithful services, we the great Lord and Czarian Majesty were pleased to order the said Lieutenant General to be a General, He being worthy of that Honour through his Merit ...

The patent concluded with the assertion that Dalyell would be welcome back at any time for further service, and would be given 'safe passports', an implication that his further option of departure would be open.[4]

Their experience in Muscovy appears to have given both Dalyell and Drummond a reputation for severity. The Covenanter Kirkton wrote of Dalyell as a man whose 'rude and fierce natural disposition hade been much confirmed by his breeding and service in Muscovia, where he hade the command of a small army, and saw nothing but tyrranie and slavery'. Sir John Lauder recorded popular murmurs against the 'Muscovian rigour' of Dalyell's military administration. He also told how a Covenanter, brought before a committee of the Privy Council, denounced the members as 'bloody murderers and papists', and railed at Dalyell as 'a Muscovia beast who used to roast men'. Sir John Lauder also observed about the use of torture by thumbscrews in September 1684 that 'the authors of this invention of the thummikins were General Dalyell and Drummond, who had seen it in Moscovia'. However, he conscientiously added, 'it is also used among our coilyiars in Scotland, and is called the pilliwincks'. Bishop Burnet gave his view of Drummond that 'he had yet too much of the air of Russia about him, though not with Dalziel's fierceness'. 'Old Tom of Muscovy', as he was sometimes called, died in Edinburgh in August 1685. Drummond was created Viscount of Strathallan in 1686, and died two years later, in 1688.[5]

How should Dalyell and Drummond be assessed now? Could it be argued that their conduct was such that they helped to bring on the more momentous events of the year 1688? Certainly, they were both placed in positions of influence: indeed, Drummond followed Dalyell at the latter's death in one of the highest positions in Scotland, commander-in-chief of the royal forces there. Dalyell was most active in his harrying of the Covenanters, routing them at Rullion Green in November 1666, scouring the shires of Ayr, Dumfries and Galloway. Drummond's performance as hanging judge and merciless soldier was scarcely less draconian. And so a brief perusal of their post-Muscovite service suggests that their record was indeed severe enough for them to deserve their reputation.[6] The conclusion therefore follows that, however great their purely military skills, they lacked the political leadership that goes to make up the full complement of a good general's attributes. Possibly other adherents of the Stuart cause who could not be present to render service to James in his hour of need might have possessed these attributes. If he had found a better commander for his army than Feversham, if Hugh Mackay could have been persuaded to come over from the Netherlands with his Scottish regiments or even without them, is it not possible at least to conjecture that the course of events in late 1688 and 1689 might have turned out differently?[7] And what of Patrick Gordon? If his efforts to release himself from Muscovite service had been more successful, could he perhaps have helped James to avert disaster either in England or in Scotland?

As Gordon attempted to leave Romanov service for Stuart, James himself appears to have believed that Gordon would be an asset to him, as did supporters of James who were also friends and relations of Gordon in Scotland. These included some of the highest-placed men in the land, James the Earl of Perth, Chancellor, and his brother, Lord Melfort, one of the Secretaries of State, and his cousin and brother-in-law, George, the First Duke of Gordon, Captain of Edinburgh Castle, and also Patrick Gordon's kinsman. Patrick Gordon was also in touch with the other Secretaries of State, Alexander, Fourth Earl of Moray, and Charles, Second Earl of Middleton, and in constant communication until their deaths with Dalyell and Drummond. Except possibly for the last two, all these other contacts were Roman Catholics or had become converts by the reign of James VII and II.

After the departure from Muscovy of Dalyell and Drummond, Gordon was not always attempting to secure his own leave to depart permanently. For example, in October 1669, while on a visit back to his homeland, he wrote from Edinburgh to another well-placed correspondent, Joseph Williamson, Secretary to Lord Arlington, who was a member of the entourage of Charles II, as follows:

> ... I go into the country to my parents wher wintring, I intend to return for Russia in the Spring and hoped to go by the way of Polland, if in this journey I find no grounds for settlement anywher els, I intend to continue in Russia sometime longer, albeit God knoweth the pay ther yeelds us but a very bare subsistence as things go now. Even in Scotland souldiers of fortune can attaine no honourable employment for Nobles and persons of great quality. In England Aliens ar seldome employed, so that necessity (who was never yet a good pilot) constrained us to serve forraigne Princes when notwithstanding if with honour wee could be any wayes steddable to our Native countrey it would be some comfort ...[8]

Here, arguably, are expressed not only the frustrations of Patrick Gordon but also some of those of some of his fellow Jacobites.

This letter was written during the course of Patrick Gordon's second trip home, and one about which we know far less than the first, which was at least partly official in nature, and which took place from 1666 to 1667. Gordon gave the reasons for his selection to a tsarist diplomatic mission in his diary entry for 23 June 1666 as follows:

> ... with the Russes unwillingnes to allow any minister so much money as to maintaine him at any court, and also loth to offend the Hollanders (who had now engrossed all the trade almost here) by a publick message, it was resolved to send some stranger, and me especially, because I had petitioned to go thither the year befor, and being one of his Majesties subjects, might haply have ffriends at court.

Gordon's mission, which we will not describe in detail here, was essentially to smooth over the difficulties between Romanov and Stuart arising out of the embassy to Moscow of Sir Charles, Earl of Carlisle, Viscount of Morpeth, Baron Dacre of Gillesland, etc. Gordon's journey went reasonably smoothly. He was able to develop some of the contacts that would stand him in good stead in later years, and enjoy some of the delights of Restoration London. A last-minute hitch before his departure arose from the use of the word *Illustrissimo* rather than *Serenissimo* in the superscription of the letter that he was to carry back with him to the tsar — a similar error had been one of the causes of the difficulties of Carlisle's embassy. The most important part of the contents of that letter concerned naval stores, since the British government wanted its Dutch enemy to be cut out of the Russian market in naval stores and its own officers given free access to it.

Gordon managed to get Charles to write a letter to the King of Poland on behalf of his father-in-law, a Dutch officer in Polish captivity. The King in turn asked Gordon to do what he could to secure the release from Muscovite service of one Gaspar Calthoffe or Kalthoff. It may have been this latter request that led to Gordon incurring the tsarist government's displeasure on his return to Moscow. There follows the largest gap in Gordon's *Diary*, from June 1667 to January 1677, and apart from a few letters published by the late Professor Konovalov of Oxford University, we have little information on his service during that period, which seems to have been carried out largely in the Ukraine, apart from the visit back to Britain from 1669 to 1670. In 1678 Gordon renewed his efforts to leave Muscovy, but was unsuccessful, finding distraction in the defence of the fortress of Chigirin, one of his greater exploits. Another gap in the *Diary* ensues, from 17 August 1678 to January 1684, and again we know little of his career during this period. Small pieces of information can be extracted from the letter of supplication that he submitted to the government in the spring of 1685. This letter, composed just before 16 May 1685, the date of his own translation,[9] was preceded by preliminary enquiries, for example on 8 January 1685: 'I did writt to Mosko to kniaz Vas. Vas. desiring an answer of my business as to my going out of the Countrey, and that if I cannot be let out for altogether and with all, that I may be let of for a tyme'. On the same day, Gordon wrote to Mr. Vinius, a Dutchman, 'desireing him if I be not let out of the country, to send me the lend of *Theatrum Scotia*'. On 23 January, Gordon wrote again 'to the Boyar Vas. Vas. a petition to be let off to my own country for a time'. The Boyar Vas. Vas. was Prince V. V. Golitsyn, close adviser and possibly lover of Sophie, self-appointed Regent during the minority of her brother Ivan and half-brother Peter, the future Peter the Great, from 1682 onwards. Above all others, it was Golitsyn whom Gordon would have to placate if he were to get temporary or permanent leave to go back home, and the letter must be read in this context, which also includes the desire of Golitsyn and Sophie to hold on to power through a war against Turkey, on which Gordon's advice had been sought at the beginning of 1684.

Gordon was summoned to Moscow, where he arrived on 1 January 1686. On 18 January, 'I sollicited the Boyar about my going out of the countrey, and was bidd bring a petition'. On 19 January, 'I gave up my petition to be lett out of the countrey for a tyme; and had orders to be lett off, my wyfe and children staying in Mosko in pledge'. Before his departure, Gordon had one of his first meetings with the two tsars, 'receiving a charke of brandy out of the yongest his hand, with a command from him to returne speedily', and he also had an audience with the Regent Sophie, 'who required me to returne speedily'.

Having reached Novgorod by 4 February, Gordon was waylaid by customs officials, who demanded to inspect his effects. Gordon wrote:

> I did not allow it. They assured to have the orders to sight persons of all quality, charge, and condition. I told them that that was to be understood as to merchants and others, and not to military persons, especially of such quality as myself, and instanced them diverse examples of late. They pretended an order of some few dayes old, and I referred my self to the Governours raport or verdict, who declined to medle into it, yet gave me his dispatch as to what concerned himself.

On 5 February, the Governor gave Gordon two musketeers as an escort, but refused to restrain the customs officials from confining him to his quarters, adding the explanation that they would have received their orders directly from Moscow and that therefore he could not interfere with their activities. He advised Gordon 'that I might do as I thought fitt'. Gordon duly decided to set off and force his passage through the town, in spite of all opposition. The diary continues:

> The Customer, haveing notice hereof, came to me, and desired that, since I would be gone, and not suffer my baggage to be visited, I would let them be sealed, and put in a church or some secure indifferent place, untill order should come from Mosko; which, indeed, rather as be detained, I had offered at first. But now being encouraged, or rather connived at, by the Governour, I declined; and haveing sent a petition under my hand to the Governour, complaining upon the Customer and his fellowes for affronting me in putting a watch to my baggage and me, and detaining me from my jorney, to my great losse and prejudice, desired it to be written in here and sent to Mosko. Which being accepted, I marched out, and without offering or haveing any violence offered to me, I passed through the towne ...

On 6 February, early in the morning, as Gordon set out from the small village where he had spent the night, a 'gentleman' from Novgorod overtook him and told him that the 'Customer' and his associates had with great importunity obtained from the Governor an order for an official and a number of musketeers to pursue him, search his goods and seize any merchandise that they found. If Gordon resisted the search, he was to be taken back to Novgorod, or held on the spot. On hearing this news, Gordon drove on 'like Jehu' and passed through Pskov to the frontier without any further untoward delay. And the rest of the journey passed smoothly enough.

When he arrived in London in mid-April 1686, Gordon soon had a series of meetings with another monarch, James VII and II. It is interesting to note the King's questions:

> 15 April — 'His Majestie asked many questions concerning the Tzars, the countrey, the state of effaires, the militia and government ... '
> 21 April — The King 'was pleased ... to speake with me about halfe a houre, enquiring particularly armes, and manner of warring, the business of Czegrin, and many other things.'
> 27 April — ' ... he asked me many more things, as what armes we used in Russia? and what discipline? as also what family of the Gordons I was of? if of the Aberdeens family? and many other things.'

It is possible to draw the conclusion from these remarks that, as the king was trying to get recognition from the Scottish Parliament for Roman Catholics, his mind was also turning to the thought that Patrick Gordon, a skilled, experienced and articulate Roman Catholic professional soldier, would be able to play an important part in his plans for the new standing army. On 14 May, at their last meeting, the King said to Gordon, 'You must not stay long there, and wee shall write to the Tzaars about you'.

Gordon then went off to Scotland to see his friends and kinsmen, to be fêted and honoured by the College in Old Aberdeen and the Lord Provost and Magistrates in New Aberdeen. On 14 July, he received from London a copy of the King's letter to the tsars, including the passage:

> ' ... and wee haveing use for the service of such of our subjects as have been bred up in military employments, wee do, therefor, desire of your Imperiall Majexties that you would dismiss the said Patrick Gordon, with his wyfe, children, family, and effects, out of your dominions, which wee rather desire, because wee know that your great vertue hath procured from God the blessing of an universall peace with all your neighbours. The doing this, will be an encouragement for men of honour to repaire to your service, whenever you shall have occasion for them; and whenever the opportunity is given us of doing you the lyke pleasure, wee shall heartily embrace it.

Gordon was also furnished with a letter from his kinsman the Duke of Gordon to the 'Boyar' Golitsyn.

On his return to Moscow, Gordon wrote in mid-September: 'The King's letter to the Tzaars in my behalfe was delivered by the Hollands Resident ... I hope for a good answer and to be gone from hence once in November or sooner ... '[10] He had been warmly received, according to his diary, by the tsars, Golitsyn and the Regent Sophie, who said to him on 14 September, 'God reward thee for keeping thy word'. Gordon was sufficiently encouraged to send his servants to Kiev to fetch his wife. Two months later, however, the diary took a turn for the worse by far:

> 16 November. 'I was told by some Russes, who pretended to be my ffriends, that if I did not petition for favour or grace, some severe methods were resolving on, as to send me, with my family, in some remote place of their empire.'

17 November. 'I was told by the Hollands Resident, who altogether declined to medle in my business, telling me that the Russes had from the avisoes conceived an evill opinion of our King, as favouring the Turkes too much.'

18 November. 'I was by some of the great persons, some whereof told me that the Princess was very much incensed against me for my obstinancy, as it had been represented to her, and that she was enclined to have a harder sentence put upon me.'

After further advice from friends, and after Golitsyn had lost his temper with him, on 22 November, Gordon:

> ... caused writt a very circumspect petition, acknowledging that, seeing my petitioning to be out of the countrey, I had offended their Majesties, I desired pardon, and promised to serve as formerly. This petition being read above, was not thought sufficient, as not being penned in humble enough tearmes; so that, being forced, and threatened to be sent, with my family, to the remotest places of their empire, I told them they should sett down, or give, a copy of such a one as they desired, and so parting I came to the Slobod.

Further embarrassment for Gordon arrived on 29 November in the shape of a letter from Middleton informing him that the King had honoured him with the appointment of 'Envoy Extraordinary to their Czaarish Majesties'. Acknowledging this letter of 3 December, Gordon apologised to Middleton for his long silence, explaining: 'I petitioned for my pass, which was interpreted so high a misdemeanour (though never so befor) that I have been and am still under a great cloud and albeit I have used all possible and usuall meanes, yet nothing can prevaill for obtaining of my liberty'.[11] And on 9 December, he was obliged to record in his diary that the Earl of Middleton's letter and his own remonstrance were read 'above', that is at court, and 'had no other effect but a confirmed deniall of letting me go', the order being written that:

> The Czaars and Princess, with the Boyars, have heard these writeings above in the Privy Chamber, and have ordered that Livetennant Generall Patrick Gordon cannot be Extraordinary Envoy from the King to the Tzaars, because he is to be in the great army in this expedition against the Turks and Tartars.

On 11 December, Golitsyn informed Gordon:

> that the Czaars had graced me, and had remitted my fault, and ordered me to be in my former charge. And so thus ended this stage play. The justice and equity which I had on my syde, may appear from the many remonstrances which I gave in; which, because they could not answer, they passed all over, and told only all were tales or fables.

On 7 January 1687, Gordon wrote to Middleton confirming that he would not be able to depart from Muscovy, and went on in this letter and his next of 25 January and 26 July to discuss commercial and military matters, the tobacco trade and the campaign against the Turks and Tartars.[12]

But on 26 September 1687, he wrote to Middleton: 'As to my being freed from this service, my only hopes now are that the Tzaars being joined in the League with the other Christian Princes and States, a generall peace will be concluded ere long; and then I may be so happy as to be freed of this service'. And on 10 May 1688, while recommending one of his sons to Middleton's patronage, he declared: 'As for myself ther is nothing more I desire in this world as to be in a capacity of serving his Sacred Majesty which I hope to be ere long ... '[13] But 1688 did not come to an end as Gordon would have wished, either for himself or for the cause that he had tried to serve back home. The year 1689 brought revolution to Russia, with Peter overthrowing the Regency of his half-sister Sophie and assuming the position of senior tsar for himself. He now wrote to his kinsman the Duke of Gordon on 15 November 1690:

> If there were any likelyhood of doing any good, and that I had a commission, I am ready still to hazard lyfe and all I have in his Majesties service, and for the maintaining of his just right, and that in any place where his Majestie shall command, and in whatsoever quality I may be thought capable of. I may have some difficulty getting of from hence, yet being so near the Tzaar as I am now (for I have access to his Majestie every day), I doubt not but to obtaine licence, if it be but for a tyme.[14]

Unfortunately, Gordon's service turned out to be just as necessary for the future Peter the Great as it had been for the disgraced Golitsyn and the Regent Sophie, and he spent the rest of his career and life in Muscovy. But by helping to make Russian absolutism more secure, both in the Revolution of 1689 and the *streltsy* Revolt of 1698 when Peter was away on his first Embassy to the West, Gordon helped to make conditions of service for other mercenaries more agreeable. In the eighteenth century, as Russian absolutism went from strength to strength, while its Stuart counterpart made a few posthumous attempts at revival, Scots and other foreigners entering the Russian army and the navy as well found it almost as easy to leave Russia as to enter it.

During the seventeenth century, problems concerning the departure of Scots from Muscovy fell into two main groups, minor and major. The less important — although irksome enough — confronted Dalyell and Drummond in 1665 and Gordon in 1686, when they ran into difficulties with lower-ranking officials concerning the actual mechanics of leaving. These could not have occurred without permission to depart having been granted from a higher level — even the highest level — of government, whether for the permanent honourable discharge of Dalyell and Drummond, or the more temporary visit home of Gordon. It is difficult to detect any consistency in the policies of the government in this sphere. Intercession from the Stuarts failed for Gordon, but succeeded for his two comrades. All three had entered Muscovy on limited service contracts: Gordon's was not adhered to, those of the others were. It seems from his own account that Gordon had the option of quitting the service of the tsar in 1669, but decided not to pursue it because of lack of opportunity anywhere else. From 1685 onwards, when James VII and II would have liked him to return for important duties back home, the Muscovite authorities were putting such a high value on his contribution to their welfare that they would not contemplate letting him go. Beyond all doubt, this contribution in the last fifteen years or so of the seventeenth century was immense.

NOTES

1. For a general introduction, see A. Francis Steuart, *Scottish Influences in Russian History: From the End of the 16th Century to the Beginning of the 19th Century* (Glasgow, 1913); J. W. Barnhill and Paul Dukes, 'North-east Scots in Muscovy in the seventeenth century', *Northern Scotland*, Vol. 1, No. 1 (1972). On the War for Smolensk in particular, see Paul Dukes, 'The Leslie Family in the Swedish Period (1630–5) of the Thirty Years War', *European Studies Review*, Vol. 12, No. 4 (1982).

2. See Anna Lubimenko, 'A Project for the Acquisition of Russia by James I', *English Historical Review*, Vol. 29 (1914), 247.

3. Some of this diary was published from a copy made by Dr. M. C. Posselt and edited by Joseph Robertson as *Passages from the Diary of General Patrick Gordon of Auchleuchries, AD 1635–AD 1699* (Aberdeen, 1859). However, unless otherwise stated, the material in this essay is taken from the original, which is to be found in the Central Military Historical Archive (*TsGVIA*) in Moscow.

4. *SRO*, GD 22/1/95. See also *Ninth Report of the Royal Commission on Historical Manuscripts*, Part II (London, 1884), 236. A translation of a letter from Tsar Alexis to King Charles II, dated 23 February 1666, and bearing testimony to the distinguished military services in the Russian army of General Thomas Dalyell and Lieutenant-General William Drummond is to be found in Charles Dalton, *The Scots Army, 1661–1688* (Edinburgh, 1909), 191–2.

5. The preceding paragraph taken from Robertson, *Passages*, 78–9n.

6. This estimate made on the basis of Dalton, *The Scots Army*, and Charles Sanford Terry, *John Graham of Claverhouse, Viscount of Dundee, 1648–1689* (London, 1905).

7. These conjectures made after a reading of John Carswell, *The Descent on England* (London, 1969); John Childs, *The Army, James II and the Glorious Revolution* (Manchester, 1980); and several pamphlets of the late 1690s on the 'standing army' controversy by John Trenchard and Captain Orme.

8. S. Konovalov, intro. and ed., 'Sixteen Further Letters of General Patrick Gordon', *Oxford Slavonic Papers*, Vol. 13 (1967), 81. I have changed the punctuation slightly for easier comprehension. It was during the visit back home of 1669–1670 that Patrick Gordon and his servant Alexander Lumsden were made burgesses of Aberdeen on 6 May 1670. See 'Burgess Register of Aberdeen', *New Spalding Club Miscellany*, Vol. 2 (Aberdeen, 1908), 75.

9. See Appendix.

10. Konovalov, *Oxford Slavonic Papers*, Vol. 13, 85.

11. *Ibid.*, 85.

12. *Ibid.*, 86–9.

13. *Ibid.*, 93–4.

14. Robertson, *Passages*, 170.

Note: I am grateful to Professor William E. Butler of the Faculty of Laws, University College, London, for his scrutiny of the legal aspects of this paper.

APPENDIX: PATRICK GORDON'S LETTER OF SUPPLICATION TO THE RUSSIAN GOVERNMENT, MAY 1685

Being descended of Honourable parentage, I travelled from my native Country into forraigne to purchase honoure and meanes to maintaine it with.

Haveing served diverse Monarchs honestly and faithfully, when my occasions called me to quite their service, I was never detained, but upon my desire, I had my liberty granted, being dismissed in favour, and with ample testimonies of my fidelity and service.

I came into Russeland in an honourable charge, not out of necessity but rather of dartleness and not poor but rich according to my quality.

I came into Russeland, to serve only for a tyme, hoping when my occasions should serve, to have my liberty, as I had in other Countreys, and as others of my quality have here formerly had.

In the tyme of my service here, I have always served truly and faithfully neither sparing pains nor my head from hazard and danger or shunning danger or spareing labour.

In an dni 1670 returning out of my owne countrey and finding the pay redacted to a third part of the former, I petitioned to be dismissed from this service, which being denyed, I was sent with others to Shewsky [Shuia], his Matie of glorious memory dismissing us graciously, and oute of his owne mouth telling us that we should have bread there, and if we should stand in need of anything, we should petition for it, and our wants should be supplyed.

In an dni 1677 being at his Maties service by Czehrin [Chigirin] in the army against the Turkes, his Royall Matie of great Brittaines extraordinary envoy John Hebdon Esquire, by orders from his Royall Matie gave a memoriall into the Ambassade office desireing my dismission and liberty to returne to my owne Countrey: to which he received answer, that when this Campagnia should be ended, and I desire to be dismissed, I should be let go; to which purpose an order was sent into the Stranger Office.

In an dni 1678 I coming to Mosko in hopes according to his M. gracious promise to be dismissed, found that I was ordred with my regiment to go to Czegrin, so that being unwilling to shun such dangerous service, I went without troubling his Tz. Matie for my dismission, only remonstrateing that I might have my liberty if it should please God to bring me from that service in health.

In the same yeare having lost all I had in Czehrin, I came to Mosko, in hopes againe to be dismissed, when also his Tz: orders for me to go to Kyow [Kiev] anticipated me, and because it was expected that the Turkes would attaque that place, lest it might be thought that I shunned such dangerous service, I went with alacrity to that service.

Haveing the last year gott notice of the deceasse of my parents, and that in my absence they will not give me entry to heritage which my Father hath left me, I petitioned their Tz: Maties for licence to go to my owne countrey with my Family and if that should not be granted, that I alone might have liberty for a short tyme.

My grievances.

The former Generalls Thomas Dalyell and William Drummond, who in my tyme served his Tz M of glorious Memory, had not only full monthly meanes and pay, but for maintenance of their honour, and that they might live according to their charge, had villages given them with great rents.

Genll. Lt. Athanasious Trawrnicht after the Czehrin's siege, where he did not loss anything hath been graced from one Government to anor.where he hath enriched himself.

For my heavy beleaguering in Czehrin where I lossed all I had there, to the value of about 700 rubles, I have received but 200 rubles no more, as my Comorads who were in the army, and not only not lost any thing, but had great gaines by booty and other wayes.

The other Generall persons have great advantages beyond me, living in garrisons where they have profitt, and in peace, and have diverse children graced in very yong yeares with honourable charges.

Two of my sonnes, who in ordinary, and by his Tz M of gracious memory approved and allowed, yeares were graced with Ensignies places, were careered or exauterated, so that being destitute of moye meanes to give them subsistance and breeding, I was forced to send them to my owne countrey to my parents to be maintained and educated.

Albeit I am alwayes at service in great danger, paines and labour, yet am I forced to struggle with wants and necessities.

Being by many wounds, labour and yeares become valetudinary, I would gladly be at a resting place in my owne countrey where I may looke to the ordering of my affaires, and the admiration of my children, and the care of my health.

Frequent sicknesses being as it were sumonses and warnings from death, the often use of the sacraments are the more needfull and here all occasions of much spirituall helps and comforts are taken away.

Being alwayes struggling with wants and not being able to provide any thing for my wyfe and children, it cannot but grieve me to think of leaving them upon my death in poverty among strangers.

In a tyme of Generall peace with all their Tz M's enemyes being denyed my pass or liberty to go to my owne countrey without giveing me any reason for it or imagine in what condition I am.

Redresses.

Nevertheless if it be not to their Maties pleasure to let me to my native Countrey for good and all, I humbly desire that the underwritten points may be taken in consideration.

I am so farr from desiring to live in ease, or eat the bread of idleness, that I am willing to stay here or in any place where my service may be acceptable to their Maties, or where I may have occasion of doing their Maties service.

Liveing here among strangers, where I must buy all things at a dear rate, even wood and hay, my expences in keeping servants, horses and many things extraordinary, ar greater than my pay.

Therefor that I may serve cheerfully, and live in some manner according to my quality and charge, it is requisite that I have such a constant pay or other helps for my maintenance that I may subsist and not be in necessity.

In tyme of necessity and once or twice in the year at the principall Feasts, it may be free for a priest of my Religion to come to Kiow out of the nearest townes of Polland, so long as the peace or truce continueth with them.

Because of my frequent sicknesses, that a doctor or any other understanding person may be entertained and remain here in Kyow with medicines, which will not only be necessary for me but for the Governours, and all sorts of their Maties subjects.

I have here few soldiers under my command, and no wayes conforme to my charge or other Generall persons, so that I have not attendants nor watches equall with a Colonell.

There must be more souldiers sent hither, which will not only be necessary, but very advantageous for their Maties service.

If it shall be their Maties pleasure to continue me still in Kyow and that warres be and are expeditions against their Tz Maties enemyes, and that there be no fear of the enemyes advancing to attack this Garrison that I may be employed in the Fields with a comand agreeable to my charge.

In the meane tyme that their Tz Mat would be pleased in such a tyme as the Neighbour armyes are retyred into their quarters, and when no attempts or attaques of enemyes ar to be feared, to give me licence to go to my owne Countrey for the tyme of six months, that I may order my affaires there.

10

A NOTE ON THE SCOTS IN POLAND, 1550–1800

Anna Biegańska

Scots in the early modern period were particularly drawn to Poland, due to certain factors that distinguished that country from others which they also found attractive such as France, Germany, Denmark, Sweden and Russia; firstly, although Poland was Catholic, she readily offered shelter to those of other persuasions, and was equally hospitable to Calvinist and to Catholic Scots; secondly, because in Poland participation in trade was regarded as degrading for a gentleman, there was an obvious opening for immigrants with a flair for peddling; thirdly, the Polish army consisted mainly of cavalry, so Scottish foot soldiers, who had an unrivalled reputation, were highly valued. Commercial relations between Scotland and Poland went back as far as the end of the fourteenth century. The inflow increased in the fifteenth and sixteenth centuries, reaching its peak in the second half of the sixteenth and the first half of the seventeenth centuries.

As far as can be ascertained, the Scots emigrating to Poland originated from over 140 localities situated chiefly in the east and north-east of Scotland. They arrived mainly by sea at Gdańsk (Danzig) and the other Baltic ports, though some came by land from Germany or Bohemia. They moved southwards from the coast, initially to localities situated on the main roads and rivers. They showed preference for settling in private towns, in 'latifundia' of the aristocracy, in gentry or monastic properties within the royal towns, and in the country estates of the nobility, but were also more generally residents in the royal towns. They have been found in over 420 localities in Poland.

The vast majority of the immigrants were pedlars and small itinerant tradesmen, particularly weavers, cutlers and shoemakers. Those of some financial standing even became merchants, or established artisans. The mercenaries were either directly transported from Scotland or recruited in Poland from the pedlars and itinerant tradesmen. Spytek Wawrzyniec Jordan, a well-known captain in Stefan Batory's army, stressed that when need arose pedlars put aside their baskets and girded on their swords. He highly praised their qualities as foot soldiers saying that 2,000 Scots were better by far than 6,000 Polish infantry.[1]

There were also a few immigrant clergy, both Reformed (e.g. J. Dury) and Catholic (e.g. R. Abercrombie), and some erudite scholars, such as the physician W. Davidson and the lawyer W. Bruce, but these were infrequent.

The pedlars refrained from paying taxes and remained outside the bounds of guild organisation, carrying out their business illegally as they sold goods 'ulna et libra',[2] gained direct access to customers' homes both in town and country,[3] and provided goods on credit or in direct barter for agricultural products and raw materials.[4] They were thus serious rivals to those who had to bear municipal and guild burdens: the latter therefore objected to the illegal ways by which the Scots earned their bread.

National and municipal authorities promulgated a series of edicts against the vagrant Scots. As early as 1562 and 1565 the Seym (Diet) enacted laws against the Scottish pedlars,[5] and in granting privileges to towns the kings frequently forbade them to admit Scots to municipal rights unless they also had domicile. Casimir Jagiellończyk did so in respect of Gdańsk in 1457; Sigismond August, following a writ of the Prussian estates dated 1537, issued a general edict in 1551,[6] and one respecting Międzyrzecz in 1556;[7] Stefan Batory issued an edict in respect to Poznań in 1576,[8] and a manifesto in 1580;[9] Sigismond III one in respect to Kcynia in 1594,[10] and a manifesto in 1600 that differentiated two categories of Scots — pedlars and traders — of whom only the latter might be granted municipal rights under certain safeguards.[11] In 1616 the same king promulgated a decree against Scottish pedlars.[12] The problem was also raised several times by the Prussian estates.[13]

Various municipal instructions and resolutions[14] also aimed at eliminating vagrant Scottish pedlars and itinerant tradesmen, forbidding purchase of goods[15] or offers of hospitality to them,[16] limiting their sojourn in the town after the end of fairs,[17] interdicting them from organising illegal societies,[18] ordering them to remove their signboards[19] and restricting the number of craftsman-tailors residing within a cloister to one man.[20]

The same policy is revealed in statutes of the small traders' guilds, for example in Bydgoszcz in 1568, 1581, 1622 and 1635,[21] though here four resident Scots were granted fellowship.[22] The regulations of several crafts protected their members against Scottish pedlars, viz. shoemakers,[23] bellowsmakers,[24] harnessmakers,[25] glovers,[26] tailors,[27] cutlers,[28] smiths,[29] pewterers[30] and linen drapers.[31]

Nonetheless, the country was swarming with immigrants. Their number was estimated in an intuitive and subjective way by contemporaries at from 15,000 to 40,000 people or even 30,000 families.[32] Placenames such as Nowa Szkocja, Skotna Góra, Szkockie Wzgórza, Sckotowo, Sckotówka, Szkoty, Szotniki, Szoty and, in Gdańsk, Szkocka Grobla (Scottish Jetty, Pasaz Szkocki (Scottish Passage), Brama Douglasa (Douglas' Gate) and others embodying a family name, like Ramzy,[33] also bear witness to the important inflow of the newcomers.

How many Scots actually lived in Poland, and when did they arrive? There is no way of computing the number accurately, but some impression may be gained from careful investigation of the sources of the scale, and more especially of the timing, of the movement. The statistical appendix presents the results from 1550 onwards: a Scot was regarded as having 'arrived' when his name was entered for the first time in the documents. The largest numbers of names are concentrated in the period 1570–1690, but because there is no way of distinguishing between an immigrant and his descendant, many, especially at the end of the period and in the eighteenth century, must be regarded as being second or third-generation Scottish immigrants, not genuine newcomers to Polish society. It is therefore reasonable to assume that the main arrival of Scots occurred in the last three decades of the sixteenth century (especially the 1580s) and the first half of the seventeenth century (especially in the 1610s). The figures themselves, however, should not mislead us. On the one hand, the sources generally relate to adult males: we do not know what families they brought with them, or acquired in Poland. On the other hand, only a fraction of the names actually appear in the sources. The 'vagrant' Scots were generally untraceable, as were many settled immigrants. Well-to-do citizens formed so-called 'silent societies', concealing several countrymen as pseudo-factors so that neither their names nor number can be precisely discovered. Attempts to solve the problem are not fully satisfactory. For instance, at first sight the most comprehensive list of Scots in Poland is contained in the subsidy list of those ordered to contribute to the cause of Charles II in 1651, giving 461 names,[34] but other sources give the names of another 141 Scots who must have been in Poland in that year. And how many were there who escaped entry both in the subsidy list and in the other sources?

The Scots' full assimilation into Polish society generally occurred in the second or third generations, although this did not mean that the offspring of the immigrants were not aware of their origin; they often knew and used the language of their fathers both in speech and writing.[35] On the whole, the immigrants were loyal toward their new country, though under the stress of war some of them regarded it as more advantageous to support Poland's invaders and others returned to Scotland mostly to invest money they had earned in Poland such as John Turner and Robert Brown. More enterprising individuals, like the wine monopolist Robert-Wojciech Portius, the corn merchant Daniel Davidson, the banker Peter Tepper and the manufacturer Thomas Dangel, became very rich people and contributed to the economic life of the country of their choice.

By the end of the eighteenth century the process of polonisation was complete. Several descendants of the Scots were completely devoted to the Polish cause, some participating in risings against the partitioners of Poland and thereby proving their patriotic devotion to the country where their ancestors had settled. Nowadays a number of people with Scottish names take an active part in Polish social, economic, cultural, religious and political life.

Scottish immigration to Poland differed from that of the Italians in the first half of the sixteenth century, of the Armenians in the sixteenth and early seventeenth centuries, of the Saxons at the turn of the seventeenth and eighteenth centuries, and from that of the English as well. The Italians arrived in Poland in Bona's suite, to the number of about 350 persons; they appeared predominantly at the royal court in a large range of occupations from dignitaries to servants, and had among them outstanding representatives of intellectual life and artisans of high skill. The Italians contributed to closer relations between Italy and Poland and transmitted the art and spirit of the Renaissance. The Armenians resembled the Scots in that they too were mainly pedlars, tradesmen and craftsmen, but the territory where they settled was limited to the south-east of Poland, and the number far smaller than that of the Scots. The Saxon immigration was largely military, related to the policies of August II Wettin as Polish king and Saxon elector; and that of the English was largely restricted to the representatives of rich merchants and their companies.

The Scots, however, had few advantages. They were not, like the Italians, bound to the throne, and they had therefore to make a special effort to penetrate Polish society, particularly in the economic field. Their trade differed from that carried on by the English in being small-scale and without the backing of extensive capital. It must be stressed again that the Scots were in the majority pedlars who obtained direct access both to producers and customers, buying and selling small quantities of cheap goods of low quality. Regardless of their financial status they were engaged in credit transactions. One feature above all characterised the Scots: they were readily responsive to market needs and knew how to make the best of any situation.[36]

NOTES

1. Arckiwum Główne Akt Dawnych (hereafter AGAD) Warszawa, Archiwum Radziwiłłów V 6123.
2. Consularia civitatis Leopoliensis 102 f. 146, *passim* — after L. Charewiczowa, Lwów na przełomie XVII i XVIII wieku. 'Studia z historii społecznej i gospodarczej poświęcone prof. dr F. Bukakowi', (Lwów, 1931), 360–361.
3. A. Grabowski, Starozytnicze wiadomości o Krakowie (Kraków, 1852), 232; — M. K. Radziwill, Peregrynacje do Ziemi Swiętej. Ed. J. Czubek. in: Archiwum do dziejów literatury i oświaty w Polsce. (Kraków 1925), 15, part 3, 81. — J. I. Kraszewski, Wilno od poczatków jego do roku 1750. (Wilno 1840),2, 49. — A. Zaleski, Konfraternia kupiecka miasta Starej Warszawy. (Warszawa 1913), 67. — Wojewódzkie Archiwum Państwowe (herafter WAP) Gdańsk 300, 10/21 f. 287. — WAP Toruń II II 2 f. 137: — *ibidem* II II 4 f. 151.
4. AGAD Metryka Koronna (herafter MK) 123 f. 226. — WAP Poznań Depositum Unitatis 7254; *ibidem* 9788. — WAP Bydgoszcz, Nowe 12 f. 112. — WAP Lublin 16 f. 532; — *ibidem* Kazimierz 3 f. 4. — M. Bogucka, Gdańsk jako ośrodek produkcyjny w XIV-XVII wieku. (Warszawa 1962), 187.
5. Volumina Legum. Ed. J. Ohryzko. (Petersburg 1859), 2, 20, 51.
6. AGAD MK 82 f. 394.
7. A. Warschauer, Die städlichen Archive in der Provinz Posen. (Leipzig 1901), 14.
8. WAP Poznań D 260.
9. AGAD MK 123 f. 223.
10. A. Warschauer, *op. cit.*, 38.
11. WAP Kraków Wawel Relationes civitatis Cracoviensis 27 f. 1510–1514.
12. Polska Akademia Nauk (hereafter PAN) Kórnik 1540 f. 5. — WAP Kraków Wawel Relationes Castrensis Cracoviensis 42 f. 478.
13. Akten der Ständetage Ost- und Westpreussens unter der Herrschaft des Deutschen Ordens. Ed. M. Toeppen. (Leipzig 1874), 1, No. 175; (1879), 2, No. 148; (1886), 5, Nos. 90, 125, 142. — Akta Stanów Prus Królewskich. Ed. K. Górski, M. Biskup. (Toruń 1955), 1, Nos. 109, 148, 242, 247, 269, 530; (1957), 2, Nos. 3, 74, 85–86; (1961) 3, cz. 1, Nos. 87, 202; (1963). cz. 2, Nos. 92, 418; (1967), 4, cz. 2, No. 218; Ed. M. Biskup. (Warszawa Poznań 1973), 5, cz. 1, No. 131. — Inwentarz aktów sejmikowych Prus Królewskich 1600–1764. Ed. K. Górski. (Toruń 1950), Nos. 1034, 1036–1038, 1118–1121. — WAP Toruń 2280 II 4 f. 266. — Preussische Sammlung allerley bisher ungedruckter Urkunden, Nachrichten und Abhandlungen. (Danzig 1747), 1, 40–47. — G. Lenglich, Geschichte des Preussischen Landes Königlich-Polnischen Antheils. (Danzig 1726), 4, 189. — G. Löschin, Geschichte Danzigs von der ältesten bis zur neuesten Zeit. (Danzig 1822), 1, 155. — Ein Litauisches

Mandat von J. 1589. Ed. A. Bezzenberger. 'Altpreussische Monatsschrift' 1878, 15, 119–123.
14. E.g. WAP Poznań I 273f. 104. — WAP Gdańsk Akta Elblaga 45f. 42.
15. WAP Gdańsk 300, 58/120 ff. 591, 616.
16. PAN Gdańsk 740 f. 86. — WAP Gdańsk 300 R/Bb 32 f. 68. — Zaklad Narodowy im. Ossolińskich, Wroclaw 1771 II f. 5.
17. WAP Toruń II II 3 f. 116.
18. WAP Toruń II II 1 f. 140; ibidem II II 2 f. 137; ibidem II II 3 f. 112; ibidem II II 4 f. 151. — AGAD MK 170 f. 214. — WAP Przemyśl 473 f. 49; ibidem 548 f. 25.
19. AGAD Warszawa Ekonomiczna 537 f. 55.
20. WAP Gdańsk 300, 5/74 ff. 64a, b.
21. WAP Bydgoszcz Liber Privilegiorum No. 1 ff. 139–141 §§ 8, 10.
22. Ibidem § 2.
23. WAP Poznań I 51 f. 313.
24. WAP Gdańsk 300 C/2501. — WAP Poznań I 36 f. 6. — Lauda miejskie lubelskie. Ed. J. Riabinin. (Lublin 1934), 10.
25. WAP Gdańsk 300, 30/329.
26. WAP Gdańsk 300 C/162. — WAP Kraków 3038.
27. WAP Kraków Wawel Castrensis Cracoviensis 99 f. 995. — Biblioteka im. H. Lopacińskiego Lublin 1393 f. 54.
28. WAP Poznań I 35 f. 182 — WAP Gdańsk 300, 1/62 f. 145. M. Bogucka, op. cit., 180.
29. WAP Poznań I 52 f. 460.
30. WAP Poznań I 50 f. 735. — WAP Gdańsk 300, 59/10 f. 546.
31. WAP Gdańsk 300, 58/120 f. 591. — Neu-revidierte Willkür der Stadt Danzig aus Schluss sämmtlicher Ordnungen. (Danzig 1761), 78.
32. W. Borowy, The Scots in Old Poland. (London, Edinburgh 1944), 10. Public Record Office State Papers 88/10 ff. 54, 142. — J. Webster, White Devil, in: Ancient British Drama. (London 1810), 1, 132. — Public Record Office State Papers 14/120 f. 38. — Calendar of State Papers Domestic 1619–1623. Ed. E. Green. (London 1858), 10, 237. — W. Lithgow, The Totall Discourse of the Rare Adventures and Painefull Peregrinations of long Nineteene Yeares Travayles from Scotland to the most famous Kingdomes in Europe, Asia and Africa. (Glasgow 1906), 9, 422.
33. Slownik geograficzny Królestwa Polskiego i innych krajów slowiańskich. Ed. B. Chlebowski, W. Walewski, F. Sulimierski. (Warszawa 1888), 9, 524; (1889), 10, 392–393; (1890), 11, 923–924; (1892), 12, 23–25. — S. Rospond, Slownik nazw geograficznych Polski zachodniej i pólnocnej. (Warszawa 1951), 1, 324, 384; 2, 690. — T. A. Fischer, The Scots in Germany being a Contribution to the Scots Abroad. (Edinburgh 1902), 71. — Neumann's Orts-Lexikon. (Leipzig, Wien 1894), 808. — W. Stephan, Die Strassen Danzigs. (Danzig 1911), 86.
34. AGAD Archiwum Skarbu Koronnego I 134.
35. E.G. Archiwum Konsystorza Katolickiego Przemyśl 88 f. 83. — WAP Lublin Zamość 22 f. 149. — Muzeum miasta Tarnowa 71 f. 265, passim. — Biblioteka Uniwersytetu Warszawskiego Synodalne 17, passim; ibidem 475 f. 8–13. — Biblioteka Narodowa Warszawa Biblioteka Ordynacji Zamoyskich 2912 f. 5.
36. The author would like to express her appreciation to the editor of the volume who assisted her with the English text, and to Dr Stanislaw Biegánski, who helped with the maps.

APPENDIX. THE ARRIVAL OF SCOTS IN POLAND, 1550–1799

Years	Number
1550–1559	46
1560–1569	76
1570–1579	341
1580–1589	518
1590–1599	401
1600–1609	615
1610–1619	899
1620–1629	634
1630–1639	550
1640–1649	625
1650–1659	586
1660–1669	356
1670–1679	346
1680–1689	364
1690–1699	246
1700–1709	251
1710–1719	122
1720–1729	115
1730–1739	85
1740–1749	40
1750–1759	64
1760–1769	39
1770–1779	36
1780–1789	25
1790–1799	28
Total	7,408

Note: A Scot was regarded as having 'arrived' when the name of an individual immigrant, or his descendant, was entered for the first time in the documents. It is often impossible to distinguish clearly between a new arrival and his son or grandson, so many in the later seventeenth and eighteenth centuries in particular must be regarded as the descendants of an earlier wave of immigration.

Sources: This table is based on research in a number of archives, mainly in Poland: viz. Archiwum Główne Akt Dawnych (hereafter AGAD) in Warszawa; Wojewódzkie Archiwa Państwowe (hereafter WAP) in eight towns, i.e. Bydgoszez, Gdańsk, Kraków, Lublin, Poznań, Przemyśl, Rzeszów and Toruń, where sources concerning seventeen smaller towns are also kept; Muzeum Narodowe i Biblioteka im. Ks. Czartoryskich and Biblioteka Jagiellońska in Kraków; Zaklad Narodowy im. Ossolińskich in Wroclaw; Biblioteka Narodowa in

Warszawa; Biblioteka im. H. Lopacińskiego in Lublin; Ksiaznica in Toruń; Biblioteki Uniwersytetów Warszawskiego in Warszawa and Wroclawskiego in Wroclaw; Polska Akademia Nauk (hereafter PAN) in Gdańsk, Kórnik and Kraków; Muzeum Historyczne in Warszawa; Muzea miast Krosna and Tarnowa; Archiwa Konsystorzy Katolickich in Lublin and Przemyśl; Archiwum Konsystorza Ewangelickiego in Kraków; Archiwa zakonów Dominikanów, Franciszkanów and Jezuitów in Kraków; Archiwum kościola Aniolów Strózów in Wegrów.

Outside Poland research was carried out in the Public Record Office and British Library in London; and the Scottish Record Office and National Library of Scotland in Edinburgh. Additional data were also obtained from the New Register House there and the Bibliothèque Nationale and Biblioteka Polska in Paris.

The names of the Scottish immigrants occur first of all in the municipal registers of twenty-six towns in WAPs (advocatialia, consularia, alba civium, guild registers) and in AGAD (inscriptions, Metrica Regni, sigillata, chancellery registers, libri legationum, paper and parchment documents, Archiwum Skarbowo-Wojskowe, Archiwum Skarbu Koronnego, Stara Warszawa, Warszawa Ekonomiczna and the Radziwills', Potockis', and Zamoyskis' archives). AGAD contains a vast range of documentation concerning decrees, individual and group privileges, appointments for servitoratus, legitimatio, ennoblement (nobilitatio), indigenatus, donations (the so-called 'caduc', i.e. intestate and heirless estate), delegations, documentation related to the levies, as well as all kind of municipal sources for Warszawa, and moreover some data concerning immigrants settled in the 'latifundia' of the aristocracy. A particularly interesting register is the Subsidy for His Majesty the King of England which was paid in 1651 by the Scots (and the English) living in Poland. Supplementary information on the number of Scots is available in Church archives.

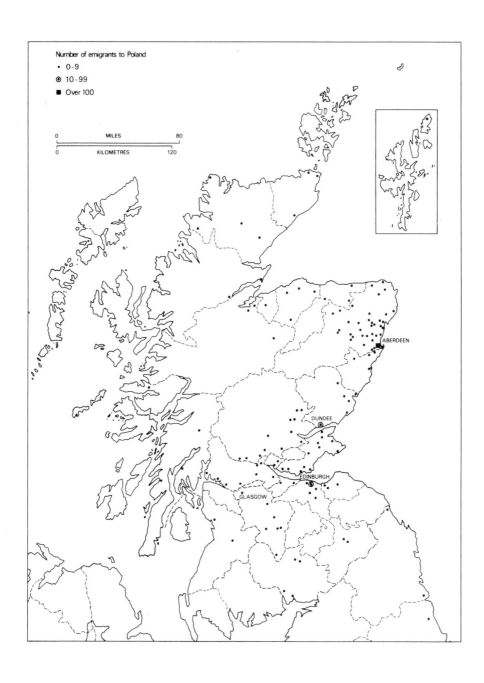

Number of emigrants to Poland
· 0-9
◉ 10-99
■ Over 100

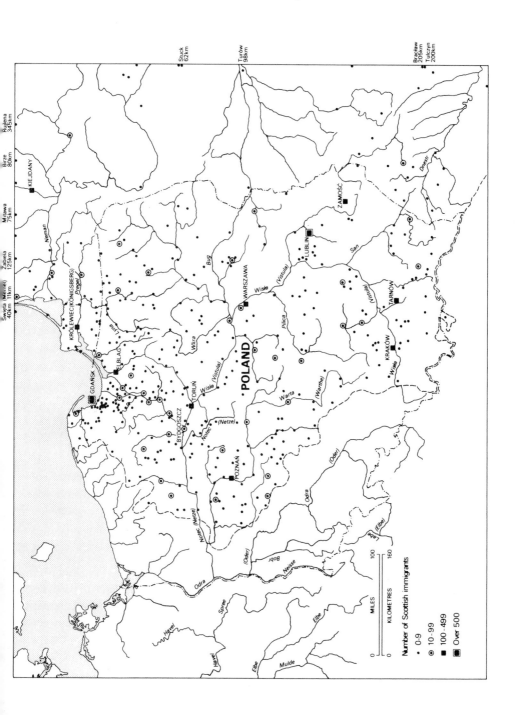

11

SCOTLAND IN THE LIFE OF THE POLISH COUNTRY ESTATE, 1790–1830

Katia Kretkowska

If one were to locate villages like Berwick, Linton or Longwood, a Gothick palace amidst them, with the pinnacles of Roslyn Chapel adorning it and a Robertson, Burns or Stewart clattering around in the light, two-wheel Scots cart, or peacefully tilling the soil with James Small's iron plough, one would perhaps not immediately think of early nineteenth-century Poland. Yet it is there that we find them: at Dowspuda, close to the north-eastern Lake Wigry, the country residence of General Ludwick Pac. Moreover, they appear there neither as literary fancy nor as the isolated and somewhat wild venture of an eccentric. There were other Dowspudas in Poland during the period, roughly between 1790 and 1830 — undertakings that were deliberate, pragmatic and, at the same time, intensely Polish. Their origins, conditioning factors and diverse manifestations are the subject of this essay.

Scottish thought had pervaded Poland since the introduction of Duns Scotus into the curriculum of the Jagiellonian University at Cracow. In the days of the seventeenth-century scholastic revival the Scot was, in fact, the only philosopher whom it was 'permissible to cite against the ways of St. Thomas'.[1] Simultaneously, Edinburgh and Aberdeen students were reading Martinus Polonus, the thirteenth-century historian and Dominican preacher.[2] Still, it is doubtful whether this could be counted as evidence of the students' awareness of each other's countries ranging beyond the scholars' names.

The coming of the Scots into Poland in the sixteenth century opened a period of cultural exchange of a different calibre. Economic and military historians might see it in terms of a 'Scottish invasion'. Yet, though the period abounds in vital and delightful episodes, often undeservedly neglected today, its significance for future cross-cultural inspiration should not be overestimated.[3] The colonies of Scottish tradesmen and religious dissenters came as alien communities and remained as such; the troops of mercenary soldiers in the Polish or Swedish army, constantly on the move and happily crossing over to the opposite ranks upon capture, could hardly be said to have gained a cultural foothold. Did any of them pave a path to the country estate of the late eighteenth century? If at all, it was at best a round-about one. Though there were allegedly 30,000 of them in their day, and the 'Scots pedlar's pack' was a familiar sight in the countryside, and though we come across Scottish garrisons stationed at many noblemen's residences and Scottish dissenters who sought powerful protectors there (for example, at Kiejdany, home of the powerful Radziwill magnates[4]), their impact was transitory, and did not

166

foreshadow the nature of future contacts. By the end of the eighteenth century, 'here and there, in Polish farms and manors, you could still meet a Douglas, a Lendze or an Ogilvy, who, though he has no papers to prove it, says he knows his forbears came from Caledonia'.[5] Some of those had by then become ennobled, like the Watsons in Warsaw, some reappear as architects and garden designers, like the two Kramers or William Mier, or as financiers, like the Fergussons, owners of the Tepper Bank in Warsaw, the great Court bank which 'failed disastrously' owing to the bankruptcy of King Stanislaw Poniatowski after the third partition of Poland in 1795.[6] But by and large, the Scots immigrants had either been culturally absorbed or had abandoned the country. Around 1795, their imprint upon Polish culture was tangible in three respects — in surnames and place-names; in a few cases of blood relationships which stimulated later contacts; and, most pertinent to our enquiry, in a general awareness of the distinctiveness of the Scottish nation, the early disassociation of the image of the Scot from that of the Englishman, clearer, perhaps, than in other Anglophile societies of eighteenth and nineteenth-century Europe.

Scottish influence penetrated the Polish country estate through different media — Scottish literature, read in the original or in Polish or French translation; articles on Scotland in the Polish and British press; and the cultural tour across Europe, which in the last few decades of the eighteenth century had begun to include Scotland. The latter factor was crucial. Though Scottish literary works at times inspired Polish artistic adventures in architecture and garden-planning, it was mainly through the medium of the tour that direct transformations began to be undertaken on Polish estates. Furthermore, the tour often produced an additional factor for change — the appearance of the Scot on the estate, in the capacity of mechanic, farmer, gardener or artist, who arrived with an invitation, a letter of introduction or a ready business contract.

The character of life upon a country estate is a reflection of the character of its inhabitants. What sort of men were they, the owner and his family, financiers and patrons, with their circle of acquaintances, flavouring the social and intellectual climate?

In one of the few British publications pertaining to the period of British influence in question, Brian Knox, discussing the English garden in Poland, concludes that: 'like much of the art of the Enlightenment, these gardens were made for a tiny group of well-travelled aristocrats, the most important of them in fact closely related; one family tree of the Czartoryski and Poniatowski families embraces almost all of them. From the first, their leaders called their landscape gardens 'English' '.[7] The opinion is unfortunately all too true not of the art of the Enlightenment in Poland and its patrons, but of the standard academic approach to the reception of British Sentimental and Romantic culture in Poland, with the related assumption that it was transmitted in a mutated and rudimentary form through France and Germany. This approach has only recently been questioned.[8]

Knox's 'tiny group' of English garden owners in Poland in reality amounted to at least three hundred, to consider only those listed in a five-volume gardening book of 1824;[9] aristocrats, moreover, constitute only one class of owners and, even then, their family trees extend comfortably beyond those of the Czartoryskis and Poniatowskis. A cursory glance at Polish Englightenment periodicals widens the circle of average recipients of British culture beyond the blue-blooded and well-travelled. It must be borne in mind that the openness of Polish society to foreign cultural influences was the driving force of the Enlightenment upheaval of the second half of the eighteenth century. 'Englishness' was the rage. Society press screamed of 'everything English', from 'English curls and spencers' to porter and greyhounds. Amidst the fashionable Warsaw gardens and music-halls, the 'English dandies' swung their way in 'English gigs' to the delighted ridicule of cartoonists and satirists.

But there was also a different Anglophile on the scene. Whether of peasant or aristocratic origin, he was both cosmopolitan and patriotic, of wide horizons and ambitions, alert and critical, essentially a man of the Enlightenment. He was a common figure at the country estate, and sometimes chose to travel to Scotland. When he did, he could be classified in various ways: as the landed gentleman of leisure; the reader; the scholar or scientist and the industrial or agricultural improver, the latter usually being also a politician.

The gentleman of leisure, and of means ample enough to permit travel, appeared in Scotland armed with letters of introduction from English acquaintances or the Polish envoy in London. He restricted his visit to Edinburgh and Glasgow, occasionally venturing beyond the Lothians to view the Falls of Clyde or some other sufficiently 'sublime' spot. Most often, though, he abandoned his intention of seeing Scotland at the card-table in London or Brighton. The Poles who did ride on north usually sought experiences other than sheer pleasure.

The reader was a frequent species of traveller. He set off determined to 'get a wiff of Ossian'[10] or to stumble upon a Fingal's cave. With the blind bard or Rob Roy to guide him, he 'discovers Scotland' and the tones of landscape, park or ruined castle that touch the strings of a sentimental or romantic sensibility might echo in the design of his residence or park at home.

The reader is thus important, as his literary fascinations form the matrix of all other works of art. Polish culture in the years 1790–1830, whether in its Enlightenment, Classicist, Sentimental or Romantic phase, was essentially a literary one. Architecture, painting, garden design, were the expressions of a literary programme, the projections of a sensibility aroused by verbal images. Ossian's misty melancholy would thus descend into the sentimental garden to isolate the walker in a hermitage or crag, the novels of Walter Scott would be perpetuated in some of the follies of the Medieval Revival.

How far were Scottish authors known in eighteenth and early nineteenth-century Poland and what impact, if any, did they make? To attempt such an assessment here could only result in an over-simplification. We shall limit it to a few facts.

The total number of Scots authors known and translated at the time in Poland was not large. As elsewhere on the continent, these were James Thomson, Henry Mackenzie, James Macpherson, Walter Scott. Yet, with Edward Young and Byron, they were the most popular British authors in Poland, and each of them left a mark upon the literature of the period. They were read in the original or, more often, in French translation. Their Polish versions were usually derived from the English ones. Sometimes these would be delayed, as was the case with Mackenzie's *The Man of Feeling*, which appeared in Polish only in 1817;[11] at other times, their popularity was instantaneous, as with Thomson's *The Seasons*, which inspired a leading Enlightenment poet to write *Pulawy*, a descriptive poem, incidentally, about an estate dealt with in the present analysis.[12] Macpherson was first read in Le Tourneur's translation of 1774, and from 1782 in a number of Polish ones. The pan-European Ossianic epidemic swept the country, leaving native Celtic bards in its wake — Derwid, Bojan, Wajdelota, Wernyhora. They appear in the poetry and dramas of the great Romantics Mickiewicz and Slowacki, and in a host of lesser poets, while the quest for a native pre-Christian literature that Macpherson in part inspired accelerated early Polish antiquarian research. Walter Scott, held in high esteem by all early Romantics, served as a model for a new school of historical novelists.[13]

The originals of Scottish authors could be read by those of the educated classes who knew English; their Polish versions by the inhabitants of the larger towns with ready access to new translations. The provinces relied on magazines and periodicals. There, we come across instalments of novels like the anonymous, stylised *Ben Gruyanan, a Caledonian Tale*[14] and a wealth of articles on Scottish themes. Scarce until the second decade of the nineteenth century, they rapidly multiplied in the 1820s and 1830s, till whole journals like *Rozmaitościszkockie* (*The Scottish Miscellany*) appear on the scene of the 1840s. The span of the Scottish topics is imposing, ranging from advice on how to tan leather in the best 'Scots fashion'[15] to bird catching in the Shetlands, Pictish symbol stones or descriptions of the Edinburgh prisons.[16] A fashion magazine dictated to 'the middle-aged lady' in 1839 'a cap à la Marie Stuart, decorated with flowers and golden studs, and a dress of white muslin with a woollen checkered sash called Lammermoor'.[17] That an interest in Scotland had been stirred in the provinces by 1829 is brought out in a review of the first book on Scotland to be published in Poland, the three-volume *England and Scotland: Recollections of a Journey, 1820–1824* by Krystyn Lach Szyrma, termed 'captivating' and 'illustrious', with its copies sold within two years of publication and fragments of it brought out in instalments in a national periodical 'for the benefit of provincial readers'.[18]

The scholar and the scientist travelled to Scotland to study political economy, philosophy or medicine. There were some, though, who broke the rule. The eccentric folklorist, orientalist and writer Jan Potocki explored Orkney in 1787 to find traces of the poem 'Oceania', which the Polish monarch of the time considered irresponsible, as 'he would do better to be studying subjects like law and economy from which the country might derive benefit',[19] while General Jan Komarzewski traversed Glasgow and Edinburgh 'in search of telescopes'.[20] Such episodes, however significant in themselves, did not mould the life of the country estate. Future agrarian improvers stopped at Edinburgh mainly to attend agricultural courses and to listen to lectures on Political Economy.

In early nineteenth-century Poland, Adam Smith was 'the demarcation line between backwardness and progress'.[21] To be anti-Smithian was at the same time not only backward; it was unpatriotic. It was characteristic that the Russian Minister of Finance of the time, Kankryn, publicly attacked the Scots economist. *The Wealth of Nations* was brought into the curriculum of Warsaw University by the economist Dominik Krysinski. In 1818, Count Fryderyk Skarbek, economist, writer and social worker, published his treatise *The National Economy, the Elementary Principles Being a Polish Lecture on the theories of Adam Smith*; in 1828, he published an economic encyclopedia which, though based upon K. Ganilh, the author himself admitted was 'in reality all Adam Smith'.[22]

In the years 1820–22, there were six Polish students attending MacCulloch's lectures on Smith at the University of Edinburgh — the author of the book on Scotland already mentioned, the librarian of a country court, two future agrarian and social reformers (one of them would later head the Polish Agrarian Society) and two sons of Lithuanian landowners.

What ideas of change on the estate could the Scottish tour suggest? Improvement was the main concern. Agricultural reforms were to raise both the income of the proprietor and the level of artistic design with which he was surrounded: house and gardens were to conform to fashionable principles, while fresh subscriptions of English books and journals were to keep the inhabitants in touch with the latest British cultural and technological developments. There was also an element of snobbism, of satisfying a whim for a British gardener or governess.

The final object of the tour was a visit to the Lothian farms and attending courses on agriculture in Edinburgh. Parks and palaces were visited on the way, but as aesthetic experiences gratifying an interest additional to the economic one.

Most of the Polish agrarian improvers only came to Scotland after 1815. The economic and cultural reforms of the Polish Englightenment had been stopped short by the third partition in 1795. The downfall of Kosciuszko's insurrection of 1796 brought about the banishment of the patriots to Russia, and the confiscation of their estates. During the Napoleonic Wars, Polish-British contacts once more came to a natural standstill. In 1815, with the establishment of a Polish Congress Kingdom subservient to Russia and the withering of hopes of regaining the *status quo ante* through a military effort, patriots turned either towards conspiracy or to reviving the economy. The improver, on looking around him, realised that European agriculture had, in the intervening years, progressed by leaps and bounds. He crossed over the border to Germany to be told that 'it was all English',[23] on arriving in Norfolk he would learn that he was late by half a century, as it was the Lothian farmers who were setting the pace. And thus he arrived in Scotland.

Scotland transmitted to Poland not only native inventions and ideas, but also those which her farmers had at one point imported from Norfolk — crop rotation, enclosures, new crops and machinery. The travelling landlord was aware of the dependencies; his villagers back in Poland were less so and they usually attributed the havoc their laird created upon return to 'all those Scots he had gone to'.[24]

Despite such protests, in the years 1815–1840, in particular areas in Poland, on the instigation of particular landowners, Scottish farming rapidly became the respectable and accepted model. Changes progressed by fits and starts, with some areas switching completely over to the new methods and technology, others remaining obstinately old-fashioned, with a near-feudal relationship between landlord and peasant, villainage, the three-field system with one field lying fallow, traditional implements etc. One of the main problems that the improvers faced was to induce the gentry to switch over from serfdom to the tenant system. The progress in British economy, they claimed, was sufficient proof of the system's advantages. Its introduction at certain estates came, therefore, as part of the Scottish inspiration. More generally, its advent in Poland, though, was part of a wider phenomenon occasioned by a variety of forces.

Around 1815, the decision to travel to Scotland was in some cases reached on the spur of the moment when the estate was threatened with bankruptcy; in others it was part of a longstanding family tradition. The latter example is afforded by the Zamoyskis.

The Zamoyski family were one of the oldest and most prosperous noble families in Polish history. In the second half of the eighteenth century, Count Andrzej Zamoyski, Great Royal Chancellor in the reign of the last Polish monarch, Stanislaw August Poniatowski, attempted to introduce rents in place of serfdom in the Polish village. He was fully successful only in his own domains. His son and heir in tail, Stanislaw, continued the programme of reforms. In 1803 he travelled to Britain. In 1805, the first factory of grain machinery in Poland was set up on his estates — staffed by Scottish and English mechanics and producing tools and equipment to British designs. *The Dziennik Ekonomiczmy Zamoyski* (*Zamoyski Economic Diary*) was a national agricultural periodical initiated by Zamoyski and published in the years 1803–04; it printed numerous articles on British farming methods and inventions.[25] It proposed, for instance, introducing a new type of homestead for peasants based on the British 'cottage'.[26]

In 1810, Count Stanislaw Zamoyski organised the Agricultural Society of which he became President. Two of his sons, Andrzej and Konstanty, were despatched to Edinburgh in 1820 to study the Scottish political economists and to take agricultural courses. In Scotland, they visited Lowland tenants and their landlords to whom, among others, Alexander Douglas, Duke of Hamilton, an old friend of the family, gave them letters of introduction. Upon return, Andrzej presided over the Agricultural Society (1858–61), while Konstanty experimented on his estate at Gruszczyn by turning the economy 'upside-down' to introduce the Scottish version. The success of the venture led to the introduction of the Scottish system in the entire Zamoyski estate. Its income tripled.[27]

In the meantime, a third brother, Wladyslaw, was supplying Andrzej and Konstanty with seeds, machines, even a stallion, despatched from Britain, where he was living after the unsuccessful November Insurrection of 1830–31.[28] Some years later, Konstanty himself settled in Scotland — and when he revisited his Polish estates, a peasant delegation, bidding him farewell, said to him: 'You had better go back to those Scots, master, from whom you said you had gained the knowledge by which we have profited so'.[29]

The agricultural policy adopted on the estate at Dowspuda in the years 1815–30 by General Ludwik Pac provides another instance of highly intensive farming through extensive borrowings of Scottish methods, ranging from farm implements and machines to immigrant Scottish farmers and mechanics, who then set up tiny Scottish agricultural communities in that part of Poland. Unfortunately, the origins of the experiment are very poorly documented. No known private diaries of the General have survived, most of the estate archives having been lost, destroyed or removed to Russia as early as 1831, following the November Insurrection when the estate was confiscated by the Tsarist authorities. Other papers, stored in the archives of the local county court and at the Town Hall, disappeared to the Soviet Union at the end of World War II, though a small quantity was returned in 1964. Information about the fate of the rest is inaccessible to Polish scholars. In 1968, J. Bartyś unearthed a number of forgotten estate documents among the Zamoyski papers in one of the Polish libraries. It is solely from this find that we can gain clearer insight into the social and economic politics of the general.[30]

Ludwik Pac was the son of a landed proprietor and general of the Army of the Grand Duchy of Lithuania. He was educated in Poland, England and France (his father had travelled to Scotland and England in the 1770s). In 1807 he joined the army of Napoleon, to rise to the rank of General of Division. After Napoleon's downfall Pac refused to serve in the forces of the Polish Congress Kingdom (as it was dependent upon Russia) and, upon leaving the army, settled at his country estates of Dowspuda and Raczki. He had inherited both from a distant relative. Finding the farming backward and unproductive, and the estate on the verge of bankruptcy, he embarked upon a two-year journey to the most modern farming estates and schools of agriculture in Great Britain, France and Holland. Upon return, he decided to remodel the entire agricultural structure of Dowspuda on Scottish examples. It is interesting to note that this particular approach was shared at the time by a number of patriotically and pragmatically inclined ex-army men, who conducted energetic and effective campaigns on their estates (lands impoverished by successive years of unrest and wars) in order to uplift the economy in the spirit of General Chlapowski's motto: 'From the plough to the horse, from the horse to the plough'. The concept of a steady grip on the country's economy as the next best way of facing up to occupying governments and of preserving a healthy native core raised imaginative farming to a fundamental patriotic duty. Scotland seemed an attractive example by virtue of its own progress and, possibly, its parallel history in other ways.

Ludwik Pac remained in Britain for two years: 1814–16. The lack of documentation pertaining to this period is acute. Judging by the character of his later farming activities, we can assume that the men and places he visited were roughly those frequented by other Polish travellers. We can map them in the case of General Chlapowski, a pioneer from Central-West Poland, who toured Norfolk and the Lowlands four years later. There is evidence of Pac's presence at a Lothian farm in the recollections of one Muir, a tenant farmer from Kirkcudbright, at whose farm Pac stopped for three days. Mr. Muir found it hard to believe that there were 'no stones' at some of Pac's estates, and that there was 'an alley straight as a rod, and lined by trees, leading from Dowspuda right down to the Prussian border'.[31]

On his return Pac immediately set about the task of reforming the old-fashioned farming. Contrary to other Polish pioneers who attempted to encourage Polish peasants to switch to enclosures, crop rotation and practical foreign implements like the 'Scots plough', and who more often than not encountered steadfast hostility on the part of the peasants ('Our master has gone mad', Chlapowski's farmhands sighed, shook their heads and gave up their jobs[32]), Pac had the foresight to embark upon a more daring but potentially more successful scheme — he decided to people his estate with Scottish tenant farmers who would not have to be additionally instructed.

The first joint Scottish–English settlements appear at Dowspuda in 1815. The immigrants did not know Polish, which at first was a hindrance. Though Pac himself knew English, his Polish staff did not and thus mediators were required — John Lohman, the general's private secretary, and a Peter Stewart. The two names are present on all the contracts signed at the time. The terms of those contracts were advantageous to the colonists. Tenant holders were exempted from rent in the first two years, and received free farmsteads and other farm buildings. After that, their rent was lower than the local average. Later, due to the general fall in produce prices, these were lowered even further.

The first to arrive were English craftsmen, specialists in the construction of machines, tools and other farming equipment, two tanners and two Scots stewards, experts in rational crop cultivation and selective breeding. From 1816, a stream of tenant farmers began to appear, mostly from Scotland — Berth, Andrew, George and James Broomfield, William Burns, John Dickson, Dobe, Douglas, Walter Govenlock, William Hay, Pritzer, Riad, Robertson, Peter Stewart, Thompson are the names that have come down to us.[33] Altogether there were about fifty Scottish and English families living at Dowspuda. Some of them set up a new village, which they named New Scotland (set about half a mile from the palace at Dowspuda, it is today still called Scotland); others settled at farms like Govenlock (or New Havelock according to some sources), New York in the village of Wielka Pruska, Longwood and Broomfield at contemporary Ludwinowo, and Linton and Berwik at Korytki.

The foreigners' technological skills and general education earned them respect in the neighbourhood and their assimilation appears to have been smooth. Still, they retained their native custom and language. According to contemporary sources 'their habits ... are exemplary. They enjoy Polish spirits, though they dilute them with beer, water and other liquids, and they are altogether very thrifty ... in the field they are much more hardworking than the local peasants ... and although they pursue the most common tasks about the farm, every one of them knows how to write and calculate, and some of them have collections of different kinds of books, and they sometimes read them'.[34] By 1865, their descendants had become naturalised, but nevertheless retained some distinctive Scottish features: 'A delicious cheese, ... called Chester', and other farm products inherited from their ancestors.[35] There is only one family of Scots descent living at Dowspuda today, but bearing the rather evocative name of Burns (today Borms) after William Burns, who settled at Berwik in 1817.[36]

The fundamental change Pac desired his Scottish and English settlers to bring about was to displace the old three-field system in favour of modern crop rotation. Most of the fields were lying fallow at the time for shortage of farm hands. Pac rented half of his lands to the foreign settlers. New crops began to appear, heretofore unknown in the Suwalki area — the potato, the so-called Swedish turnip (or mangel), white and red clover, and a wide assortment of vegetables.

The new potato crop was of particular significance. Until then, it had been cultivated only in the gardens of the more affluent gentry as a speciality vegetable. Due to its popularisation by Scots farmers, it soon became a common and cheap product, the basic ingredient of both country and town diet. The effects were similar to those attained in Scotland in the first half of the eighteenth century when the potato was first transplanted there. There had been no famine in Poland, but nutrition among the peasant classes had often been dismal. General Pac made further use of the potato, applying it in industry, and in the production of vodka and bleaching powder. The Scottish ways of harvesting and storing it caused a sensation not only among the local villagers, but also among the graduates of the Vilno Agronomic Institute. However, the Scottish implement for picking the potato was not adopted (neither was Lawson's). On the other hand, the Scottish storage system — mounds of earth and straw — has survived in Poland till today.[37]

As the fields had been lying fallow and the settlers could not always afford expensive fertilisers, they introduced new crop rotations gradually. In New Scotland, six-course rotation was introduced, in Planta, four-course, in Dowspuda, a five-course one.

New breeds of imported cattle were milked to produce Scottish 'Chester cheese' and a high-quality butter. Besides 7000 Merinos, horses were bred and kept to draw the light, two-wheeled, multi-purpose Scottish cart.

In 1816, Pac opened a factory of agricultural implements and machinery where the tenants obtained iron ploughs, iron harrows, machines for sowing different vegetables and cultivators. The factory was operated by Scottish and English mechanics of different specialisations, for example the mechanics Douglas and Robertson, the wheelwright Pritzer and a blacksmith and ironmonger. It was the third factory of that kind in Poland, the first being Stanislaw Zamoyski's 'English' factory at Zwierzyniec in 1804–05, the second Antoni Trembicki's at Lomza, set up in 1811. In 1817, Meikle's threshing machines were produced there and were reputed to save six thousand working days in the year when compared to the older flails system. The factory produced the complete technical equipment for a distillery, a brewery, an oil mill, a tannery, and a linen and cloth workshop, all set up in 1816–1821. A mechanical sawmill was constructed in 1817. Orders for all sorts of implements were received from other neighbouring landed proprietors, and for the richer farmers.

Thus, by the second decade of the nineteenth century Dowspuda had become the greatest centre of agricultural mechanisation in the area, radiating over the whole Congress Kingdom. Confiscated by the Russian authorities in 1831, it soon underwent a decline, and by the 1840s all of Pac's social and economic achievements had been ruined. The Scots mechanics and craftsmen left to seek employment elsewhere.[38]

In their own day, news of Pac's novel agricultural activities spread rapdily. At the nearby University of Vilno, Pac was soon nicknamed 'the English Count'. As a propagator of Scottish and English achievements in the area, though, he had a rival in the Supervisor of the school district of Lithuania, Prince Adam Jerzy Czartoryski, a man of royal connections and considerable influence, whose court at Pulawy was the foremost cultural centre in the country. In line with a family tradition, he had travelled to England and Scotland where he had relations, and then in different ways had attempted to transplant the British economic, judicial and educational systems onto Polish soil.[39] His knowledge of Scotland and its economic take-off is mapped in the route of his travels over the country in 1790,[40] which led through factories, farms, canals, iron-works and the scientific departments of universities.

In the 1820s, Prince Adam Jerzy Czartoryski despatched several scholars to the University of Edinburgh to study Scottish political economy, agriculture, moral philosophy and literature. The young men were instructed to keep a sharp lookout for innovations and possible improvements, which is made evident from the three-volume account (already mentioned) published by one of them, Krystyn Lach Szyrma, a graduate in philosophy from the University of Vilno, who came to Edinburgh as tutor of Konstanty Czartoryski, Prince Adam Jerzy's nephew. This detailed and vivid account is a compendium of knowledge about contemporary Scotland, with frequent excursions into history. Though Szyrma himself was primarily interested in the humanities, and received a doctoral degree in moral philosophy from Edinburgh (he would later lecture on moral philosophy at Warsaw University where his students called him 'the Scots philosopher'), he also studied political economy and recorded manifold aspects of Scottish agriculture. In his travels across the country, he took note of the state of the farms and the occupation, level of education and social condition of the people, from obscure Highland hovels to the prosperous farms around Edinburgh. Of the latter, he describes at length a visit to the farm of a Mr. Oliver at Lochend, tenant farmer to Lord Murray, where he was taken by Professor James Pillans, Prince Konstanty's Edinburgh host and tutor.

Among the guests present at dinner, Szyrma recalls Maclaren, the editor of *The Scotsman*; John Morton, the agronomist; Professor MacCulloch, whose lectures on political economy all the Poles attended; and the farmer Muir from Kirkcudbright, whom Count Pac had visited. The conversation at the table was all about farming and political economy, and he went on to describe in detail the system of rents and income on the estate, comparing it to the new tenant system being introduced in Poland.

A few days after that, Szyrma visited Morton's display of farm machinery and described the various types of modern equipment he saw there. It was the revolving harrow that most captured his fancy, and considering it particularly well-suited for Poland, he printed an engraving of it.[41]

Another Pole resident in Edinburgh at the time was Karol Sienkiewicz, librarian to Prince Adam Jerzy Czartoryski; his purpose in the city was to study political economy and to purchase books for the Pulawy library, but he also travelled extensively around Scotland and was deeply impressed by the state of the Lowland farms, particularly at New Lanark, which he visited in 1821. In his letters home, he encouraged his father, a provincial squire, to reorganise his small country estate in the Scottish manner.[42]

The reforms discussed so far all occurred in North-east, East and Central Poland. Their greatest number, however, and the most lasting impact, occurred in the Central-west region of Wielkopolska (Great Poland) around its capital, Poznań. The man responsible for their intensive introduction and rapid spread was General Dezydery Chlapowski.

Upon his return home in the summer of 1815 Chlapowski, like General Pac, 'decided to teach himself farming, as the possibility to serve the country has been left us in this sole occupation'.[43]

General Chlapowski's agricultural education mirrored the popular assumption of what a reformer's teach-yourself manual should consist of. He set about the task by importing the works of John Sinclair, Arthur Young and Brown (probably Andrew Brown), which he read in English, together with the German writings of Albrecht Thaer, A. Block and J. G. Koppe. Having studied them, he decided to meet the authors themselves and seek practical instruction.[44]

In the spring of 1817, he travelled to Albrecht Thaer's renowned school of agriculture at Möglin near Berlin. At the time, it was frequented by other Polish pioneer agriculturalists such as Michal Oczapowski and Jan Nepomucen Kurowski. The information Chlapowski acquired there on the benefits of fertilisers stirred an interest in crop rotation.[45] He crossed the Channel. The geographic nature of the Polish farmlands, their flat and wide open character, seemed to him ideally suited to the introduction of British enclosures.[46] Chlapowski knew England, as he had lived there in the years 1814–15, whiling away the aftermath of the Napoleonic wars in the social life of London and Bath, and in the proceedings of Parliament, which he followed with a keen interest, particularly the Corn Law issue.

Upon arrival in London in the summer of 1818, the General made his way to John Sinclair, whose writings he had admired, and who gave him letters of introduction to various English and Scottish farmers. The first of those was William Coke at Holkham in Norfolk. Later, Chlapowski would recall that he was received very politely and taken around four farms. At one of them in Warren, he studied the irrigation system and learnt how to put up stacks.[47]

On the coach to Scotland, he met Lord William Benthinck, the future Governor of the East India Company, who invited him to his house at Lynn. In Edinburgh, he came across an old friend from the Napoleonic days, General Flahaut, who had since married the daughter of Lord Keith and was living in Scotland. Lord Murray explained to him what the system of instruction of future tenant farmers and economic staff at the Edinburgh agricultural courses was like,[48] and Chlapowski was surprised to find that no economic theory was taught, but that the students, having been instructed in those branches of general science that agriculture might draw upon, were sent for several months' practice to well-known farmers.

Chlapowski interspersed his stay in Edinburgh with trips to some of the Lowland farms. He stayed longest at Phantassie, where he learnt how to handle the Scots plough and put up round stacks, and where he finally understood the principles of crop rotation. Among others, Chlapowski visited the Duke of Roxburghe at Mollenden. Everywhere he went, he conducted long interviews with the farmers and keepers, studied the new machinery, the organisation of work, cattle and sheep breeding and the new industries. In the course of his eighteen-month stay, he purchased machinery, ploughs and seeds, hired a Scots mechanic and in 1819 returned home to Turew.

Chlapowski's reforms began at his estates at Turew, Wronowo, Rabinek and Podborze (in those days part of the Grand Duchy of Prussia), which were all in debt. He introduced enclosures, crop rotation, Scots drainage, strips of green bushes and trees between fields to raise microclimate conditions, and sheep, cattle and horse breeding on selective principles. He opened new home industries — a distillery, an oilmill, a sugar-refining plant — the wastes of which were used as fodder. He began to stack the harvest in the fields instead of stowing it in barns, thus changing the visual aspect of the farms in Great Poland, in a way different from that brought about by the introduction of the monumental farm buildings in the Prussian style, which had by then begun to appear quite frequently. He introduced subsoil ploughing with the new Scottish invention, trying to popularise it elsewhere with the claim that 'to deepen one's soil is equal to buying a second farm'.[49] Only the more well-to-do farmers introduced it, however, as the Scots subsoil plough was expensive to import, with no Polish firm responsible for it and no home factory producing it.[50] Next, Chlapowski imported a threshing machine with a British thresher to operate it. The machine was very rare at the time: there was only one other, at a neighbouring estate. By the 1840s it had become very popular in the area.[51]

In the years 1831–34, all the equipment bought in Britain for Chlapowski was handled by Karol Marcinkowski, a Polish doctor, social worker and philanthropist then in exile. At home, the General embarked upon a campaign popularising his economic and social reforms. A hospital and a school were built for the employees, supervised by his wife Antonina. He organised an agrarian exhibition, became one of the founders of the Central Economic Society, and wrote articles for farming journals on various aspects of agriculture, with detailed descriptions of the estates he had seen during his foreign travels.[52] Such Scottish 'novelties' became part of the Great Poland landscape, with the consequence that the farms, and peasant holdings, attained a good European standard by the end of the century.[53]

The examples analysed here do not exhaust the problem of the Polish debt to Scottish farming. Those and similar attempts created a climate of alertness to any Scots or English agrarian novelty encompassing an impressive part of society, men of differing social standing and varying affluence. The Zamoyskis were a noble family of considerable influence; Pac and Chlapowski were landed gentry and ex-army men of leisure; Sienkiewicz was the son of a provincial civil servant living on an impoverished farm of a few hundred acres of land; Szyrma, finally, was the son of a peasant and a tenant farmer and had no land of his own. Their common denominator was readership of farming journals and manuals, or only the heterogeneous daily press and magazine 'miscellanies' which often touched upon agriculture. Scottish and English farming were the backbone of all such articles. Alojzy Prosper Biernacki's 'In What Ways Knowledge of English Country Estates Is Important for the Polish Farmer'[54] is a typical title.

The author, a pioneer of crop rotation (which he introduced in 1802) was the co-editor of the *Gazeta Wiejska* (*Country Gazette*) of 1817-1819. The paper abounded in similar articles. The one mentioned was an introduction to the translation of J. C. Landon's treatise: 'On the Setting Up of Farmsteads in the Scottish Style', which Biernacki published in Berlin in 1819.[55] Another pioneer, Michal Oczapowski, inserted a series of articles in the *Dziennik Wileński* (*Vilno Daily*) in 1819-1820, entitled 'On the Social Significance of the Farm and the Means of Perfecting the State of It in Every Country — by Sir John Sinclair'.

John Sinclair had himself been to Poland, and was later, as we have seen, read and visited by travelling Polish improvers. W. Niepokojczycki was an economic envoy of Prince Ksawery Drucki Lubecki, the Minister of Finance in the Congress Kingdom. In 1825 he came to Scotland to prepare accounts of the economic and technological achievements — meticulous analyses of the Edinburgh water system, of the new canals and wagonways, all down to minute detals — to be utilised in Polish cities. One of his reports was about agriculture. It was the translation of a letter written by M. Mathieu de Dombasle to the Agricultural Institute at Loville. The letter is full of minute descriptions of Lothian farms and Scottish implements, and begins with an extensive summary of the views of John Sinclair.

We have observed how English technology was being transmitted to Poland through Scotland. It would be interesting to compare the two processes that led up to this. Was the import and adoption of Norfolk farming in the Scottish Lothians analogous to the import and adoption of the resultant Lothian farming in Poland? Both processes were characterised by fits and starts, by an uneven distribution in various parts of the countries. What mainly differentiates the Polish attempts from the earlier Scottish ones is the depth of their sense of mission, not absent in Scotland either, but which was more radical in Poland owing to the drastic political situation with its gloomy prospects for the Polish economy.

Perhaps men like Zamoyski, Pac or Chlapowski were closest to John Cockburn of Ormistoun, who 'burst upon the high walls of tradition on his estate', in a manner not untypical of the first generation of Scots improvers: he was 'a gentleman ... an Anglophile ... his interest in agriculture was a cultural one rather than an economic one. This was his bit for Scotland, his way of dragging her into the Britain of the eighteenth century'.[56] The Polish gentleman and Anglophile did this and more. He took the best from Norfolk and Lothian achievements to withstand the encroachment of other foreign economies — the Russian and Prussian ones — which were backed by the alien policy of depolonisation and the erasing of native culture and traditions through a financial, economic and cultural dependence. The agricultural take-off placed rural Scotland among the advanced commercial societies of the nineteenth century. In Poland, the results were not as uniform. In some cases the process brought about lasting changes, in others there was a return to old ills — as has been observed in the case of Pac. The nature of the three occupying states and their different policies was a hurdle in the path to progress, a hurdle which at times could not be taken.

Next, let us consider a totally different kind of traveller, whose influence on the Polish country estate was artistic rather than practical, but substantial nevertheless. Princess Izabela Czartoryska was no economic reformer, self-righteous in the sense of social mission. She toured Britain with her son, Adam Jerzy, in 1790, but when he rushed to foundries, mills, factories or canals which all captivated him, she would at first trudge along reluctantly until, as she admits in her diary, she got the 'migraine' and henceforth on such occasions kept to the inn. Their trip across Scotland illustrates the dualism of the traveller's purpose — the economic and social one versus the subjective and purely aesthetic. The latter does not necessarily imply a dilettante. Czartoryska, well-educated, well-read and well-travelled, ambitious and sensitive to novelties, would not only later become the author of the first Polish printed treatise on garden-planning and the instigator of significant architectural designs, but would play hostess to a country court that vied with Warsaw for intellectual and artistic supremacy. Her tour, mapped in her diary, is a good example of the aims and fascinations of a contemporary patron of the arts.[57]

Izabela entered Scotland through Berwick and, having admired the landscape park in the grounds of the Haddington estate at Tyningham near Dunbar, she halted at Edinburgh and went round the city in the company of William Robertson, John Clarke and a Mr Coward, a paper manufacturer. Holyrood, the Physicians' Hall, the Royal Infirmary, a city park 'with a pleasant stream' and the Botanic Garden all caught her attention. John Playfair and a Mr Gibson, whose two sons traded in Gdańsk, guided her round the art galleries. She rode into the country to see Newbattle, 'campagne de Marquis de Lothian', Melville Castle and Dalkeith, where the Duke of Buccleuch entertained her. She was received politely everywhere, as the Czartoryskis, cousins of the Polish monarch, Stanislaw August Poniatowski, were among the first aristocrats in Europe, and, in addition, they had a drop of Scottish blood in their veins through Lady Catherine Gordon, daughter of the 2nd Marquis of Huntly, who married the poet-noble Andrew John, Count Morsztyn, in 1683,[58] and whose daughter became the grandmother of the last King of Poland, while their son became the immediate ancestor of the Czartoryskis. Relations in Britain remembered the alliance and were proud of it. Lady Mary Coke (neé Campbell), daughter of John, Duke of Argyll, wrote in 1768: 'The Polish Prince Czartoryski ... is our cousin ... The King of Poland is the same relation to Us'.

Having stayed for some time at Hopetoun House, where the Carracci in the art collection particularly caught her fancy, she visited Linlithgow Palace and Stirling, and from there, embarked upon a tour of the Highlands. Dunblane she found 'romantically situated' and Scone, the most beautiful of Scotland's palaces, but it was Dunkeld, with its park, ruined cathedral and, most dear, Ossian's Hall, that occasioned a long and effervescent description of the 'rustic bridge', the wild rocks and roaring waterfall, 'de beaux arbes, arbustes, plantes et fleur', and 'sur les rochers des inscription d'ossian'.

Blair Atholl, its park, grottos and cascades was the next stop, the journey enlivened by the ruins, mansions and gardens along the way. Lord Breadalbane invited mother and son to Kenmore at Taymouth, where the lake, mountains, park, crenellated castle at Dains and particularly 'une petite île avec l'hermigage de Fingal' were viewed with delight. At Inveraray, Lady Louisa Campbell and Lady Augusta, daughter of the Duke of Argyll, entertained her with choice family gossip. Next Loch Linnhe, Loch Lomond, Dunbarton, and then Glasgow, where Adam Jerzy finally coaxed Izabela into the 'grande fabrique de gare' at Paisley and the College of Physicians, after which experience she regaled herself at the Hamilton art gallery with Alexander Douglas as guide. After two months of travel, she set off for the 'vieux chateaux' by Carlisle. The mountains and valley were 'pittoresque' and still more so the 'temple des druids' at Keswick.

Upon her return to Poland, Izabela set busily about the task of turning Pulawy into the romantic, picturesque park that would surpass her earlier garden, the sentimental Powazki, and make up for its destruction in the Prussian siege of Warsaw in 1794. She recruited British gardeners — the English James Savage and the Irish Denis McClair (who would later design countless parks in the Polish Ukraine) and replanted and remodelled the grounds to the point of redirecting the course of the Vistula to make it more irregular and craggy-banked.

These practical activities were supplemented by a treatise on gardens, written around 1800 and published in Wroclaw in 1805, *Varied Thoughts on the Way of Designing Gardens*.[59] The book deals mainly not with the layout of gardens, but with their elements — trees, plants, clumps, with a few pages devoted to monuments and buildings. How far did the parks and gardens of Scotland nurture the *Thoughts* and their Pulawy manifestation? Despite the 'English stairs' in the garden, and the Gothick House, its portico following Batty Langley in spirit and its crude representation drawn on the back of Izabela's diary of the tour, the garden at Pulawy was eclectic in mood. It was at the same time a reflection firstly of the English Picturesque (for example the river bed and its application, the steep cliff upon which the Temple of the Sibyl was situated, the stairs, the stone bridges, the heterogeneous garden buildings), secondly of the Rousseauvian, sentimental 'jardin anglois' (the grave slabs, tombstones, inscriptions commemorating, among others, the French poet Delille), and, finally, of a Polish literary and patriotic programme (the Temple of the Sibyl, its contents, the national overtone of its motto: 'The Past to the Future'). Despite unquestionable incitement, no part of the Scots tour can be pinpointed as direct precursor of the garden elements at Pulawy. At the Gothick House, however, along with 'English canonballs from Gdańsk embedded into the front wall' were 'stones from the castles of . . . Mary

Stuart, Holyrood and Fortheringhay, recently made famous by Walter Scott . . . '
Inside, in the Foreign Collection, there were views of Scotland, ('Fingal's Grave'
and 'Ossian's Tomb') by John Payne and, 'beneath glass, a blade of grass from
Fingal's tomb'.[60]

The Scottish garden had established its name in Poland at the time mainly as a
botanic one. It had been proclaimed already in the works of John Johnston
(1603–1675), the seventeenth-century court doctor and botanist, a Scot born and
living in Poland, who published a number of treatises on vegetables and plants.
The five-volume garden manual of 1824 already quoted does not describe Scottish
landscape gardens, but does present the Edinburgh Botanic Gardens. Polish
magazines of the period often advertised seedlings of the 'Scots rose' or other
flowers. The reformer, Antoni Tyzenhauz, had imported the seedlings of trees
from a Keith Richmond in Edinburgh as early as the mid-eighteenth century.[61]

Robert Adam was a Scottish architect whose influence is traceable in a number
of Polish palaces and residences. His ideas were made familiar in Poland not only
through British books of architectural design. Princess Izabela Lubomirska, for
instance, commissioned Adam to design a villa for her during her stay in England
in 1787. The design is at present in the Ashmolean collection.[62] Unfortunately, the
villa was never constructed, though it was probably intended for the estate at
Krzeszowice. The Princess was both a patron of art and a designer herself. It was
she who founded the park at Mokotów, one of the earliest English sentimental
landscape parks in the capital. She visited England (there is no evidence of any
excursion to Scotland) in 1787, her carriage packed with other Polish travellers,
viz. her nephew, Prince Henry, and his tutor, the Abbé Piattoli, her son-in-law
Prince Stanislaw Kostka Potocki, the poet Niemcewicz and the scientist Lamotte.
Having been presented at Buckingham Palace by Lady Pembroke, she visited
Horace Walpole at Strawberry Hill. Upon her return to Poland, Izabela
Lobomirska invited the well-known classicist architect Peter Aigner to dress the
Baroque Eastern elevation of her palace at Lańcut in a Gothick costume. An extant
painting of the Gothick elevation (which was later removed) shows marks of
British influence. So does the Romantic Castle in the park, built by Aigner in 1807.
As Aigner disapproved of the Gothick and did not design it himself, he must have
derived his ideas from books of design (which remain to be discovered). The
interior of the palace was furnished with Sheraton, Chippendale and even, later,
'an English bath-tub' (produced by an English firm in Vienna), and a cosy,
panelled 'English library'; it displays, however, clearly Adamesque colour
schemes and motifs in the overall décor and in the fireplaces.[63]

Robert Adam prototypes are identifiable in a number of eighteenth and early
nineteenth-century residences. What is derived from him is the realisation of the
facade, accentuated on the axis by a great columned portico, and clasped by huge
recess towers to the sides, differentiated from the facade, as at Crome Court
(1750).[64] Typical Polish counterparts are found in the Wielkopolska residences of
Siedlce and Gultowy,[65] the latter also with Adamesque interior decor. The design
of the interior itself is more traditionally Polish, with a big, oval drawing room on
the axis, and a multilateral projection upon the garden elevation.

Both General Chlapowski and General Pac were determined to reside in Gothick residences upon their return from England and Scotland. Chlapowski began to reconstruct his Baroque palace at Turew around 1830. The left projection was rebuilt to house a crenellated tower, punctuated by lancet windows. The whole building was buttressed, and wooden porches and roof were added, also in the Gothick style. Around 1847, a Gothick chapel was built in the east of the building.[66] The architect is not known, but Chlapowski himself was responsible for the conception of the design, if not for its actual realisation. What books of design or models he used in the process is an open question.

General Pac began to build the palace at Dowspuda in 1820 from scratch. At first he employed a little-known Italian architect, Peter Bosio, who did not finish it. In 1822 Pac replaced him by Henry Marconi who, unfamiliar with Gothick forms, soon left for Warsaw to study the books of design available in the library of Josef Sierakowski. It is most unfortunate that neither Marconi's designs of Dowspuda, nor any list of the books of design he might have consulted, have survived to our times. The palace is one of the most 'British' of all Polish Gothick structures — both in the Tudor arches of the arcades in the portico and the first-floor windows, in the pinnacled crenellation, its pointed helmets, and in the general symmetry and regularity. Jaroszewski associated it with Sheffield Place, Hatfield Hall and Keiler Castle, though mainly with Eaton Hall near Chester (William Porden, 1803–12 and 1820–25).[67] Yet there is no evidence that Marconi knew either Eaton Hall itself or its engravings. Another art historian, J. Baranowski, on the other hand, is convinced that the Palladian-cum-Gothick structure, though it emphasised, in many ways, historic Polish features, was inspired by the architectural elements of a number of British buildings, the designs of which Marconi took from John Britton's *Architectural Antiquities of Great Britain* of 1805 and the subsequent volumes. What is most interesting from the point of view of our enquiry is that the pinnacles could be those of Roslyn Chapel. Britton's publication was available at the time in the library of the royal palace at Wilanów near Warsaw.[68]

Just as the economic and agrarian activities of the General were modern, so his architecture, for all its historicism, mirrored the spirit of the day. The Gothick décor and form satisfied contemporary aesthetic predilections, but at the same time transmitted a national content, documenting the owner's patriotism. The palace combined the concept of a great British house with that of a seat of an ancient Polish family. Alongside cosmopolitan, popular Gothick forms derived from a British design book, there were other elements reaching back to a forgotten medieval Polish tradition, emphasised further by statues of Polish monarchs in the elevation, and by the interior décor, consisting of representations of Polish military victories, and the history of the Pac family, and of a family tomb in the central part of the building.[69]

It was Pac himself who was responsible for the artistic and ideological programme of the residence. It was he who engaged painters, sculptors and gardeners. One of them was John Heiton (either English or Scots), the head gardener, who was responsible for the lay-out of the landscape park surrounding the house. In the village of New Scotland, and at the farms of Berwik, New Havelock, New York, Linton and Longwood, Henry Marconi in turn constructed further Gothick buildings, the folly farms that were so familiar a sight in the landscape of the tenants' native Scotland. Unfortunately, neither the buildings themselves nor their designs have survived.

The Princesses Izabela Czartoryska and Izabela Lubomirska are examples of patrons who came into direct contact either with Scots art or artists, while the Generals Chlapowski and Pac are examples of those in whose architecture possible Scottish repercussions would have been more probably inspired by British architectural publications. There was yet another type of estate owner: the one who need not have travelled to Scotland himself, but who nevertheless strove to recapture some of the country's aura. It was the reader, often a man of letters himself, whose preoccupation with literature perpetuated itself in architectural forms.

The reader of Walter Scott sometimes built himself a Gothick phantasmagoria. General Wincentry Count Krasiński constructed a Gothick castle at Opinogóra in 1828, where his son Zygmunt would later reside. The great Romantic poet introduced Gothick castles as stage props into his early works. His father, in turn, intended to build himself an extensive Gothick residence in the form of a picturesque castle with his coat of arms, Ślepowron, above the portcullis.[70] Both father and son were avid readers of historical novels. The writer and critic Michal Grabowsli, fascinated by Walter Scott, built a castle folly at Aleksandrowka, today in the USSR. Irregular, diverse, surprising, its crenellated tower adorned by round Scots turrets, and with its interplay of lancet and rectangular windows, it is a picturesque folly, and one that instantly recalls Abbotsford and its jigsaw of antiquities.

The Scottish turret appeared again in the castle at Zagórzany, built by the architect Francis Maria Lanci over the years 1834–39 for the Skrzyński family. At the time when the castle became the property of Count Jan Ciechoński, author of the oriental novel *Al Hakim*, the periodical *Klosy* published the following anonymous description:

> Amid the greenery and shade of an English park, there arises a rough-hewn building of six towers, built in a square in the style of old Scots castles, appearing as if reproduced directly from a novel of Walter Scott. In the light of the moon the castle creates a weirdly fantastic impression, which is reflected in the transparency of the lake. The castle was built by the famous architect Lanci, and the taste in the furnishing of the interior and in the park design was certainly augmented by the two aesthetes, Joseph Kremer and Wincently Pol, who stayed here a long time.[71]

The name of the former, incidentally, is perhaps of Scots origin.

The Polish 'revived' castle, though often inspired by Walter Scott or the English Gothick novel, was at the same time set in a native historical landscape. It was neither as gloomy nor as terrifying as the Scots one, though it often housed eerie events. As Jaroszewski put it, 'it was first and foremost a monument of times gone by — times of the power and glory of a great state which no longer existed ... It evoked feelings of sorrow for the foresaken power of Poland, and the reader of a

Polish romance or historical novel could therefore go to inhabit it and raise it from ruin in the form of a historical token'.[72]

The appeal of Scotland on the Polish estate, therefore, operated at two levels: by models of the new farming, it pointed the way forward to the modernisation of the Polish rural economy; by models of Classical and Gothick building it enabled the nobility both to declare their involvement in the most up-to-date cultural modes of Europe, and to link these modes to their own resonant and patriotic past.

NOTES

1. Leon Koczy, 'Edinburgh University and Scottish-Polish Cultural Relations', *The University of Edinburgh and Poland* (ed. Wiktor Tomaszewski, Edinburgh, 1968), 18.

2. F. C. Nicholson, 'Lists of Fifteenth Century Books in Edinburgh Library', *Papers of the Edinburgh Bibliographical Society*, Vol. 9 (1904) 99, and *Ibid.*, 'A List of Fifteenth Century Books in the University Library of Aberdeen', Vol. 13 (1925), 11.

3. For an English bibliography of that chapter of Polish-Scottish contacts, see *The University of Edinburgh and Poland*, 38–40.

4. In this case, the dissenters were Socinians. F. Steuart (ed.), *Papers Relating to the Scots in Poland, 1576–1793* (The Scottish History Society, Edinburgh, 1915), XXIV, XXVII, 109.

5. *Ibid.*, 110.

6. *Ibid.*, XXV.

7. Brian Knox, 'The Arrival of the English Landscape Garden in Poland and Bohemia', in: *The Picturesque Garden and Its Influence Outside the British Isles*, (Dumbarton Oaks, 1974), 101–102.

8. Cf. W. Liponski, *Polska–Brytania 1800–1830* (Poland–Britain 1800–1830) (Poznan, 1979). For a comprehensive account of Polish travellers in Britain in the eighteenth century, consult Z. Libiszowska, *Polskie zyeie w londynie w XVIII wieku (Polish Life in London in the 18th Century)* (Warsaw, 1972). Titles and all further translations by the author.

9. S. Wodzicki, *O chodowaniu, (sic) użytku, mnożeniu i poznawaniu drzew, krzewow i ziol celniejszych*, Vol. II (supplement) (Cracow, 1924).

10. K. Lach Szyrma, *Anglia i Szkocja: Przypomnienia z podrozy roku 1820–1824 odbytej (England and Scotland: Recollections of a Journey in the Years 1820—1824)* (Warsaw, 1828), 50.

11. H. Mackenzie, *Czuly czlowiek z angielskiego na polski przelozony przez Kazimierza Hr. Wodzickiego* (Warsaw, 1917).

12. The poet was Julian Ursyn Niemcewicz.

13. Walter Scott's and James Macpherson's influence on Polish Romantic literature has been treated by several Polish literary historians, e.g. J. Kleiner, M. Szyjkowski, S. Windakiewicz, K. Wojciechowski, S. Wasylewski, J. Ujejski.

14. In the *Tygodnik Polski i Zagraniczny (Polish and Foreign Weekly)*, 1819, Vol. II, nos. 14 and 15.

15. *Izys Polska (Polish Isis)*, 1822, no. 3.

16. *Magazyn Powszechny (The Universal Magazine)*, 1832–1836.

17. *Magazyn Mód (Magazine of Fashion)*, 1839, no. 1.

18. *Rozmaitosci Warszawskie (Warsaw Variety)*, 1828, no. 38.

19. Z. Libiszowska, *op. cit.*, 222–223.

20. University of Edinburgh Library MSS, letter dated 26th June, 1792, Gen. 873/III/243-4.

21. W. Liponski, *op. cit.*, 109.

22. *Ibid.*, 108–109.

23. W. Kalinka, *Jeneral Dezydery Chlapowski*, in: *Dziela*, Vol. XI, part III (Cracow, 1900), 63.

24. *Jeneral Zamoyski* (Poznan, 1918), Vol. IV, 517.

25. E.g. nos. 1, 9, 10, 11, 16.

26. *Ibid.*, 1803, 806.

27. *Jeneral Zamoyski*, Vol. II, 514–517.

28. Ref. S. Kieniewicz, *Dramat trzezwych entuzjastow* (Warsaw, 1964), 61.

29. Jeneral Zamoyski, *op. cit.*, 517. Quoted in Liponski, *op. cit.*, 135.

30. J. Bartyś 'Dzialalnosc gospodarcza i spoleczna gen. Ludwika Paca w Dobrach Dowspuda na Suwalszczyznie w Tatach 1815–1830', in: *Rocznik Bialostocki*, Vol. IX (1968–69). All further details of the General's economic activity at Dowspuda rely heavily on the above source.

31. K. Lach Szyrma, *op. cit.*, 102.

32. W. Kalinka, *op. cit.*, 68.

33. J. Bartyś, *op. cit.*, 48–49.

34. AGAD MSS, Zamoyski Archive, no. 100, p. 802, 1821; quoted after J. Bartyś, *op. cit.*, 51.

35. K. Kaszewski, 'Ruiny zamku w Dowspudzie', in: *Tygodnik ilustrowany*, no. 276, Warsaw 1865, 4. Also quoted by J. Bartyś, *op. cit.*, 52.

36. *Op. cit.*, 53.

37. *Ibid.*, 53.

38. *Ibid.*, 55–64.

39. W. Liponski, *op. cit.*

40. I. Czartoryska, *Tour Through England* (sic), Czartoryski Library MSS, Ew 607.

41. *Op. cit.*, 107.

42. K. Sienkiewicz, *Dziennik podrózy po Anglii 1820–21* (*Diary of a Travel Through England* (sic)) (Wroclaw, 1953), 177.

43. D. Chlapowski, *Pamietniki* (*Diaries*) (Poznan, 1899), 122.

44. J. Tupalski, *General Dezydery Chlapowski 1788–1879* (Warsaw, 1983), 104–105.

45. J. Topolski, 'Nieromantyczny rozdzial zycia Generala', *Polityka*, XXIV/2.

46. D. Chlapowski, *O rolnictwie* (Poznan, 1835), 121.

47. J. Tupalski, *op. cit.*, 107.

48. *Ibid.*, 108. I have been unable to trace the 'College of Agriculture' of which Lord Murray is here said to have been Rector.

49. In J. Tupalski, *op. cit.*, 108.

50. *Ibid.*

51. Z. Pietruszczynski, *Produkcja roślinna w Wielkopolsce, jej przeszlośc i terazniejszośc* (Poznan, 1937), 89, also quoted by Tupalski, *op. cit.*, 109.

52. E.g. in the *Przewodnik rolniczo-przemyslowy* (*Agrarian and Industrial Guide*) (1836–44).

53. T. Lepkowski, *Polska-narodziny nowoczesne go narodu, 1764–1870* (Warsaw, 1967), 55; Liponski, *op. cit.*, 138.

54. *Gazeta Wiejska* (*Country Gazette*) (1817), 371–376, after W. Liponski, *op. cit.*, 137.

55. T. C. Smout, *A History of the Scottish People, 1560–1830* (London, 1972), 272–273.

56. I. Czartoryska, *op. cit.*

57. *Ibid.* All further quotations from the *Tour* ... are taken from this manuscript.

58. Ref. Steuart (ed.), *op. cit.*, XXVII–XXVIII.

59. *Mysli różne o sposobie zakladania ogrodów.*

60. L. Debicki, *Pulawy* (Lvov, 1887), Vol. II, 277, 281, 283.

61. M. Bohusz, 'Krótka wiadomosc o rolnictwie litewskim', in: *Dziennik Towarzystwa Krolewskiego Rolniczego*, 1812, no. 1, 17.

62. B. Majewska-Maszkowska, *Mecenat artystyczny Izabeli z Czartoryskich Lubomirskiej* (Warsaw, 1980), 332.

63. J. U. Niemcewicz, *Pamietniki czasów moich*, Vol. I (Warsaw, 1957), 83.

64. Z. Ostrowska-Keblowska, *Architektura palacowa z pol. XVIII wieku w Wielkopolsce*, Prace Kons. Hist. Sztuki, PTPN (Poznan, 1969), no. 2, 180 and footnote.

65. J. Skuratowicz, *Dwory i palace w Wielkim Ksiestwie poznanskim* (Poznan, 1981), 63.

66. Ostrowska-Keblowska, *op. cit.*, 49–53, 68, 79, 83, 198; and T. Jaroszewski, *O siedzibach neogotyckich w Polsce* (Warsaw, 1981), 305–306.

67. *Ibid.*, 191.

68. J. Baranowski, 'Architektura Palacu w Dowspudzie', in: *Rocznik Bialostocki*, Vol. XIII, 1976, 427.

69. *Ibid.*, 430.

70. T. Jaroszewski, *op. cit.*, 157, 158.

71. A. D. (Zagórzany), *Klosy* (1875), Vol. 21, no. 522, 8, 12.

72. T. Jaroszewski, *op. cit.*, 11.

12

SMITH, ROUSSEAU AND THE REPUBLIC OF NEEDS

Michael Ignatieff

In ancient times, when persuasion took the place of force, eloquence was a necessity of civil life. But of what use is it today, when force has replaced persuasion? Force needs neither artistry or figures of speech to say, 'Such is my desire.' What discourse then remains available to the people? Sermons? What does it matter to try to persuade people, since they are without power? Popular speech has become as useless as eloquence. Society has now set in its mould: nothing can be changed except with cannons and money; and since no one in power has anything to say to the people except 'Give us your money', they say it with official notices posted on street corners, or with soldiers knocking on our doors. There is no longer any reason to assemble people for civic purposes. On the contrary, keeping citizens apart, has become the first maxim of modern politics.

J. J. Rousseau *Essai sur l'origine des langues,*
Ch. XX, 1782 (1817 ed.).

In March 1756, a thirty-three-year-old professor at the University of Glasgow, unknown to the world but acknowledged by his friends as an 'ingenious and learned gentleman' wrote anonymously to Alexander Wedderburn's new periodical, *The Edinburgh Review,* to warn that it risked extinction unless it extended the coverage of its reviews beyond the often 'absurd' local performances of Scottish writers to include the dramatic new philosophy of the Continent.[1] After mentioning Diderot and d'Alembert's *Encylcopédie,* the first volumes of which had just appeared, the anonymous correspondent devoted the rest of his letter to a review of 'the late Discourse upon the origin and foundation of the inequality amongst mankind by Mr. Rousseau of Geneva'.

This is one of history's resonant little encounters — between Adam Smith, for this was the reviewer's name, and the already notorious Jean Jacques — in the pages of a short-lived review published on the northernmost border of the European republic of letters. With hindsight, we can understand it as the first (and only) intellectual meeting between early capitalist society's most perceptive critic, and its most penetrating theorist then unknown but already leading students in his lectures along the chain of reasoning which was to conclude exactly twenty years later in the *Wealth of Nations.* If we judge the meaning of this moment from everything they were yet to write, we could think of that little review as a paridigmatic encounter between classical republicanism and classical political economy, between a vision of the world as it might be, a utopia of small, autarchic republics of self-governing citizens, and an account of the world as it was coming to be, a society of strangers held together by the invisible hand.

On the face of it, then, the 'meeting' of 1756 is hardly a meeting of minds. When Rousseau had written in 1751, 'ancient treatises of politics continually made mention of morals and virtue; ours speak of nothing but commerce and money', he was in fact referring to Melon and Petty, and the way these political economists wrote of human labour like Algiers slave-dealers talking about their slaves.[2] He might just as well have been speaking of Smith and those still-startling sentences in the wages chapter of the *Wealth of Nations* in which labour is valued like any other commodity.[3]

Yet we would be mistaken to think that Rousseau spoke only in the ancient language of morals and virtue, while Smith spoke only in the vernacular of commerce and money. Scholars tracing the roots of both languages have followed them to the same seedbeds: the conjectural history of property found in the natural jurisprudence of Grotius and Pufendorf,[4] the ancient Stoic critique of the vanity of human wishes, revived again in the Presbyterian culture of seventeenth-century Scotland, no less than in Rousseau's Geneva; and the civic republican critique of modern citizenship, another ancient Greek and Roman heritage re-crafted into a critique of modernity and a utopia of democratic self-government by Calvin's saints, Scottish Covenanters and English Country Party opponents of the impact of modern commerce on politics after the Restoration.[5] This 'civic humanist' critique of commercial society would have been familiar to Smith, long before he encountered Rousseau in 1756: in the rhetoric of the Country Party opposition to the Walpolean ascendancy, in Andrew Fletcher's discourses against standing armies; in the Scottish militia debates of the early 1750s, all the 'Rousseauian' elements were there: the critique of luxury, and private interest; the jeremiads against the standing armies, and the attenuation of civic virtue.[6] Yet it is only in Rousseau, not in the local Scottish or English rhetoric, that the critique of luxury and corruption in modern polity attains the grandeur and scope of an inquisition of modern civilisation as such. The *Wealth of Nations* is a synthesis of the great eighteenth-century European debate on the compatibility of wealth and virtue, commercial capitalism and civic responsibility, but it is one which we now know bears the marks of a deep absorption of the terms of its civic humanist antithesis. If there is the language of commerce and money in Rousseau's discourse, there is a language of morals and virtue in Smith's.

This is usually demonstrated by citing all those passages in the *Wealth of Nations* in which Smith denounced the avarice and oppression of the rich, their delusional pursuit of 'baubles and trinkets', the employers' love of combination and hatred of competition, and perhaps most of all, the icy reproofs to those merchants who act as if their private selfish interests were identical with the public good.[7] This is obviously a Smith with whom civic republicans, even Rousseau in particular, could have found common ground: the Smith who loved the teachings of the Stoics; the Smith who admired the martial training of the Swiss republics and proposed universal primary education as a means of counteracting the mental mutilation of the poor in the modern division of labour;[8] the dying Smith who in 1790 found time to insert a new chapter to his *Theory of Moral Sentiments*, arguing that the 'great and most universal cause of the corruption of our moral sentiments' was our 'disposition to admire, and almost to worship, the rich and powerful, and to despise, or at least to neglect persons of poor and mean condition'.[9]

But these are the surface identities of allegiance which a shared admiration for Stoic teaching, a common education in natural jurisprudence and civic humanist values were likely to engender in profound minds pondering the meaning of the same society. Their deeper identity is to be found in the common structure of economic, political and moral relationships examined in the second *Discourse* and in the *Wealth of Nations*. They share the same problem: the historical relationship between division of labour, inequality and citizenship, and they tackle it in the same language: a language of human needs. Their work thus attains the rare dialogue of true antitheses: sharing the same terms, the same problem to arrive at diametrically opposed solutions. Their debate concerns us, across the centuries which divide us, because it is about a fundamental problem: is a society which is master of its needs possible in modern economic conditions?

Let us go back to the pages of the *Edinburgh Review*. Smith begins with a startling paradox: Rousseau's account of civil society resembles nothing so much as Mandeville's 'Inquiry into the Origin of Moral Virtue' in the *Fable of the Bees*, published in 1728.[10] This is paradoxical because, of course, nothing could have been more repugnant to Rousseau than Mandeville's 'private vices, public benefits'. Yet Smith persisted: both the 'profligate' Mandeville and the high-minded Jean Jacques shared the same starting point: 'both of them suppose that there is in man no powerful instinct which necessarily determines him to seek society for its own sake'. In Mandeville's case, men submit to social rules only to guarantee that their own pursuit of 'private vice' will not be endangered by the private vices of others. Only scarcity in the state of nature obliges men to agree to rules of private property and justice to prevent their competition from becoming murderous.

In Rousseau's account of the passage of man from primitive equality to civilised inequality, there is no scarcity in the state of nature: there cannot be — as long as each man's needs remain the limits of his desires, as long as each man can appropriate nature as he pleases, nature provides enough for all. Scarcity, for Rousseau, is not a natural, but a social fact: it arises only when some desire more than they need and set out to get it by appropriating nature to their exclusive use.[11] So long as men, Rousseau wrote, 'undertook only what a single person could accomplish, and confined themselves to such arts as did not require the joint labour of several hands, they lived free, honest and happy lives'.[12] In a society, in other words, in which there is no surplus, there is no scarcity; without surplus, need remains the limit of desire; no one desires more than others. Anthropologists now tell us this *is* the equilibrium position of many hunting and gathering societies: their history is an eternal present.[13]

Smith's disagreement with this picture was not, as one might expect, that it ignored the omnipresence of natural scarcity. He agreed that it was property which created scarcity. It had been Hume, not Smith, who located the original rationale for forming political or civil society in natural scarcity: in 'our numberless wants and necessities', in our natural inability to satisfy them on our own and in the necessity of rules of individuation to prevent conflict over scarce resources.[14] Smith, by contrast, argued that we were drawn into civil society, not by necessity as such — whether it be natural or social in origin — but by our 'propensity to truck, barter and exchange one thing for another'. Human beings were the only species, he argued, for whom sociable co-operation in production and exchange was entirely natural. 'Nobody ever saw a dog make a fair and deliberate exchange of one bone for another with another dog. Nobody ever saw one animal by its gestures and natural cries signify to another, this is mine, that yours'.[15] Our natural propensity to society, he argued, was a 'necessary consequence of the faculties of reason and speech'. This association of natural sociability with language contrasted sharply with Rousseau's remark in the second *Discourse*:

> ... be the origins of language and society what they may, it may be at least inferred from the little care which nature has taken to unite mankind by mutual wants, and to facilitate the use of speech, that she has contributed little to make them sociable, and has put little of her own into all they have done to create such bonds of union. It is in fact impossible to conceive why, in a state of nature, one man should stand more in need of the assistance of another, than a monkey or a wolf of the assistance of another of its kind: or, granting that he did, what motives could induce that other to assist him; or even then, by what means they could agree upon the conditions.[16]

For Smith, on the other hand, the initiation of a process of division of labour and exchange even in the hunting and gathering stage was as natural a step as, and indeed a consequence of, their speaking together:

> In a tribe of hunters or shepherds a particular person makes bows and arrows for example with more readiness and dexterity than any other. He frequently exchanges them for cattle or for venison with his companions; and he finds at last that he can in this manner get more cattle and venison, than if he himself went to the field to catch them. From a regard to his own interest, therefore, the making of bows and arrows grows to be his chief business, and he becomes a sort of armourer.[17]

From this specialisation, unique to the species, developed the other unique capacity of the human race: its ability to generate surplus, to expand the scarcity constraints of nature and thus to release human desire from the bounds of need.

Yet, with surplus came property, came the progressive individuation of the means of subsistence; by the time mankind had passed from the stage of hunters and gatherers, through shepherding, to the period of settled agriculture, the species was already divided between those who had property and those who had to sell their labour. As Smith expressed it in the *Wealth of Nations*:

> It is in this age of shepherds, in the second period of society, that the inequality of fortune first begins to take place, and introduces among men a degree of authority and subordination which could not possibly exist before.[18]

Smith was in no doubt as to civil government's essential rôle, in this and in any stage of society:

> Civil government, so far as it is instituted for the security of property, is in reality instituted for the defense of the rich against the poor, or of those who have some property against those who have none at all.[19]

However differently they understood the roots of human sociability, Smith and Rousseau were entirely at one in seeing the history of the division of labour as a history of human economic inequality. In a passage which Smith quoted in the *Edinburgh Review*, Rousseau made the connection between the division of labour and inequality explicit:

> But from the instant in which one man had occasion for the assistance of another, from the moment that he perceived that it could be advantageous to a single person to have provisions for two, equality disappeared, property was introduced, labour became necessary, and the vast forests of nature were changed into agreeable plains, which must be watered with the sweat of mankind, and in which the world beheld slavery and wretchedness begin to grow up and blossom with the harvest.[20]

The challenge of this passage is taken up directly in the *Theory of Moral Sentiments*, which Smith was already giving as lectures to his students at the time of his review of Rousseau and which he published in 1759. He accepted with Rousseau that the desire to have more than another was vanity: hadn't the Stoics taught that 'happiness was altogether or at least in great measure independent of fortune'? The restless pursuit of the 'baubles and trinkets' enjoyed by the rich was, he freely admitted, a snare and a deception.[21] But it was 'well that nature imposes on us in this manner. It is this deception which rouses and keeps in continual motion the industry of mankind'. In a passage whose choice of words is so close to those of Rousseau just quoted that it cannot be mere coincidence, Smith went on:

> It is this which first prompted them to cultivate the ground, to build houses, to found cities and commonwealths, and to invent and improve all the sciences and arts, which ennoble and embellish human life; which have entirely changed the whole face of the globe, have turned [this is the phrase speaking directly to Rousseau] the rude forests of nature into agreeable and fertile plains, and made the trackless and barren ocean a new fund of subsistence, and the great high road of communication to the different nations of the earth.[22]

Yet how was this panegyric to the human desire to accumulate wealth reconciled with the facts of inequality? How did the cunning of Nature turn men's potentially vicious desire to have more than they needed into a means of providing for those who had not enough? Smith went on:

> The rich only select from the heap what is most precious and agreeable. They consume little more than the poor, and in spite of their natural selfishness and rapacity, though they mean only their own conveniency though the sole end which they propose from the labours of all the thousands whom they employ, by the gratification of their own vain and insatiable desires, they divide with the poor the produce of all their improvements. They are led by an invisible hand to make nearly the same distribution of the necessities of life, which would have been made, had the earth been divided into equal portions among all its inhabitants, and thus without intending it, without knowing it, advance the interest of society, and afford means to the multiplication of the species.[23]

The question raised here of how the rights of property could be reconciled with adequate provision for the needs of those left out of the original division of the means of subsistence in the hypothetical passage from a state of nature had occupied Christian minds like Saint Basil, both as a problem in the ethics of charity and as a historical issue since the days of the early Church. From the Church Fathers were bequeathed to the early modern natural jurisprudence tradition a set of questions about whether property carried with it obligations to provide for the needs of those who had none, and whether these were voluntary or binding, matters of benevolence or matters of justice.[24] In the political theory of classical republicanism, too, extreme inequality at least among propertied franchise-holders had always been regarded as a threat to the longevity of the republic.[25] In a real sense, the classical political economy of Smith was an attempt to vindicate the compatibility of adequate provision for the labourer with the exclusive property relations in a free market, in the face of the challenge offered by both of these traditions, and thrust at him, not only by, but above all by, the passionate eloquence of Rousseau.

But how did Smith *know* that more equal societies provided less adequately for the poor than modern ones? On the very first page of the *Wealth of Nations*, its 'Introduction and Plan', he remarked that in the 'savage nations of hunters and fishers, every individual who is able to work, is more or less employed in useful labour', while in 'civilized and thriving nations, a great number of people do not labour at all'; and yet the former are frequently 'so miserably poor, that, from mere want, they are frequently reduced ... to the necessity sometimes of directly destroying their infants, their old people and those afflicted with lingering diseases, to perish with hunger'. In a civilised society, on the other hand, the 'produce of the whole labour of the society is so great' that the labouring poor are able to support the huge burden of non-productive labourers and still enjoy 'a great share of the necessaries and conveniences of life than it is possible for any savage to acquire'.[26] Why this should be so, why inequality in modern commercial society should be compatible with the minimum degree of distributive justice to the poor, and why in more equal but backward societies the poor starved, was *the* essential question which the *Wealth of Nations* set out to explain, and which, to judge from Smith's *Early Drafts*, he had been pondering in the 1750s, at exactly the moment he came across Rousseau's most passionate defence of the opposite proposition: that in commercial society 'the privileged few ... gorge themselves with superfluities, while the starving multitude are in want of the bare necessities of life'.[27]

Smith's answer to the question of how the productive labour of the poor in commercial society had been so increased that they could support both themselves and the mass of unproductive labourers (servants, professionals, artists, standing armies and the state) was of course the division of labour: the economy of human time which specialisation of tasks made possible. It was rising productivity per man hour which prevented the distributional conflict between rich and poor from becoming a zero-sum game: growth did not give the labourer a rising relative share of national income, but his rising absolute share in distribution was such that, however simple his standard of comfort might be in comparison to the 'more extravagant luxury of the great' in his own society, it exceeded the standard of 'many an African king, the absolute master of the lives and liberties of ten thousand naked savages'.[28]

To this day, Smith's argument remains the core of modern capitalism's defence of itself: economic growth may increase relative inequality of income, but it diminishes absolute inequalities in the satisfaction of basic needs. To this day, too, Rousseau's remains at the core of the rebuttal. He did not, as one might expect, deny that the material prosperity of the poorest members of the population was the test of the civic wellbeing of a society. Just as Smith had said that 'no society can surely be flourishing and happy, of which the far greater part of the members are poor and miserable', so Rousseau maintained, in the *Social Contract*, that the end of all political association could only be the 'preservation and prosperity of its members'.[29] But he insisted that even if absolute inequalities in the satisfaction of need were overcome for the poorest, relative inequalities would corrupt morals and threaten citizenship by enslaving the poor in craving for the luxuries of the rich. In his reply in 1753 to the King of Poland's strictures against his *Discourse on the Sciences and Arts*, Rousseau said, 'the words rich and poor are relative; wherever men are equal, there are neither rich nor poor'.[30] By accepting that luxury was relative, a social rather than a natural fact, Rousseau also accepted a society of abundance, provided its distribution was equalised, and men's virtues were thus safeguarded from the temptations of invidious desire and envy.

It was in his *Discourse on Political Economy*, an article for the fifth volume of the *Encyclopédie*, which appeared in November 1755, that Rousseau sought to explain how the legislator could create an egalitarian but affluent society. Once again, Rousseau shared his starting premise with Smith, indeed with every defender of the existing order of commercial society. Any polity, whether it be a democracy, aristocracy or monarchy, had no other *raison d'être* than that of 'assuring the property, life and liberty of each member by the protection of all'.[31] If a modern government's first task was to prevent 'extreme inequality of fortunes', it ought not to do so by 'taking away wealth from its possessors, but by depriving all men of means to accumulate it'.[32] How then was this to be accomplished? Rousseau was cautious. He left the right of the living to bequeath property to the dead untouched: nothing, he said, 'is more fatal to morality and to the Republic than the continual shifting of rank and fortune among the citizens'.[33] Voltaire thus had misread Rousseau when he scribbled indignantly in the margins of his copy of the *Second Discourse*, 'What! he who has planted, sown, fenced in, has no right to the fruit of his labour! What!'[34] As Rousseau made clear, justice required absolute equality in the law's application: seizure of some people's property for the sake of other people violated this principle. 'The Sovereign has no right to touch the property of one or several individuals',[35] just as the general will could only legislate justly if its laws applied to every single one of those who comprised it. This left only one alternative: 'it may legitimately take possession of the property of all'; but even the redistribution of such property would have to observe strict equality among each of the individuals composing the general will. Rousseau left the option of communism unexplored.

Short of this primitive communism, how, Rousseau asked, could a society be created in which 'no citizen shall ever be wealthy enough to buy another, and none poor enough to be forced to sell himself?'[36] This, for Rousseau, was the heart of the matter: men could only become free to determine their own needs if they could be both economically autonomous of each other and equal in fortune. The only just redistributive measure, Rousseau reasoned, would be a capitation tax on wealth and income, 'exactly proportioned to the circumstances of individuals':

> He who possesses only the common necessaries of life should pay nothing at all, while the tax on him who is in possession of superfluities may justly be extended to everything he has over and above mere necessities.[37]

Here Rousseau's reversal of the same propositions used by Smith is obvious. Smith used the argument that a rich man's needs were no greater than a poor man's to argue that extreme inequality in an affluent society would not deny the poor their minimum due, since the rich could not physically consume all of the available surplus. Rousseau used the same argument — 'a grandee has two legs just like a cowherd, and like him, again, but one belly' — to justify the redistribution of fortunes. He also proposed the taxation of imports of luxury goods as a measure of equalisation. Taxes raised the price of luxuries for the rich but did not violate their liberty to waste their surplus on the 'frivolous and all too lucrative arts'. Not only import duties on luxuries, but heavy taxes as well, should be laid on

> servants in livery, on equipages, rich furniture, fine clothes, on spacious courts and gardens, on public entertainments of all kinds, on useless professions, such as dancers, singers, players, and in a word, on all that multiplicity of objects of luxury, amusement and idleness, which strike the eyes of all, and can the less be hidden, as their whole purpose is to be seen, without which they would be useless.[38]

The aim of these taxes was moral and political: to 'ease the poor' and 'throw the burden on the rich'; to weaken the incentives for invidious distinction, and to hold back that relentless reproduction of inequality which menaced democratic republicanism. For Rousseau, as for Smith, inequality was the inertial direction of history, 'the natural course of things'; but, unlike Smith, he believed it was a slide which law and politics could stop: 'it is precisely because the force of circumstances tends continually to destroy equality that the force of legislation should always tend to its maintenance'.[39]

Rousseau's insight is that a community of men can only become masters of their needs, instead of slaves to their desires, when they democratically determine some form of collective constraint on inequalities of fortune. These constraints in turn are the necessary economic condition for democracy itself: for the equality of citizens without which there can be no true justice. If this is utopia, Rousseau knew as well as anyone how difficult it would be to achieve:

> How many conditions that are difficult to unite does such a government [a democratic republic] pre-suppose! First, a very small state, where the people can readily be got together and where each citizen can with ease know all the rest;

secondly great simplicity of manners, to prevent business from multiplying and raising thorny problems (which would have to be resolved by delegation to experts); next, a larger measure of equality in rank and fortune, without which equality of rights and authority cannot long subsist; lastly, little or no luxury — for luxury either comes of riches or makes them necessary; it corrupts at once rich and poor, the rich by possession and the poor by covetousness; it sells the country to softness and vanity, and takes away from the State all its citizens, to make them slaves one to another, and one and all to public opinion.[40]

If this was a utopia inspired by the Renaissance republican tradition, by the 'ancient treatises of virtue', it was one whose economic preconditions Rousseau took care to specify in the new language of 'commerce and money'. The duties to be levied on imported luxuries implied a republican economy based on agriculture, exporting food and remaining in surplus in the international balance of trade by restraining imports of manufactured goods. The taxes on domestic production of manufactured luxury goods enacted the civic humanist hostility to the draining effects of urban manufacture upon agriculture, a hostility paradigmatically expressed, of course, in the County Party rhetoric of mid-eighteenth century oppositional politics in England, but also in the 'agricultural system' of the Physiocrats.[41] Rousseau's *Political Economy* made his position on the town–country division of labour quite explicit:

industry and commerce draw all the money from the country into the capitals: and as the tax [land taxes] destroys the proportion there might be between the needs of the husbandman and the price of his corn, money is always leaving and never returning. Thus the richer the city the poorer the country.[42]

Taxation of both imported and domestic manufactured goods would stop the haemorrhage of men and capital from town to country: it would prevent 'the multiplication of idle persons in our cities, and the depopulation of the countryside'.[43] Rousseau also mused in fragments of his writing about banning machines from the republic to prevent unemployment, unrest and the shifting of economic fortunes.[44]

In the republican ideal, self-government required as much economic autarchy within the world economy as the natural resources and situation of the republic permitted. He acknowledged that republics without sufficient agricultural resources of their own would have to trade their manufactures for food. But he insisted that the futures of these republics would be short. Commerce, he agreed with the Marquis d'Argenson, enriched only some individuals or some towns: 'the nation as a whole gains nothing by it and the people is no better off'.[45] The history of such republics was bound to be short because wealth from trade would throw up a merchant oligarchy, who would subvert republican institutions to their own purposes. Only the sovereign people themselves, or even a wise and virtuous legislator acting in their name (the Lycurgus, the Solon, the Prince, the Patriot King of successive republican ideals) could shore up, by redistributive legislation, the equality of the republic against the ceaseless battering of the waves of international commerce, and the fragmentation of the population by the effects of the international division of labour. The republic, in other words, must even be prepared to risk its liberty at the hands of a legislator in order to preserve itself against the historical inertia of luxury and inequality.

If the republic was menaced from without by the impact of commerce, it was threatened from within by the tendency of its own citizens to delegate their own civic responsibilities to paid servants. Some delegation of executive, administrative and judicial functions was both necessary and inevitable.[46] The most dangerous of these acts of delegation, these exchanges of duty for money, was the handing over of citizens' common defence to the standing army. Mercenaries had been a 'principal cause of the ruin of the Roman Empire': they fought not for virtue but for cash, and they were just as likely to turn against a republic as to defend it. Rousseau realised, however, that the 'invention of artillery and fortifications', the increasing cost of armament and the resulting professionalisation of military expertise forced all commercial societies to resort to standing armies for their defence. The only alternative was a citizen's militia — a mass mobilisation — which would continually disrupt commerce and agriculture. Rousseau could see no alternative to a standing army, but he warned, in common with eighteenth-century British defenders of citizens' militias, of the danger both to liberty and to the integral civic personality of the increasing divorce between citizen and soldier.

How were the legitimate claims of the private sphere — the *oeconomia* of family, home and work — to be reconciled with the claim of public duty? This, the most ancient conflict of human claims in the civic vernacular, had been made more acute, Rousseau realised, with the coming of a market economy: in an exchange economy 'men surrender a part of their profits [in taxation] in order to have time to increase them at leisure'.[47] The size of the state grows *pari passu* with the amount of time devoted to private economic affairs, and increasing economies in the expenditure of labour time do not increase the time available for civic pursuits: the free time is ploughed back into the pursuit of new means of economising time and increasing profit. This was the core of Rousseau's answer to the claim that the productivity of the division of labour not only released men from the burden of basic need, but reduced the time men were required to expend in their satisfaction. These economies of time were the keys to a historically new type of freedom: the leisure of emancipated desire. Rousseau countered this claim with one of his own: that the free time opened up by modern prosperity was a mirage: it was entirely filled up by delusional pursuit of the baubles and trinkets of the rich. True freedom did not lie in enslavement to what was later to be called 'commodity fetishism', but in participation in the *res publica* of the city state.

Taken as a whole, Rousseau's writing is the most profound attempt to ground an egalitarian republic of citizens within the actual constraints of the international market and division of labour of an emerging capitalist economy. It represents the most sustained attempt by any thinker within the tradition of the 'ancient treatises of morals and virtue' — the Machiavellian moment, as John Pocock has taught us to call this tradition — to argue with the future proposed by the new 'treatises of money and commerce'.

Smith's reply to this tradition would be simple enough to understand were it a mere defence of private economic interest against the ideal of civic virtue. But

Smith's (and even more so, Hume's) deep concern, for example, with the issue of standing armies, and his unconcealed preference for government by the independent landed class in preference to the ascendant commercial interests make it clear how deeply he shared Rousseau's anxieties, if not his solutions.

The main burden of Smith's reply, if not to Rousseau himself, then to the civic republican language in which he spoke, was to demonstrate that any society which sought to maintain equality and virtue by constraining its needs — chiefly through import duties on luxury and taxes on domestic manufactures — would in the end jeopardise the economic growth which ensured the long-term satisfaction of the needs of its poorest members. If growth in productivity depended on the division of labour, and the extent of the division of labour depended in turn on the extent of the market, a republican economy which sought to withdraw as much as possible from the international market and the division of labour would pay the eventual price of stagnation, decline and impoverishment.[48] The most direct of the *Wealth of Nations*' engagements with a specifically republican economics comes in Smith's treatment in Book IV of the attempts by the 'antient republicks of Greece' and Rome to favour agriculture at the expense of manufactures and foreign trade and to inhibit the emergence of a class of urban artisans and proletarians. Those systems of economic policy, both ancient and modern (he was referring to the Physiocrats, but also to the ancient republicans) 'which prefering agriculture to all other employments, in order to promote it, impose restraints upon manufactures and foreign trade, act contrary to the very end which they propose'.[49] Prosperous agriculture depended on vigorous demand from an urban population dependent upon cash purchase of food. Inhibiting the growth of the urban manufactured sector would only hold back the growth of agriculture: it would replace rural depopulation with rural stagnation. The more expensive manufactures were made by taxes and duties, the less of them the agricultural sector could purchase, and the less incentive it would have to produce food. This critique of both republican and Physiocratic economies led to a famous Smithian peroration:

> All systems either of preference or of restraint therefore being thus completely taken away, the obvious and simple system of natural liberty establishes itself of its own accord. Every man as long as he does not violate the laws of justice is left perfectly free to pursue his own interest his own way, and to bring both his industry and his capital into competition with those of any other man, or order of men.[50]

In place of the republican liberty of laws collectively arrived at, then, the natural liberty of an international market, under the ruthless secular providence of the invisible hand. The crux of Smith's rejection of the republican utopia is not, to repeat again, that he did not share an allegiance to their vocabulary of civic virtue, but that he became convinced of the almost entirely perverse and unintended effects of all attempts to order the 'natural course of things' by legislation: perverse in the double sense that they did not achieve the economic ends intended, and in the sense that legislative interference jeopardised the very liberty in the use of property which republicanism vowed itself to defend.

But what then of that active liberty — the public participation in politics? How could that be reconciled with submission to the 'natural course of things', in particular to the elaboration of the social division of labour between state and civil society, epitomised by the replacement of citizen militias by standing armies? Like Rousseau, Smith believed that the social division of labour — the separation of private and public spheres — was as much a cause of the distinctive productivity of modern labour as the division of labour within industry. Yet by a paradox which Rousseau had understood no less than Smith, the more time was economised in production — in the private sphere — the less time was available for the public. All economies of time achieved in the private sphere were then re-invested, as it were, in redoubling the productivity of labour. Thus:

> A shepherd has a great deal of leisure; a husbandman, in the rude state of husbandry has some; an artificer or manufacturer has none at all. The first may, without any loss, employ a great deal of his time in martial exercises; the second may employ some part of it; but the last cannot employ a single hour in them without some loss, and his attention to his own interest naturally leads him to neglect them altogether.[51]

The increasing dependence of commercial societies on paid mercenaries and on officers of justice and revenue was the very secret of their distinctive productivity. 'Men of republican principles have been jealous of a standing army to liberty', Smith wrote, citing Caesar's destruction of the Roman republic, and Cromwell's turning the Long Parliament out of doors, but in many modern republics standing armies had become essential to the defence of liberty — against factions within and barbarians without. Yet, characteristically, Smith did not leave the matter there, for he worried aloud that whereas in 'barbarous societies' every man was in some measure a warrior, a citizen and a statesman, and therefore capable of forming a 'tolerable judgement concerning the interests of society', it was otherwise in a 'civilized society'. Only philosophers, whose trade was thinking, had the time and leisure for a synoptic view of the public interest. The rest of the population were divided and segmented by their position in the division of labour, and indeed were divided within themselves, unable to reconcile their rôles as producers and citizens, public and private men.[52] Yet the solution, if there was one at all, could only lie in further elaboration of the division of labour itself: in the formation of a system of education, staffed by paid teachers specialising in martial and civic instruction. Only the reproduction of common belief through education could re-forge the social linkages atomised by the division of labour. The invisible hand was evidently no substitute for the conscious ties of allegiance and belief known as civic virtue. For while the invisible hand did tie men's real economic interests together, in what Durkheim would have called 'mechanical solidarity', a market society of strangers lacked the means to know its general interest as such. Hence commercial society's unique vulnerability to faction, to deluded conflicts between economic interests which while seemingly antithetical in the short term were identical in the long term, if only the participants could be torn apart long enough to see it.[53] Rousseau's solution to this problem — restricting the size of republics, so that the identity of interests could be transparent to each citizen — may have ignored the actual geography of national states, as well as the logic of the international division of labour; but the solution of one who did take these obdurate realities into account was no less the substitution of a pious wish for empirical inference than Rousseau's. Smith and Rousseau's faith in civic education was indeed faith in something larger: in the capacity of a society of strangers to build a common language of trust and civic commitment.

If we wish to understand why Rousseau's assessment of the future of civic virtue in commercial society was, in the end, so much more pessimistic than Smith's, we need to return to our starting point — those pages in the *Edinburgh Review* — and to their fundamental disagreement about the psychology of human sociability.

The common threat to virtue in market society, they both agreed, lay in the desire for invidious distinction — in the envy and emulation — which an unequal distribution of property caused men to acquire in civil society. In societies without surplus, therefore without inequality and without scarcity, envy was absent. Men were possessed of natural *amour de soi*, a natural self-knowledge and self-regard which was based in their instinct for self-preservation. This sense of self was autonomous because no individual had the possibility of desiring more than he needed; natural equality deprived him of any incentive to compare his satisfactions with those of any other. But with the emergence of surplus, with the emancipation of desire from the limits of universal and equal need, men lost their natural *amour de soi*, and came instead to have a knowledge of self derived only from relative comparison with others. Their identities came to be grounded instead in *amour propre*, in competitive and emulative self-definition against others. In a famous passage from the second *Discourse* which Smith quoted in his review, Rousseau wrote:

> ... the savage lives in himself; the man of society always out of himself; cannot live but in opinion of others, and it is, if I may say so, from their judgment alone that he derives the sentiment of his own existence.[54]

Men's inner enslavement to the opinions of others, their dependence on others even for the sense of their own being, derived, Rousseau said, not from men's intrinsic nature, but from their emerging historical dependence upon each other for subsistence in the division of labour:

> Thus man, from being free and independent, became by a multitude of new necessities subjected in a manner, to all nature, and above all to his fellow creatures, whose slave he is in one sense even while he becomes their master; rich, he has occasion for their services; poor, he stands in need of their assistance, and even mediocrity does not enable him to live without them. He is obliged therefore to endeavour to interest them in his situation, and to make them find, either in reality or in appearance, their advantage in labouring for his.[55]

The pathology of this interdependence was that each man was seized by an 'insatiable ambition, an ardour to raise his relative fortune, not so much from any real necessity, as to set himself above others'. Market relations were thus a theatre of duplicity, in which men served each other's needs only to satisfy their desire of superiority over each other:

> To be and to appear to be, became two things entirely different; and from this distinction arose imposing ostentation, deceitful guile and all the vices which attend them.[56]

Smith's account of moral identity in commercial society rebuts the Rousseauian position point by point, first from the economic viewpoint. In free exchange processes, he argued, while each party might, in the process of 'higgling' seek to cheat the other, the freedom of the parties to withdraw from any transaction which failed to approximate equivalency, guaranteed that market transactions could not be *only* theatres of duplicity. This was especially true in the crucial market transaction — the buying and selling of labour. 'Nothing', he quite agreed with Rousseau, 'tends so much to corrupt and enervate and debase the mind as dependency, and nothing gives such noble and generous notions of probity as freedom and independency.' But it was precisely in commercial society that the labouring poor had become free to contract for their wages, to leave harsh conditions and seek better ones. It was commerce which had dissolved the dependency relations of patronage, serfdom and clientage of the feudal age.[57]

But what was such freedom worth, Rousseau might well have replied, if the poor had no desires but those of the rich, if they had no way of distinguishing need from fetishes? At this point in the argument, Smith made use of his initial pairing of Mandeville and Rousseau: if the dominant motive at work in the poor's emulation of the rich was 'vanity', what in fact was so bad about vanity? As Hume had said, the desire to earn the praise of others — whether it be through the pursuit of wealth or any other activity — could be a motive to virtuous action.[58] Not all self-regarding, self-interested action, motivated by vanity, was immoral, as both Mandeville and Rousseau supposed.[59] If this were really the case, why then did men commonly praise many self-regarding virtues including the quintessential Protestant economic values: 'oeconomy, industry, discretion, attention and application of thought'?[60] Such virtues were certainly in Rousseau's pantheon, no less than in Smith's, so how could he consistently call them vicious?

Moreover, and here we get to the heart of the matter, neither Rousseau nor Mandeville had distinguished, in their critique of vanity, between 'our desire of acquiring honour and esteem by really deserving those sentiments' and our 'frivolous desire of praise at any rate'.[61] Only the latter was properly called vanity. The phrase 'to be and to seem become two different things' presumed that men so lose touch with elementary moral discriminations that they would do anything, no matter how duplicitous, to earn praise. What follows in turn is that in capitalist society vanity obliterates each individual's capacity to make personal choices between needs and desires: what anyone else desires, the self desires by that very fact. Yet this was clearly at odds with the detachment and 'self-command' which stoics believed men were capable of and which certainly the 'wise and virtuous few' in commercial society continued to hold dear. The very fact that we are sociable beings, Smith argued, guaranteed that we did not understand our moral commitments only from within our own interest: by processes of detachment within the capacity of any ordinary mortal we could discern what an 'impartial spectator' might command us to do in any situation of profound moral conflict with another. If this capacity for self-command and self-detachment was indeed a feature of human personality, then it followed that men were able not only to seek praise, but to deserve it; they were capable in turn of distinguishing between their *amour propre* and their *amour de soi,* between those desires for distinction which served no end but vanity, and those desires for autonomous self-regard which grounded true self-knowledge. Some men moreover *knew* that money could not buy them happiness, knew that 'the chief part of human happiness arises from the consciousness of being loved'.[62] They knew this and they could act accordingly, keeping a virtuous detachment from the 'great scramble of human society'.[63] And what the 'wise and virtuous few' could do, humans in general could do.

This is a language of the will, a Stoic's language. If, as I have argued, crucial passages in the *Theory of Moral Sentiments* are to be understood as refutations of both Mandeville and Rousseau's conception of capitalist economic man's moral alienation, they are refutations which attempt to turn Stoic premises against two of their most ardent advocates. For as many scholars have pointed out, the Stoic definition of man as a creature distinguished, not by his passions, but by his will, ordered all of Rousseau's thought.[64] As he wrote in the second *Discourse* itself, 'Nature lays her command on every animal and the brute obeys her voice. Man receives the same impulsion but at the same knows himself at liberty to acquiesce or desist'.[65] Indeed, it was only in the social world of men that this capacity to choose the good, instead of merely following natural instinct, could exercise itself:

> The passing from the state of nature to the civil society produces a remarkable change in man; it puts justice as a rule of conduct in the place of instinct, and gives his actions the moral quality they previously lacked. It is only then when the voice of duty has taken the place of physical impulse, and right that of desire, that man who has hitherto thought only of himself finds himself impelled to act on other principles, and to consult his reason rather than study his inclinations.[66]

In the language we have been using, man only becomes himself when he can choose between what he needs and what he desires. In the state of primitive simplicity, where need is the limit of desire, there are no choices to make, there is no virtue, not even consciousness of self:

> So the sweet voice of Nature is no longer an infallible guide for us, nor is the independence we have received from her a desirable state. Peace and innocence escaped us for ever, even before we tasted their delights. Beyond the range of thought and feeling of the brutish men of the earliest times, and no longer within the grasp of the 'enlightened' men of later periods, the happy life of the Golden Age could never really have existed for the human race. When men could have enjoyed it they were unaware of it; and when they could have understood it they had already lost it.[67]

Without society, without others, men would have no mirror in which to see themselves, and without others' desires, they would feel no lack, no desire of their own. Without the other, men would have only such needs as animals have; 'bring him into society', said Smith adopting the metaphor of his mentor, Hume, 'and he is immediately provided with the mirror he wanted before'.[68] Bring him into society, and he acquires the capacity to choose between his needs and his desires; in acquiring that capacity he makes himself a moral agent, capable of evil, but also of good.

Rousseau's account of how men enslave themselves to the opinions and desires of others is the first specifically modern theory of false consciousness: the first to take the ancient Stoic account of moral corruption and link it to the economic conditions of modern capitalist society: inequality, acquisitive envy and the division of labour. Smith's reply is paridigmatic of all critiques of theories of false consciousness since: if men are creatures of will, they can choose; if they can choose, they can preserve the immunity which self-commands affords from the alienation in the 'great scramble of society'. The weakness of theories of false consciousness is not merely that they are true only for some, but not for the 'wise and virtuous few': it is that in derogating the capacities of the individual human will, they remove from their theories the very possibility of human liberation for which they speak: for liberation, whether individual or collective, is an act of will, a choice of need against desire, which begins with the self.[69]

As the French say, fundamental political choices are '*choix de sociétés*': choices between societies. The encounter between Rousseau and Smith in 1756 is such a choice, the most fundamental legacy of political choice bequeathed to the nineteenth century, and through them to us, by the Enlightenment. It is a choice between two languages of reflection upon politics, and two different utopias. We must say utopia in both cases, because Smith's 'system of natural liberty' no more described the world as it was than did Rousseau's republican ideal.

Rousseau's utopia is a *republic of needs*, a society which by democratically limiting its size, its contact with the world outside, and most of all the domestic consumption of its citizens, reduces inequality, envy and competition. It constrains desire within a set of democratic and consensual limits on need, and it does so for the sake of social solidarity, civic virtue, and the primacy of public over private life. It does so at a cost. Societies which constrain the economic desires of their citizens, which guard their political integrity within an international division of labour by an economic strategy of autarchy, and which seek to make the distribution of wealth and income a matter of collective choice, risk economic stagnation. That is, they risk becoming unable to meet the first requirement of a just society: that it satisfy the basic needs of all. Moreover, the apparatus of constraints upon individual desire which is necessary to restrain inequality and to promote civic virtue potentially jeopardises the liberty which is the republic's *raison d'être*. As Rousseau so profoundly understood, citizens can only be free in a republic of need if the constraints to which each submits are willed and chosen by each. Less *is* only more in such a society if each citizen consents that it be so. Such a republic requires heroic displays of Stoic self-command by each citizen: each individual, to remain truly free, must consent, in the deepest recesses of his self, to the yoke of collectively determined constraints upon desire: each must refuse the temptation which passion offers to desire more than one's fellow citizens. Over time, Rousseau held out hope that the experience of civic equality itself would remove the temptation to compete: virtue would become natural, that is, fully social, because society would remove the incentives for envy. The greatness of his reflection, however, is that he did not seek to hide the intense demands which his utopia demanded of the civic virtue of its inhabitants. Were citizens to relax their guard, were they to entrust the choice of virtue to others, were they to renounce their sovereignty, both over their own passions and over their polity, the republic would surrender its freedom. It would terminate in a dictatorship of need.

If Rousseau speaks for a republic of needs, Smith envisages the society of the future as a *market in desire*, as a collectivity whose economic dynamic is based in the unlimited expansion of desire. Neither natural scarcity, nor satiation of desire were ever likely, Smith argued, to place limits on either the spiral of human desire for commodities or the capacity of the system to deliver.[70] To the degree that he anticipated the problem of Malthusian limits on the expansion of a commercial economy, Smith dismissed them by means of the division of labour argument.[71] As long as productivity per man hour could be kept rising in tandem with population, and as long as the market could continue to expand to embrace the whole planet, these demographic and ecological constraints could be pushed back indefinitely. The specific historical property of a commercial society, he insisted, was that it was no longer threatened by the cycle of expansion and decline which has brought earlier modes of subsistence, earlier empires, to their term: the extension of the division of labour to the world market made permanent economic expansion possible for the first time in human history.[72] The fourth stage — commercial society — was thus the last stage of historical time, the apotheosis of a history of progress which had begun in the mists of ancient time, among the first hunters and gatherers.

Yet if a market society was not threatened by stagnation and backwardness which menaced a republic of needs, and if it guaranteed private economic freedom more effectively than in a needs-constrained system, it too was menaced by the very features which a republic could avoid: inequality, envy and competition. Inequality, Smith argued, in a growing economy would not threaten the subsistence of the poor: a commercial society could discharge its minimum obligations in terms of distributive justice. But inequality posed a threat both to civic and private virtue. A society given over to the unlimited satisfaction of private desire was always endangered by the economic and political despotism of the rich, and by the privatisation of the poor. It purchased prosperity at the potential price of virtuous government: it potentially traded public liberty for private liberty, active citizenship for private, passive freedom to enjoy one's property.[73] In this sense, if the freedom of a *republic of needs* risked degenerating into a dictatorship of needs, the freedom of market society risked degenerating from a blind scramble between competing economic interests into a despotism of the rich.

In the end, for this to be a utopia at all, Smith had to make as austere a set of demands on the virtue of its participants as did Rousseau. A market society could only remain free and virtuous if its citizens displayed the Stoic self-command all too often displayed only by the 'wise and virtuous few'. Without this self-command, competition would become a deluded scramble, politics a war of factions, and government a dictatorship of the rich. Smith was optimistic that none of this was fated to take place, but it was an optimism based on a Stoic wish: on the human will, on each individual's sovereign capacity to know the difference between what he wants and what he needs. In this, the demands of a virtuous market society were no less austere than those of a republic of needs. With perhaps one crucial difference. For Rousseau, civic morality was always a matter of collective public choice. If men are to be freed of the slavery of desire, they must make democratic choices of need together. If there *is* an individualism in Smith it is here, in the relative neglect of politics as the realm in which the choice between need and desire must be made. For Smith it is a choice made 'by the impartial spectator within the breast'; for Rousseau, a choice to be made in the forum of politics.

NOTES

1. Adam Smith, *Essays on Philosophical Subjects*, ed. W. P. D. Wightman and J. C. Bryce (Oxford, 1980), 242–256.

2. Jean Jacques Rousseau, 'A Discourse on the Arts and Sciences', in *Social Contract and Discourses*, ed. G. D. H. Cole, revised by J. H. Brumfitt and J. C. Hall (London, 1973), 16.

3. Adam Smith, *An Inquiry into the Nature and Causes of the Wealth of Nations*, ed. R. H. Campbell, A. S. Skinner and W. B. Todd, 2 vols. (Oxford, 1975), I. viii. 23–4. Hereafter cited as WN.

4. Duncan Forbes, *Hume's Philosophical Politics* (Cambridge, 1975), *passim.*

5. John Pocock, *The Machiavellian Moment: Florentine Political Thought and the Atlantic Republican Tradition* (Princeton, 1975), Chs. x–xii; Quentin Skinner, *The Foundations of Modern Political Thought*, 2 vols. (Cambridge, 1978), Vol. 1, 162–8.

6. Donald Winch, *Adam Smith's Politics: An Essay on Historiographic Revision* (Cambridge, 1978), 30–46; John Robertson, 'The Scottish Enlightenment at the Limits of the Civic Tradition', in Istvan Hont and Michael Ignatieff (eds.), *Wealth and Virtue: The Shaping of Political Economy in the Scottish Enlightenment* (Cambridge, 1983), 137–179.

7. WN. III. iv. 10–16; WN. I. viii. 13; WN. I. xi. 10.

8. WN. V. i. f. 6.

9. Adam Smith, *The Theory of Moral Sentiments*, ed. D. D. Raphael and A. L. Macfie (Oxford, 1976), I. iii. 3. 1. Hereafter cited as TMS.

10. Bernard Mandeville, *The Fable of the Bees*, 2 vols., ed. F. B. Kaye (London, 1924), Vol. 1, 42.

11. Rousseau, 'A Discourse on the Origin of Inequality', in *Social Contract and Discourses*, 76.

12. Rousseau, *Ibid.*, 83.

13. Marshall Sahlins, *Stone-Age Economics* (London, 1972), 1–39.

14. David Hume, *A Treatise of Human Nature*, ed. L. A. Selby-Biggs, 2nd edn., rev. P. H. Nidditch (Oxford, 1979), 484–495.

15. WN. I. ii. 2.

16. Rousseau, 'A Discourse on the Origin of Inequality', in *Social Contract and Discourses*, 63.

17. WN. I. ii. 3.

18. WN. V. ib. 1.

19. WN. V. i. b; Adam Smith, *Lectures on Jurisprudence*, ed. R. L. Meek, D. D. Raphael, P. G. Stein (Oxford, 1978), Report of 1766, hereafter cited as LJ(B); report of 1763 hereafter cited as LJ(A). LJ(B). 20; LJ(A). iv. 21.

20. Rousseau, 'A Discourse on the Origin of Inequality', in *Social Contract and Discourses*, 83.

21. TMS. III. 3. 30.

22. *Loc. cit.*

23. TMS. IV. I. 10.

24. Richard Tuck, *Natural Rights Theories* (Cambridge, 1979); Istvan Hont and Michael Ignatieff, 'Needs and justice in the Wealth of Nations', in Hont and Ignatieff (eds.) *Wealth and Virtue*, 1–44.

25. Pocock, *Machiavellian Moment*, 468–486.

26. WN. (I). 4.

27. Rousseau, 'A Discourse on the Origin of Inequality', in *Social Contract and Discourses*, 105.

28. WN. I. i. 11.

29. WN. I. viii. 36; Rousseau, 'The Social Contract', in *Social Contract and Discourses*, 231.

30. As quoted in S. Harvey *et al*, *Re-Appraisals of Rousseau: Essays in Honour of R. A. Leigh* (Manchester, 1980), 268.

31. Rousseau, 'A Discourse on Inequality', in *Social Contract and Discourses*, 123.

32. *Ibid.*, 134.

33. *Ibid..*, 39.

34. Quoted in Lester Crocker, *Jean Jacques Rousseau*, 2 vols. (New York, 1974), 271.

35. Rousseau, 'Emile', in *Social Contract and Discourses*, 302.

36. Rousseau, 'Social Contract', in *Social Contract and Discourses*, 204.

37. Rousseau, 'A Discourse on the Origin of Inequality', in *Social Contract and Discourses*, 146.

38. Rousseau, 'A Discourse on Political Economy, in *Social Contract and Discourses*, 152.

39. Rousseau, 'Social Contract', in *Social Contract and Discourses*, 204.

40. *Ibid.*, 217.

41. R. L. Meek (ed.), *The Economics of Physiocracy* (Cambridge, 1963), *passim*.

42. Rousseau, 'A Discourse on Political Economy', in *Social Contract and Discourses*, 149.

43. *Ibid.*, 151.

44. Jean Jacques Rousseau, 'Fragments Politiques', in *Oeuvres Complètes*, 3 vols. (Paris, 1961), Vol. 3, 525.

45. Rousseau, 'Social Contract', in *Social Contract and Discourses*, 205.

46. *Ibid.*, 217.

47. *Ibid.*, 231.

48. WN. I. iii. 1–8.

49. WN. IV. ix. 49.

50. WN. IV. ix. 51.

51. WN. V. i. a. 15.

52. WN. V. i. f. 51.

53. WN. V. i. f. 50.

54. Smith, *Essays on Philosophical Subjects*, 253.

55. *Ibid.*, 252.

56. *Loc. cit.*

57. LJ(A), 333.

58. Hume *Treatise*, 491.

59. TMS. VII. ii. 4. 8.

60. TMS. VII. ii. 3. 15.

61. TMS. VII. ii. 4. 9.

62. TMS. I. ii. 5. 1; J. R. Lindgren, *The Social Philosophy of Adam Smith* (The Hague, 1973), 20–21.

63. LJ(A) 263.

64. Patricia Springborg, *The Problem of Human Needs and the Critique of Civilization* (London, 1981), 36–43.

65. Rousseau, 'A Discourse on the Origin of Inequality', in *Social Contract and Discourses*, 54.

66. 'Social Contract', in *Ibid.*, 177.

67, 'Geneva Mss.', in *Ibid.*, 156.

68. TMS. III. I. 3; Hume *Treatise*, 365.

69. Springborg, *Human Needs*, 119.
70. WN. V. ii. k; WN. II. iii. 28.
71. WN. I. viii. 23–27.
72. WN. II. iii. 36.
73. J. H. Hexter, *On Historians* (London, 1979), 255–303.